To: SEBASTIAN and EMMA.

Hopefully this will not only ~~will~~ be of help
On your Honeymoon and will be a happy remembrance.
Of a wonderful and magical 10 days

With love and every wish in the world
From
Robert and Mummy

THE DORDOGNE

Stephen Brook

THE DORDOGNE

Photography by Charlie Waite

GEORGE PHILIP

British Library Cataloguing in Publication Data

Brook, Stephen
The Dordogne.
1. Dordogne (France) —— Description and
travel —— Guide-books
I. Title
914.4'7204838   DC611.D7
ISBN 0–540–01106–1

Text © Stephen Brook 1986
Photographs © Charlie Waite 1986

First published by George Philip,
59 Grosvenor Street, London W1X 9DA

Reprinted 1988, 1990

Printed in Italy

Half-title illustration **It's a climb of 100 metres or so to the top of Nontron from the road twisting through the gorges at the foot of the town.**

Title-page illustration **The riverside houses at Terrasson contemplate their own reflection.**

Contents

To Maria,
worth her weight in truffles

Beaulieu. A Madonna and Child looks tenderly at a
shop much frequented by local parishioners.

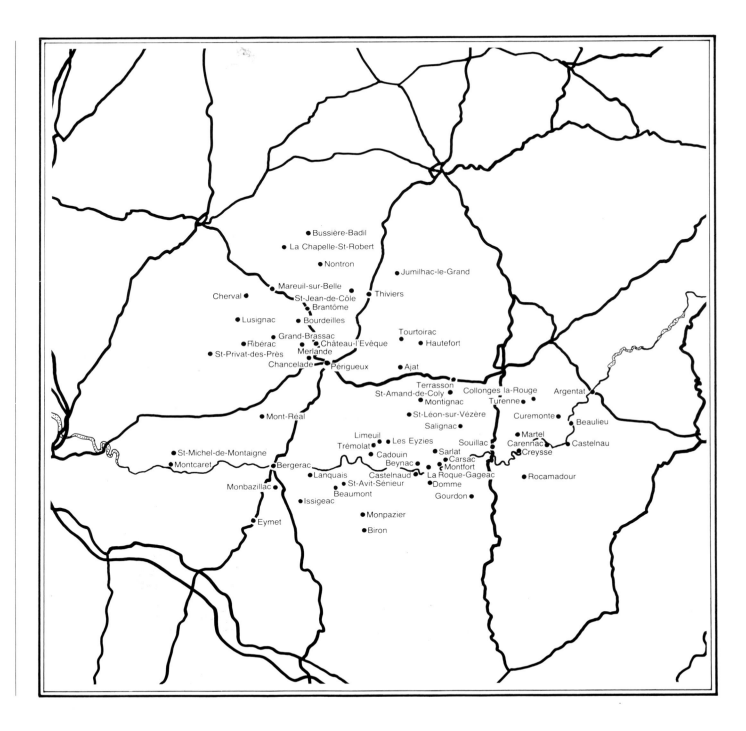

Introduction

When English-speaking visitors refer to a beautiful region of southwest France as 'the Dordogne', any Frenchman listening would be baffled. For the same area is known to the French themselves as *le Périgord*. True, there is a *département* known as the Dordogne, but to the French the Dordogne is not an administrative region but a river. Moreover, no two people have the same precise area in mind when they speak of the Dordogne. When a friend of mine kindly offered to rent me his house in 'the Dordogne', I was most surprised when it turned out to be located on the River Lot many kilometres to the south. So in writing this book about the Dordogne, I too have had to draw my own boundaries.

This is less wilful than it appears. I have tried to meet what I take to be most readers' expectations. Many guides to the Dordogne do not step over the boundaries of the department. This is logical but not sensible. Although this book discusses the entire department, it also follows the river upstream for about 70 kilometres from the administrative boundary. This enables me to include such marvels of the region as the towns of Souillac, Turenne, Martel, and Beaulieu, the great castles of Castelnau and Montal, and the natural wonders of Padirac and the *causses*. I have followed the Dordogne valley as far upstream as Argentat and explored the surrounding countryside, stopping well before Brive to the north and the valley of the Lot to the south.

It can be argued that the hills of the Corrèze beyond Beaulieu and the wooded slopes of the region known historically as Quercy south of the river have little in common with the landscapes of the Dordogne. On the other hand, the department of the Dordogne is itself marked by great diversity – flat forests to the west, rolling farmland to the north, dramatic riverscape to the east. These differences are easily discerned, for the edges of the department seem to be nodding deferentially towards their neighbours. Much of the north resembles the Limousin, the large verdant region that encompasses a number of departments to the north of the Dordogne, while the west resembles the flatter Gironde and Charente. The elements that unify the region are less easy to define. Yet the attempt is worthwhile, for the Dordogne does have its own strong personality, and though the features that mark the region are not unique to it, they are more strongly expressed here than elsewhere in France.

Its agriculture, for instance, is distinctive, with the cultivation of walnuts and the elusive truffle, and the rearing of poultry, especially ducks and geese. Its architecture is emphatically regional; remarkable domed Romanesque churches and lovely galleried farmhouses with their dovecots speckle the landscape. It is a region of châteaux; no other corner of France has such a wealth of medieval and Renaissance domestic and military architecture. The cuisine, heavily reliant on fresh local produce, is among the finest in France. Duck and goose preserves are ubiquitous, walnut oil and truffles are used in the best

Above **A weathered but dignified galleried farmhouse at Autoire.**

Left **Morning mists rising from the river add to the dramatic beauty of the valley at Loubressac.**

jagged cliffs and some remote valleys, but by and large the landscape is settled and domesticated. The department has lost a quarter of its population since the mid nineteenth century, and depopulation is a serious local issue. Villages that seem at first glance to be charming, picturesque examples of rural living turn out to be half-deserted; nevertheless, the occupation of earlier decades has left its mark on the region, both in its buildings and in the layout of farms and pastures.

The Dordogne has long been regarded with great affection by north Europeans. The Dutch and the British in particular demonstrate this not just by invading the region's hotels and campsites every summer, but by purchasing houses in such numbers that some villages are now dominated by foreign residents. These secondary homes, rarely occupied year round, constitute a kind of gentrification. Farmhouses occupied by farmers are cluttered: ploughs and tractors and tobacco sheds and yapping dogs are evidence of people at work. Those inhabited by foreigners are far more neat: masonry will be repointed and earthenware tubs filled with plants will be lined up on the open balcony. One reason for the influx of foreign residents is the French inheritance laws. With property repeatedly subdivided between many heirs, farms dwindle in size until they become unworkable. Agricultural reforms have reorganized many such farms, combining properties so as to make them economically worthwhile. Such reorganizations mean that many farmhouses become redundant and are sold off, usually to town dwellers, whether from Paris or Birmingham or Rotterdam. Purists may lament this development, but had it not occurred the result might well have been a severely rundown rural economy. As it is, tourism and its offshoots – campsites, secondary homes, the food industry – have saved the Dordogne from economic decline without seriously compromising its character.

I suspect that what draws north Europeans to the Dordogne is the fine balance the region maintains between the alien and the familiar. The Dordogne is French, utterly French, and its historic links with England have rarely been happy ones. The evidence of the devastation caused by the Hundred Years War is pervasive, though those dreadful days are too buried in time for visitors to need fear any hostility from their French hosts. The English made no

cooking, and meals, even in a region so heavily visited by tourists, are generous and astonishingly cheap. The proliferation of caves and grottoes has given the Dordogne the greatest concentration of prehistoric sites in the world, as well as caverns of outstanding beauty and drama. Here, too, are most of the great bastides, those remarkable examples of thirteenth-century town planning, some of which remain virtually intact (see p. 105). Based on a grid system as rigid as that of midtown Manhattan and enclosed within fortifications, the bastides offered military bases to the French and English rulers as well as a refuge to local peasants.

Though the landscape is infinitely varied, it has throughout a gentleness, a lack of true wildness, that makes the Dordogne accessible and enjoyable. True, there are

lasting stylistic impact on the region: an English bastide is indistinguishable from a French one. Yet for all its Frenchness, there is a cosiness to the Dordogne that appeals to those who, if one can attempt this kind of generalization, are as a nation shy of the flamboyant, the loud, the self-dramatizing. The landscapes are less wild than the gorges of the Tarn or the Auvergne; the summers, though hot, are rarely as blistering as those of Provence; the landscape has a domesticated density, a proliferation of villages and churches. The Dordogne is sufficiently different to be exotic and endlessly interesting, but it never alarms by its unfamiliarity. Its profusion of tourist facilities and the warm welcome (*bon acceuil*) of its natives contribute to making the visitor feel at home while being abroad. Visitors do appear to be genuinely welcomed by the Périgordins, and not just for their money. The Dutch in particular, who have long had trading links with Bergerac and also sheltered many refugees from that Protestant city during the Wars of Religion, are popular in the area. Perhaps it is the relish that north Europeans display for the region that endears them to its natives. That relish is well founded, for the lovely summers and long mild autumns, the delectable food and excellent wines, the abundance of rivers, and the historical richness of the Dordogne combine to make it an inexhaustible pleasure ground. Cyril Connolly thought its appeal came from 'a certain climate, a certain relationship between man and nature, a special blend of landscape and architecture, which, taken together, form a complete and self-dependent little world somehow different in time from our own and exercising an extraordinarily soothing effect on all who stay there more than a week.'

The department is, roughly, diamond-shaped, with its capital Périgueux at the centre. The area around Périgueux is known, appropriately enough, as Périgord Central, demarcated by Brantôme to the north, Neuvic to the west, Lalinde to the south, and Thenon to the east. This is a region

---

Near Lacave the Ouysse river cuts deeply through the thinly-populated high plateaux known as *causses*.

of wooded hills and broad valleys that nurture light industry. This landscape is intensified to the northeast in the Périgord Vert, with its dense woods and lush meadows and commanding little towns such as Thiviers and Nontron. To the northwest of Périgord Central, around the towns of Ribérac and Verteillac, is the Périgord Blanc. Its gently undulating hills encourage farming on a more commercial scale than elsewhere in the Périgord; the scale is broader, the trees less abundant, the vistas wide and, occasionally, dull. West of Périgord Central are the Double and the Landais, two forested areas, a moist misty region of oak and pine and chestnut, of small lakes and widely scattered villages. South of Bergerac is the prosperous Bergeracois, with its farms and vineyards, quite flat in places yet less bleak than the Périgord Blanc.

Finally, to the southeast lies Périgord Noir with Sarlat at its centre. This is the most picturesque corner of the department, dominated by the meandering River Dordogne and the swifter Vézère, by limestone cliffs and clusters of dark woodland. East of Périgord Noir, over the department borders, are the limestone plateaux of the ancient region of Quercy known as *causses*, and beyond lie the hills of the Corrèze. The attraction of the Périgord Noir, and of the region to its east, does not rest solely in the beauty of the landscape. The area is blessed with lovely ochre building stone, and at sunset entire villages are bathed in a golden glow. Roofs are not only built from tiles or slates but from thin, roughly hewn slabs of limestone called *lauzes*, that darken with the passage of time and become dotted with lichen and moss.

It is this generous use of local materials that gives the domestic architecture of the Dordogne such charm and dignity. On the shortest journey, especially in the Périgord Noir, you'll pass dozens of fine old farmhouses, all built in the same basic style. It's a style based on practical considerations, with the ground floor reserved for animals or storage of hay and farm implements. An open staircase leads not to a forbidding front door, but to an open gallery, often supported on wooden struts, and from this area, so well suited for washing lines and the sipping of aperitifs, one enters the main living area. Attached to the side of the house there is likely to be a square or octagonal dovecot, or *pigeonnier*. Shutters frame the large windows of the main

Billowing *lauze* roofs at Martel, showing how beautifully time has mellowed the texture and colour of these rough-hewn limestone slabs.

parlours as well as the hooded dormers of the bedrooms above.

Almost as common are the châteaux and manor houses that pepper the entire region. If one includes the more modest, but often very beautiful, *manoirs* (manor houses or country seats) and *gentilhommières* (homes of the gentry), there are at least 1500 great houses in the Dordogne—a feast, not just for the castle and stately home enthusiast, but for all visitors with an interest in history. Most of the castles originated in medieval times, and have a long, complex and frequently bloody tale to tell. Dozens of these châteaux, including most of the grandest, are open to the public, though you are required to tag along on the guided tours.

Certain architectural elements keep recurring. Many of the châteaux still retain their original keep, or donjon, a severe square pile usually dating from the twelfth or thirteenth centuries. In some villages only the donjon remains, a stark reminder of former feudal authority. You will see fat round towers, invariably machicolated and with a sentry walk beneath a conical roof that enabled the defenders to survey the surrounding countryside; these round towers often date from the fourteenth or fifteenth centuries. Even châteaux that are essentially Renaissance structures of the sixteenth century, such as Puyguilhem or Monbazillac, retain a fortified appearance, though they were built as country mansions rather than as castles. The less military styles of the Renaissance introduced a wealth of ornament to the châteaux, in the form of moulded mullions and transoms in the windows, fantastically elaborate dormers (*lucarnes*), tall chimney-stacks, and corbelled turrets. The châteaux of subsequent centuries tend to be in a restrained classical style, or adopt an anachronistic Renaissance design, or, in a few cases, the local equivalent of High Victorian. Manor houses, being less grand than châteaux, often occupy a prominent location within the village rather than just outside it. They are easier to take care of than a draughty forty-room château, and these lovingly maintained old houses greatly add to the beauty of Périgordin villages and towns.

If the domestic and military architecture of the Dordogne is its greatest man-made glory, the hundreds of marvellous churches and abbeys in the region offer strong competition. Of the 800 or so churches in the department, 500 are in the Romanesque style of the twelfth century. About 100 are pure Romanesque; the remainder have been altered or added to at various times. There are two features of the Romanesque style which make a strong claim on our attention. First, there is the wealth of carving to be found in modest churches as well as in major abbeys. Capitals at the heads of columns are frequently carved on all sides. Often the carving consists of no more than a leaf or tendril design, though these can be very beautiful. In other cases, the capitals are historiated – decorated with figures that depict a

The château above Gintrac, a pastoral view of a warlike spot.

Left **Looking down from the hills onto Montal, the most perfect Renaissance château of the Dordogne.**

Above **This church at Jaurès, much altered since the twelfth century, is forbidding rather than beautiful.**

17

The great south porch at the abbey of Beaulieu contains some of the finest carvings in the Dordogne.

scene from a biblical or legendary story – or carved with birds and animals. In grander churches, such as Carennac or Beaulieu, the main doorway is adorned with a tympanum, a carved group of figures above the main door; most tympanums depict a Christ in Majesty or a Last Judgment. Other surfaces lend themselves to carving and ornament, such as the corbels that project from the walls of a church in order to support the ribs of a vault; corbels are often carved as heads that peer down onto the congregation.

The second major appeal of Romanesque architecture is its purity of form, and this is harder to define. It is mostly a question of the organization of space within the church, the balance of height to width, the way in which the worshipper's eye is drawn down the nave towards the chancel, the colour and texture of stone surfaces. It is not that purity of form is lacking in Gothic churches, but rather that the comparative austerity of the Romanesque style presents fewer distractions to the eye and, some would maintain, the spirit.

In its architecture, domestic as well as ecclesiastical, the Dordogne is extremely conservative, and styles persisted long after they were displaced in less remote parts of France. Some Romanesque-style churches were built as late as the thirteenth century, when northern France was busily erecting its great Gothic cathedrals. Indeed, Gothic architecture has made little impact on Périgord and Quercy. The reasons are historical as much as architectural. The Middle Ages found the Périgord plunged into a series of wars, and this was hardly a suitable time for initiating extensive building works, even though enormous damage had been done to its churches and châteaux. There are some fine Gothic churches dotted about, such as Issigeac and the bastide churches, but the Dordogne is rightly celebrated more for its Romanesque heritage. Here and there you will find examples of the late Gothic style known in France as *flamboyant*. As the name suggests, this style is far removed from the pure lines and simple tracery patterns typical of thirteenth-century Gothic. Flamboyant architects seemed to have loved excess for its own sake. No line is left unornamented and tracery flows and curls in the most fantastical way. A number of châteaux as well as churches have doorways in this style, and they too are embellished with crockets and shields and all the other ornamental paraphernalia that the fertile imagination of the fifteenth and sixteenth centuries could devise. There are many who find the flamboyant style over the top, vulgar and decadent. So it can be, but it can also be invigorating and hugely enjoyable, especially in a region such as the Dordogne that is so filled with austere and sober architecture.

Two characteristics of Dordogne church architecture lend it special distinctiveness. Neither is unique to the Dordogne, but both are so frequently seen that they are inevitably associated with the region. The two cathedrals of Périgueux are spanned by enormous domes, and other churches, such as Cherval or Trémolat, are vaulted with a series of domes filing down the nave. These domes give an air of delicacy and suspension to the spaces over which they hover, a sensation particularly marked at the great abbey church of Souillac. Fortifications are the other feature of Périgordin churches. At Paunat or Saint-Amand-de-Coly, the walls rise

The Dordogne at Castelnaud. This stretch of the river is overlooked by numerous castles, all keeping an eye on each other.

sheer to an enormous height; the few window openings are tiny, so as to deter would-be attackers. Trémolat, with its massive boxy shape, could easily be taken for an oversized donjon rather than a church. Belfries bristle with fortifications. The naves of churches such as Saint-Privat-des-Près are topped with loopholes and crenellations, just like a castle. Machicolations are equally common in the castles and churches of the Dordogne. They are projections from the outer wall, often close to the roofline, and their bases are perforated with large holes through which defenders could hurl missiles or pour boiling liquids down on their attackers. In many smaller churches, defensive chambers were built over the main body of the church. At Prats-du-Périgord, there's a chamber over the chancel, an arrangement by no means uncommon, but it does look most peculiar, since the chancel rears high above the nave. In times of war or siege, the entire local population would take refuge in these defensive chambers, where they were less likely to meet a sticky end than by remaining in their houses, though it is quite common to find fortifications on modest town houses and manors too.

Regional boundaries are not barriers and some architectural styles more commonly seen elsewhere in France are frequently found in the churches of the Dordogne too. In the northern Périgord, which borders the department of the Charente to the west, you will see features characteristic of the Saintonge Romanesque, named after the region north of Bordeaux where the style is extremely common. It can be recognized by the bands of blind arcades (that is, arches placed against walls of masonry rather than over an open space) marching across the west façades, and/or flanking the central doorway, of even quite modest churches. The west entrances are often elaborately decorated, and the doorway itself will be surrounded by numerous arches formed by wedge-shaped stones (voussoirs). In many instances each stone of an arch will carry different ornamentation, either of an abstract kind such as nailhead, or representational, such as the signs of the Zodiac. Further decoration will often adorn the moulded undersides of the arches (the archivolts). Many fine examples of Saintonge Romanesque will be described in Chapter 1.

It would be a mistake to view these buildings in isolation. The presence of fortified churches speaks volumes about the localized ferocity that must have dominated the countryside during medieval times. No building, however minor, stands isolated from its history. From the grassy platform alongside the half-ruined castle of Castelnaud a splendid panorama unfolds: the Dordogne river meanders below, and straight across, on an outcrop behind the loop of the river, stands the Château de Marqueyssac, while to the right the dramatic profile of the Château de Beynac juts over the river 150 metres below. It's possible to enjoy this view as an aesthetic experience independent of all other factors, but how much more rich that enjoyment becomes when you realize that for many years Castelnaud and Beynac were owned by opposing forces and that this brief stretch of river was bitterly contested by the English and French. Every corner of the Dordogne is steeped in history, mostly a history of conflict, prolonged over decades. Even the most avid amateur historian would have some difficulty sorting out the exact course of events along the Dordogne river during, say, the Hundred Years War, when it was not unusual for fortresses to change hands half a dozen times. The details are incredibly complex, yet the broad outlines are not difficult to grasp.

In a very real sense the history of this part of France is more ancient than the history not just of other parts of France, but of almost every other part of the world. Around the village of Les Eyzies lies a wealth of prehistoric remains: archaeological sites, painted caves, graves and shelters. Nowhere else in the world will you find such a concentration of prehistoric sites (see p. 111). Not only has the Dordogne been continuously inhabited for tens of thousands of years, but traces of that habitation remain to this day and, indeed, constitute one of the principal reasons for visiting the region. All over the area you'll find dolmens, prehistoric structures in which two vertical slabs of stone support a flat horizontal slab, marking the presence of Neolithic burial chambers.

Curiously, it is easier to reconstruct the daily lives of Neolithic men and women than the activities of the far more recent Celts, who left fewer remains. Stone huts, known as *cabanes*, are frequently found throughout the region, and for some of them a Celtic origin is claimed, though other historians and archaeologists are sceptical and suspect they date from medieval times. Only with the Roman occupation did man begin once again to leave a mark on the landscape. Modern Périgueux was founded as a Roman city in 16 BC and named Vesunna. The local Celts, the Petrocorii, became dependants of the Roman Empire, and the Gallo-Roman era began. Vesunna was very much the regional capital and a web of roads stretched out from the city. Roman remains have been discovered elsewhere in the Dordogne, but by far the most substantial are at Périgueux. That Vesunna was a major city is immediately evident from the size and extent of the Roman remains still visible there.

The Barbarian invasions towards the end of the third century AD marked the beginning of the Roman decline in the region, and by the early fifth century the Visigoths were in control. The following century, after the death of the king, Alaric, the Franks became top dog, but the history of the area remains tortuous until the reign of Charlemagne,

A helping hand from a few centuries ago.

who died in 814. Early medieval France did not bear much resemblance to the united country we know today; it was more an agglomeration of warring factions and unstable alliances. Charlemagne, however, fostered the development of the region by supporting the foundation of economically powerful Benedictine abbeys that supplemented the many churches that had been built from the sixth century onwards. Charlemagne thus consolidated the Christian presence in the Dordogne, and also established the *comté* of Périgord as a geopolitical entity. Yet peace was short-lived. The Normans, who sacked Bordeaux in 848, moved on to Périgueux the following year and sacked that city too.

By the tenth century the *comté* had become allied to the dukedom of Aquitaine, and ruling families established themselves throughout southwest France by means of a bewildering series of matrimonial alliances. This feudal system inevitably spawned a plethora of fiefdoms within the *comté*, and the presence of so many warlords and nobles within a relatively small region did not encourage stability. In addition there were frequent border disputes, especially with the neighbouring Limousin to the north. Nevertheless the eleventh and twelfth centuries saw increasing settlement of rural areas and it was during this time that hundreds of churches and castles were erected. Villages and hamlets, dependent largely on polyculture and vineyards, sprang into being and paid tribute to seigneuries that in return offered them protection.

It was when Henry Plantaganet married Eleanor of Aquitaine in 1152 that the real trouble began. Eleanor had previously been married to King Louis VII of France until the bond was annulled, a celebrated instance of the flexibility of otherwise implacable Church law, which opposed divorce, when political expediency was involved. Since her dowry was the large duchy of Aquitaine, Eleanor was a splendid match for Henry, who married her a mere two months after the annulment. In 1154 Henry succeeded to the English throne, while continuing to claim sovereignty over Aquitaine, a claim dismissed by Louis VII. Conflict on a major scale became inevitable. When Richard Lionheart succeeded Henry as King of England in 1189, he continued to fight for his claim to France until his death ten years later in battle at Châlus, just north of Périgord. When the French king confiscated Aquitaine in 1202, the counts of Périgord, who had tended to support the English claim, promptly swore allegiance to France.

Meanwhile, in a brutal sideshow, the Anglo-Norman nobleman Simon de Montfort, fresh from campaigns against heresy in southern France, came storming up to Périgord, conquering most of the great fortresses, including Beynac and Biron, as he went. As a papal supporter in the battle against heresy, Montfort was able to exploit his ardent religious orthodoxy to further his territorial ambitions. However, it was Anglo-French conflict that continued to disrupt the region. Although in 1259 the French king signed the Treaty of Paris, thereby ceding Aquitaine to Henry III of England, the Count of Périgord continued to maintain allegiance to France, while hanging on to his *comté* as a kind of fiefdom from the English king. The building of the bastides helped the English in particular to consolidate their grip on the Dordogne, and formal hostilities resumed at the end of the thirteenth century.

The Knights Templar and the Knights Hospitaller, the two principal military orders of medieval Christendom, also left their mark on this war-torn region. Originally founded to offer protection to pilgrims, the Templars, with branches and huge estates throughout the Christian world, soon grew into an order of such wealth and influence that the Church authorities considered it prudent to suppress the order in 1312. A Templar tower survives at Sergeac, a fortified farm at Jumilhac-le-Petit, and a whole complex of Hospitaller buildings at Condat on the Vézère; and at Domme you can still see graffiti scrawled by jailed Templars on the walls of the towers where they were imprisoned.

Despite the continuous turbulence of medieval Dordogne, the local population did its best to maintain a network of trade and to cultivate the land. The old Roman road system was kept in order, and there was constant traffic down the River Dordogne. The wines of Bergerac were shipped to Bristol in England and other parts of France, while more rural towns, including Périgueux itself, traded mostly with neighbouring territories such as Limoges.

In 1337 Edward II of England renewed his claim to the French throne. No one, I dare say, could then have dared to guess that hostilities would continue, with brief interruptions, until 1453. We call this conflict the Hundred Years War, but it raged intermittently for well over a century. The war was never a single sustained campaign. Rather it was a lengthy series of military escapades, sieges and battles, treaties and betrayals, with the local nobles selling their loyalty to the highest bidder. In 1360 the Treaty of Brétigny returned Périgord to British sovereignty, but most of southern Périgord paid little heed and supported the French side. By 1370 war had broken out once again. To the ravages of the soldiery were soon added the rampages of brigands, not infrequently under the leadership of local nobles. A truce was declared in 1396, but early in the next century it collapsed. Gradually the English were forced onto the defensive. By 1444 they had been driven out of eastern Périgord, and in 1450 the French recaptured Bergerac. The end came in 1453 at the battle of Castillon, downriver from Bergerac. The battle saw the death of the venerable English soldier, Talbot, and led to the capture of Bordeaux. By this time, the *comté* itself had ceased to be the ruling native power; the counts had supported the English throughout the first half of the war, and in 1400 Count Archambaud VI was captured and banished.

Inevitably these decades of warfare caused immense suffering among the civilian population, hardships aggravated by a series of severe winters, bad harvests and floods. The plague too was visited on the Dordogne, though this part of France was not affected as badly as other areas of Europe. The war, and the resulting destruction of castles and peasant dwellings alike, led to depopulation, though once the war was over there was a concerted effort to rebuild the devastated villages and to restore what had become wasteland to cultivation. Tax incentives drew settlers into underdeveloped communes, and the Dordogne continued to grow despite repeated outbreaks of epidemics, such as the one that killed half the population of Sarlat. New industries began to flourish: forges and papermills were established along the fast-flowing rivers. Landholding seigneurs gradually turned into entrepreneurs.

This period of growing prosperity was short-lived. After a century-long war of politics and property, there followed a war of religion, though such an expression ought, in a better world, to be a contradiction in terms. Protestantism came late to the Dordogne, and only received its first martyr in 1542, when a Calvinist preacher was burnt at the stake in Sainte-Foy-la-Grande. Bergerac rapidly became one of the great Protestant centres of France. Despite persecution, Protestantism continued to spread up the valleys, and the movement was strengthened by the conversion of some of the nobility, especially in the Bergeracois.

The St Bartholomew's Day Massacre of 1572 destroyed many Protestant leaders but it hardly pacified those who survived. Travelling around the Dordogne, you frequently come across the name of Geoffroi de Vivans, a Protestant warrior who captured, among other conquests, Monpazier and Domme. Vivans is remembered not just because, like Simon de Montfort three centuries earlier, he left his *carte de visite* at so many places, but because his exploits displayed a full repertoire of guile and cunning. His speciality was deceiving the enemy into believing the forces he led were far more numerous than they actually were. His colourful personality and ingenious victories should not obscure the fact that the Wars of Religion were fought tenaciously and bitterly with, as usual, the civilian population inextricably

Above **A swaggering dormer window in Domme, showing how every house has the makings of a château.**

Right **A house near Autoire masquerading as a church.**

involved. In a political conflict it was possible to shrug one's shoulders and plead neutrality; in war between Catholic and Protestant there was no way to avoid taking sides. Whatever your faith, you were vulnerable. The chronicler Jean Tarde records how for two days the River Dordogne ran red with the blood of slaughtered men and horses. The end of the Wars of Religion opened the way for the Counter-Reformation. Richelieu ordered the ramparts of Protestant strongholds such as Bergerac to be dismantled, and formerly moribund abbeys, such as Chancelade, were resuscitated. The Edict of Nantes of 1598, which had granted freedom of worship to Protestants, was revoked in 1685. This led some Protestants to abjure their faith, or pretend to do so, while others fled to more friendly countries such as Holland.

No sooner had the Wars of Religion ended than there followed a series of peasant revolts, not just against the oppressive nobility, but against the bourgeois tax collectors and magistrates whose demands made the lives of the poor barely tolerable. The first revolt ended in 1595, but no improvement in the peasants' lot resulted, and the imposition of new taxes forty years later provoked fresh uprisings. An army of 5000 actually captured Bergerac, but their success was short-lived. The formal military organization of the *croquants*, as the rebellious peasants were known, collapsed, and was replaced by guerrilla activity. It is a mistake to think that these peasants' uprisings had no support from higher echelons of society; indeed, many of the *croquants'* leaders were high-minded bourgeois and noblemen. Sporadic uprisings continued even into the early eighteenth century.

If the *croquants* were attempting to stop abuses of authority, the revolutionaries of 1789 were questioning authority itself. The French Revolution came at the end of a century of stagnation. The land was no longer able to support the population, and industry soured through lack of investment. Even the wine trade began to suffer as a result of cheaper competition from the Midi. The *métayage* system, a form of sharecropping, resulted in an economy of the barest survival. Malnutrition was widespread. Even the nobility had some difficulty making ends meet; the majority of the seigneurs, although landowners, controlled relatively modest estates, while the larger estates were owned by a very few wealthy nobles.

The Revolution had many positive results, including the reorganization of local government, and in 1790 the modern department of the Dordogne came into being. The unsavoury aspects of the Revolution were less marked in the Dordogne than elsewhere in France. Nevertheless there was considerable anger against the haughty indifferent nobility, and also anti-clerical feeling directed at the prelates and abbots who, as major landlords, behaved just as oppressively as the secular lords. Peasants demanded the abolition of feudal rights and a moratorium on tax arrears. Jacobin societies kept the revolutionary flame burning and attempted to see that ideology was converted into practice: the new calendar devised by the revolutionary leaders was adopted, and the Christian heritage was replaced by a more acceptable secularism. This even extended to the renaming of villages. Saint-Pantaly-d'Ans became Pantaléon-le-Bon-Vin – an attractive name but one that didn't survive for long. Yet by and large the Dordogne was spared the excesses of the Revolution: in Périgueux only twenty heads were removed by the guillotine.

By the time Napoleon came to power, much property had been redistributed; prosperous farmers and the urban bourgeoisie had purchased many seigneurial and ecclesiastical estates. An era of law and order followed; church bells rang out and, with the restoration of the monarchy, nobles began to return to their estates. The countryside prospered as never before. In the first half of the nineteenth century the population grew by 20 per cent to half a million. New farming methods were introduced; tobacco began to be grown, and vineyards and truffle plantations were expanded. The economy remained thoroughly rural. A native son, Pierre Magne, was a prominent figure during the reign of Napoleon III in the 1850s and 1860s, and the ministries he occupied brought great benefits to the department, in particular the construction of railways which made industrial expansion possible.

As so many times before in the Dordogne, its good fortune was not destined to last. Depopulation recurred, and by 1910 the population had dropped to 437,000. The outbreak of phylloxera in the 1880s meant that winemaking, hitherto a major industry, became marginal. The depopulation continued well into this century, and indeed still remains a problem. The decline in smallholdings and the increase of larger, more efficient farms may have brought economic benefits to the region, but the need for labour has dwindled. Some of the old industries, such as papermaking and lumber, persist, and a few new ones, such as shoemaking and the food industry, have sprung up. The present population is a mere 380,000, and might well be smaller were it not for the burgeoning tourist industry.

Although the Dordogne remains overwhelmingly rural, it is not, apart from the fertile Périgord Blanc, especially suited

The broad valley near Saint-Céré provides a rare example of farming land on flat ground in this hilly country.

for arable farming. *Métayage* and French inheritance laws led to a proliferation of small family-operated farms. Each year dozens of these farms vanish, and with them a style of nurturing the land that is typical of rural France. Most of these farmers practise polyculture, since the cultivation of a single crop would not be economically viable. Such a farm, and there are still hundreds left, might well have a few cattle or a few dozen sheep grazing on a hillside meadow; some vines would provide enough grapes to keep the farm cellars stocked; corn or other grain might be grown as cattle feed; there might well be a small grove of walnut trees or tobacco-drying sheds, and there will almost certainly be a fenced-in yard with a hundred noisy ducks and geese. The earth may not be abundantly generous in Périgord and Quercy, but it certainly nurtures some choice foodstuffs.

These local products are the mainstay of the regional cuisine. Goose and duck are the glory of Périgordin cooking. Every part of these birds is prepared and consumed in an infinite variety of ways. Stuffed goose neck, for instance, appears on numerous menus. The Dordogne is famous for its conserves, a relic of harsher times when food had to be stored for the winter months. This is the basis of *confit*, a method whereby poultry is cooked and salted and then sealed in a jar after it has been couched in its own fat. When the mood or need takes you, you extract from the jar as many pieces of the defunct bird as you wish to consume. The dish is present on most menus and many butchers and markets sell *confit* by the piece. Goose and duck may be ubiquitous, but they are not cheap. *Confit* is affordable, but a *bloc de foie gras* – whether *d'oie* or *de canard* – is definitely in the luxury class.

The smallest tins of *bloc de foie gras* cost about 30 francs and only provide enough of the heavenly innard to titillate the appetites of two people. The process of fattening the birds by force-feeding (*gavage*) is both unpleasant and costly, which explains the high prices. In December the farmers' wives descend on Thiviers and other towns and set up their market stalls, and here you can see the swollen yellow livers stuffed into cellophane bags. To buy an entire liver would cost you more than your holiday. It is worth trying some of these local delicacies, however, so look out for the *Artisans Conservateurs*, butchers who specialize in pâtés and other by-products of goose and duck; a list is

At Martel the market roof is supported by a forest of timber and struts, much repaired but still sound.

available from any Syndicat d'Initiative (the grandiose French name for a tourist office). These butchers' products are fairly expensive but of first-rate quality. I never minded paying 20 per cent more for duck liver pâté when I could be sure of finding large chunks of liver embedded in the delicious mixture.

But beware. French labelling is as devious as any other country's, so check carefully before buying. For instance, some processors of *bloc de foie gras* blend together a mass of livers and then divide up the result into tins of varying sizes. This stuff, called *reconstitué*, is perfectly edible, but not nearly as good as a morsel of liver sliced off a larger piece. So ask the grocer whether the liver is *en morceau*. If the answer is yes, and if the label confirms it, buy with confidence. Many of these blocs and pâtés are sold truffled (*truffé*) and the price is increased accordingly.

Let us consider the famous truffle. These irregular rounded black fungus growths attach themselves to the roots of a certain variety of oak; despite Brillat-Savarin's description of truffles as 'black diamonds', they resemble something that more properly belongs in a lab technician's jar than on the tables of gourmets, but they are prized for their flavour and aroma. Their cultivation is difficult and chancy, and their development is the fortunate consequence of a combination of the right factors, including soil, moisture, climate, and pure luck. Discovering them isn't easy either and calls for a trained pig or hound. The sheer difficulty of their cultivation and gathering accounts both for their rarity and for the astronomical prices they fetch in the markets through the winter months. The truffle has a mystique as well as an aroma, and we punters are probably paying as much for that mystique as for the unsightly black fungus itself.

Walnut plantations such as this one near Liourdes provide revenue for farmers and nuts, oil and pâtisserie for visitors.

Once again, beware. An omelette or dish of potatoes cooked with slices of fresh truffle is, I dare say, a dish fit for Valhalla, but only tourists of great affluence will encounter these, and only during the winter months. In my experience, truffles in jars and truffles in pâtés are a waste of money. Time and again I have chomped through the most delectable truffled pâté or liver and ended up wishing the chef had left out those bits of tasteless black rubber. To make up for this anti-recommendation, let me speak more warmly of the other local delicacy, wild mushrooms. *Cèpes* and *morilles* appear on many menus and are absolutely delicious. Although these wild mushrooms are expensive to buy in markets, a little goes a long way.

A less costly speciality of the region is the walnut. A fresh walnut is a revelation: the shell is soft enough to be cracked in one's bare hand, and the flesh is delicate and sweet, quite different from the often bitter flavour of imported walnuts. Walnut oil is delicious too, and menus often specify that salads are dressed with *huile de noix*. Another by-product is a liqueur called *eau de noix* (not to be confused with *eau de noisette*, which is made from hazelnuts). If your taste runs to sweet and sticky, you may be delighted with this liqueur. Fortunately you can often taste before you buy; at Domme many shops on the main street invite you to a *dégustation gratuite*, or free tasting. The walnut also finds its way into tasty little tarts, *tartes aux noix*, available in just about every pâtisserie.

During the autumn and winter, game appears on menus. Judging by the number of hunters I saw each day during the season, it's astonishing that there is any game left to be served. Hare and rabbit are quite common, though, and pheasants are reared commercially; quail also squat on many dinner plates, though they are probably farmed, and no worse for that. Trout and *lotte* are common fish, and even inland markets offer a bewildering variety of fresh fish and shellfish. Many menus feature, often as a first course, *friture de la Dordogne*, which is simply a tasty fry-up of small, rather bony river fish.

Dining out in the Dordogne is a constant pleasure. The best bargains are to be had in small towns at lunchtime. In the centre of town you'll probably find a Hôtel du Centre or Hôtel de Commerce, which, with its bar and billiard tables, functions as a social centre. The restaurant will be packed at lunchtime, with businessmen having their midday meal, with travellers pausing on their journey, and with local farmers and workers in their blue overalls. A menu may be posted, but pay no attention. The waitress will tell you what's available: without question, a soup to start with, then a pâté or fish, then a main course (*plat du jour*), followed by cheese and dessert. A bottle of red wine, unlabelled, will be put on the table and you can drink as much as you wish. Don't worry about the bill: if it surprises you, it will be by virtue of its cheapness.

The same little hotel will probably be deserted in the evening. The French rarely eat out in the evening, and I have often found myself dining alone in a country restaurant. In grander restaurants it may be worth choosing some specialities à la carte, but there's little reason to do so in most smaller restaurants, where the freshest food will almost certainly be on the set menus, which invariably offer a reasonable choice. Many restaurants will have an in-expensive house wine, usually light but drinkable. Do not be surprised if you observe other customers tipping a small amount of wine into the soup. This is not an attempt to ginger up a bland broth (indeed the local soups are often excellent, especially the wonderful garlicky *tourain*). It is in fact a custom found in many parts of southwest France, in which wine is poured into the last of the soup in a ceremony known as *faire chabrol*. You then pick up the soup plate with both hands and drink. A picturesque ceremony, but a waste of good wine. (Some country inns offer amenities catering to other parts of the body. In *The Generous Earth* Philip Oyler reports: 'When any Frenchman from the north comes to this district and requests a room, he will be asked quite naturally and openly for all to hear whether he wants it *sans* or *avec*, meaning with or without a woman.')

Good local wines are not hard to find in the Dordogne. The great vineyards of Saint-Émilion and Pomerol lie only a few kilometres west of the department boundary, and although there are great differences in microclimate between the Bordeaux region and the slopes of the Dordogne, it's not surprising that the latter should produce wine of good quality. In the nineteenth century the Dordogne was celebrated for some very distinguished bottles, but the phylloxera epidemic of the 1880s wiped out many vineyards. Great names of the nineteenth century,

Vineyards such as these keep the *pichets* in the cafés well filled with good wine year round.

such as Jaubertie, La Bachellerie and Saint-Pantaly, simply vanished from wine merchants' lists. Eighty per cent of the vineyards were never replanted, and those that were are found on the hillsides around Bergerac. You will hear people speak dismissively of Bergerac as a thin wine. That can be true. The simple Bergerac *appellation* only requires 10 degrees of alcohol, and that doesn't encourage winemakers to produce a wine of great depth or weight. But Côtes de Bergerac, the next grade up the ladder of *appellations*, is quite a sturdy wine, not unlike a minor claret. It may lack finesse and elegance, but many of these wines have abundant fruit and generosity, which may be due to extensive planting of the Merlot grape. Bergerac Sec is a dependable dry white, made from the Sémillon and Sauvignon grapes. The best Bergerac Sec can well bear comparison with the dry whites of Bordeaux itself.

There is one *appellation* well worth looking out for: Pécharmant. The gentle hills east of Bergerac, close to the villages of Pécharmant and Creysse, produce splendid red wines. Although they cost a few francs more than other Bergeracs, they are still far cheaper than a Bordeaux *petit château* of comparable quality. The *appellation* requires a minimum of 12 degrees of alcohol, and the wines tend to be dark, intense, tannic, and long-lived. A good vintage needs ten years in bottle to reach its peak. Production is limited and Pécharmant is hard to find outside the Dordogne, so make the most of it while you are there.

The other great wine of the Dordogne is Monbazillac. Vineyards fill the river valley and hillsides south of Bergerac. On these slopes are the finest Monbazillac vineyards, some a thousand years old, and the splendid sixteenth-century Château de Monbazillac, which is owned by the local wine cooperative. Here you can taste these sweet wines. If you like Sauternes, you will enjoy Monbazillac. Most Monbazillac, the bottles that find their way into the supermarkets, are young, thin, sugary wines of no distinction. Chilled and served as an aperitif, they are agreeable enough, but these insipid wines are not the bottles that have given Monbazillac a reputation almost as great as that of Sauternes. Old Monbazillac from a great year is a marvellous wine. To find it, you must go to the vineyards. Do not despise the cooperative wine available at the château. The 1976 vintage, for instance, is as ripe and delicious as a good Sauternes of the same year, and about a third of the price. Small independent producers line the slopes near the château and the ruined windmill at Malfourat, and most of them implore passing travellers to enter and taste. I had no difficulty finding vintages dating back to the mid 1960s, still at laughably low prices. A word of warning, though. It is not unusual, in a good hot year, for Monbazillac to attain 15 degrees of alcohol or more – so treat old Monbazillac with respect.

Monbazillac is not the only area where good sweet wine is made. The nearby *appellation* of Saussignac produces some pleasant surprises, and there are good wines from Montravel too, though these tend to be dry whites. Périgord produces wine to suit every taste. It's variable in quality, to be sure, and as elsewhere, you tend to get what you pay for. On the other hand, the best costs no more than a mediocre claret.

Another wine found throughout the region is Cahors, which is made just across the southeast borders of the department in the Lot. It's a powerful robust red which, like Pécharmant, can age well in bottle.

Although the region has so much to offer visitors, their life is not always made easy by those who supposedly cater to their interests. Even the best guidebook can't remain up to date, and the only reliable source of information about opening times of châteaux, prehistoric sites and other tourist attractions is the local Syndicat d'Initiative. Guidebooks are not infallible. The Michelin Green Guide, for example, is only updated every seven years. Visiting important buildings, or attempting to do so, can be most frustrating. In numerous villages near Les Eyzies I saw posters urging the tourist to visit the château at Campagne. When I tried to do so I was greeted with some astonishment by the concierge, since the château had been closed for months. At Lascaux the excellent guide exhorted visitors to walk the few hundred metres up the hill to the site of Regourdou, where other important prehistoric finds were made. I took his advice, only to find the place closed. Some of the major sites, such as Les Combarelles, are open during the morning from 10 to 12. But this information is misleading, since the last tour begins at 11. Remember that it is possible at some prehistoric sites to book in the morning for afternoon tours. I drove 30 kilometres to visit the caves at Font-de-Gaume, arriving half an hour before the afternoon opening time, as I anticipated a queue. What I hadn't anticipated was that all tickets for the afternoon tours had been sold earlier in the day.

The worst example of misleading information I encountered was at the great Château de Fénelon, which is open most of the year. When I arrived one morning I found myself the only person there, and the guide refused absolutely to show me round. She explained that the job was only worth her while if she could collect a few tips, and clearly my solitary presence was unlikely to enrich her sufficiently. I don't blame her for this attitude, but I do blame private owners for encouraging tourists to visit their property and then refusing to grant admission! If, as at Padirac, there aren't enough visitors out of season to make it a paying proposition to keep the site open, then close it. Then at least we all know where we stand.

Churches too can be hard to visit, because so many are kept locked. However, inquiries at the nearest farmhouse or café, or at the *mairie* (town hall), will often produce a key. Still, there is no form of travel that does not involve frustrations of various kinds, and despite the irritations I've referred to, travel in the Dordogne is an overwhelmingly enjoyable experience. We who visit the region, and those who pay it the ultimate compliment of going to live there, do seem to respond to its charms with affection and respect, for who can remain immune for long to its beauties, its gentleness, its glorious food and wine, and the warmth of its *bon acceuil*?

How to Use this Book

I have devised sixteen routes that explore every corner of the Dordogne. It is not intended that they should be followed slavishly. Each one is circular and can be joined at any point, though each begins in a town where tourists are well catered for and are likely to be staying. Although each route can be driven in a day or so, there is little point in merely driving from point to point. Each village or town mentioned has some feature of interest – a cave or a view or a castle – and to explore them all would take quite some time. It would, for instance, be setting a self-defeatingly hectic pace to attempt to visit in one day the historic town of Martel, the great abbey of Souillac, the famous pilgrimage village of Rocamadour, the spectacular caves of Padirac, and the beautiful little town of Carennac, each of which is worth a half day. I have indicated in the text whenever a château or site is open to the public, but opening times vary from day to day and season to season, so it is always advisable, when possible, to obtain a current list of opening times from the Syndicat d'Initiative. There is nothing more frustrating than driving 30 kilometres only to find a château closed that day. A good road map is also to be strongly recommended. Most visitors to the Dordogne will be using the excellent Michelin

road maps, though there are also some first-rate tourist maps available which highlight the major sites likely to interest visitors. Because many place names in the Dordogne can be, and are, spelt in two or three different ways, I have used the spelling given on the Michelin maps, except on the one or two occasions, which I specify in the text, when Michelin uses a spelling not found in any other source.

Remember that the routes that follow are no more than suggested ways to enjoy the region. Allow time to wander off the beaten track; no book of this length can include every village or church of interest, and my choices may differ from your own. And if you can, take it slowly. The Dordogne is more than a collection of historic and beautiful sites. There are views to be relished, and visits to be made not just to old castles but to the local shops to stock up with picnic supplies. And when, after a leisurely picnic in a meadow, you find that an excess of wine has prompted you to doze off and that you will have to curtail your sightseeing that afternoon, don't let it bother you. Exploring the Dordogne is just as much about taking a nap under the shade of a walnut tree as it is about gazing at Romanesque carvings or prehistoric paintings. The French have constructed their everyday lives, as well as the environment in which they live them, so as to extract the maximum sensuous savour and satisfaction from the passing hours. We should join them.

This village house at Les Milandes is a perfect and probably accidental marriage of disparate elements: mellow stone, limestone roofs, ivy and sunshine.

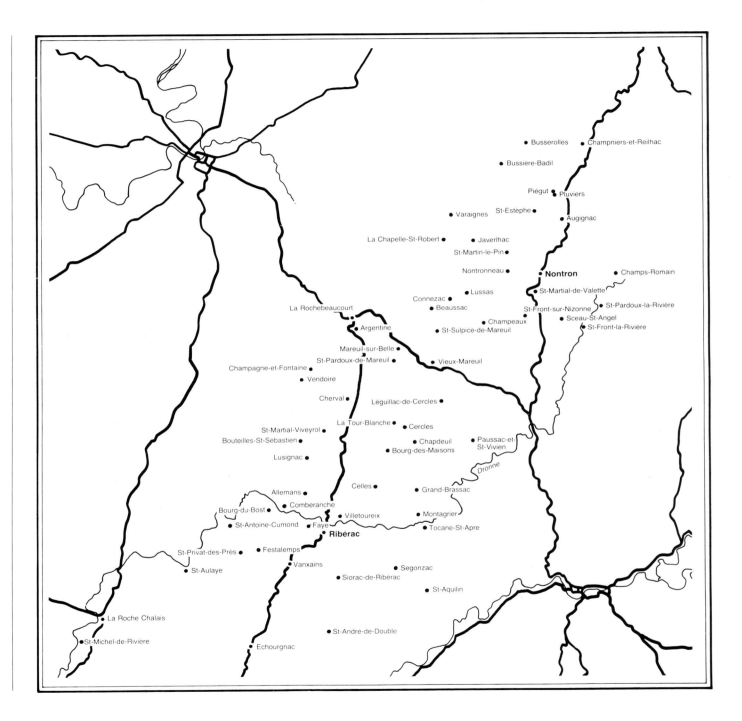

- Busserolles
- Champniers-et-Reilhac
- Bussière-Badil
- Piégut
- Pluviers
- St-Estèphe
- Varaignes
- Augignac
- La Chapelle-St-Robert
- Javerlhac
- St-Martin-le-Pin
- Nontronneau
- **Nontron**
- Champs-Romain
- Lussas
- St-Martial-de-Valette
- Connezac
- Beaussac
- St-Front-sur-Nizonne
- St-Pardoux-la-Rivière
- La Rochebeaucourt
- Champeaux
- Sceau-St-Angel
- Argentine
- St-Sulpice-de-Mareuil
- St-Front-la-Rivière
- Mareuil-sur-Belle
- St-Pardoux-de-Mareuil
- Vieux-Mareuil
- Champagne-et-Fontaine
- Vendoire
- Cherval
- Léguillac-de-Cercles
- St-Martial-Viveyrol
- La Tour-Blanche
- Cercles
- Bouteilles-St-Sébastien
- Chapdeuil
- Paussac-et-St-Vivien
- Lusignac
- Bourg-des-Maisons
- Dronne
- Celles
- Grand-Brassac
- Allemans
- Comberanche
- Bourg-du-Bost
- Villetoureix
- Montagrier
- St-Antoine-Cumond
- Faye
- Tocane-St-Apre
- **Ribérac**
- St-Privat-des-Prés
- Festalemps
- Vanxains
- Segonzac
- St-Aulaye
- Siorac-de-Ribérac
- St-Aquilin
- La Roche Chalais
- St-Michel-de-Rivière
- St-Andre-de-Double
- Echourgnac

1
Northern Périgord

Ribérac – Mareuil-sur-Belle – Cherval –
Lusignac – Saint-Privat-des-Prés – Grand-
Brassac – Nontron – Bussière-Badil –
La Chapelle-Saint-Robert

Fortress Churches of Périgord Blanc

Ribérac is not an especially prepossessing town. It's a centre for local arable and livestock farmers and a shopping town for the many foreign residents who own property in the area. The little town lies against the flank of a hillside. At the foot of this hill is the oval Place Nationale, and it's around here that you'll find the many excellent shops. Higher up stand the two churches. The older dates back to the eleventh century, while the other church is a singularly ugly twentieth-century effort. More worthwhile is the twelfth-century church in the hamlet of Faye just outside town. Above its west door a worn sculpture depicts the seated Christ within an oval of light flanked by angels. Although Ribérac, while cheerful enough, is undeniably drab in comparison with most of the region's towns, it must have been more grand in the Middle Ages, when the château, which dated from the tenth century, still survived. Here too was born the troubadour Arnaut Daniel, a poet of great technical virtuosity and with a gift for ribaldry who was praised by both Dante and Petrarch.

North of Ribérac, on the other side of the River Dronne, stands Villetoureix. Its principal attraction lies just east of the village and is visible from the road. It's the Manoir de la Rigale, an elegant eighteenth-century building tacked on to a Gallo-Roman tower. Once part of a Roman temple, this round tower is remarkably well preserved; its incongruous annexation by a seigneurial residence at least assured its conservation. Not surprisingly, it resembles a smaller version of the contemporary Gallo-Roman tower in Périgueux (see p. 51).

Continue east and then north to Celles, which contains a splendid fortified church with all the elements that will soon become familiar as one tours this region: loopholes and defensive chambers below the eaves; almost windowless walls; and the tall rectangular chancel with additional defensive chambers that raise the roofline to a height greater than that of the nave. South of the church is a *manoir* with an attractive corner turret and carvings of heads around the Renaissance windows. From Celles continue north to Bourg-des-Maisons. Its fortified church is boxy and austere, with only the narrowest windows breaking the sheer masonry of the nave. Two of the three bays of the nave are domed, and the choir, which may date from the eleventh century, is barrel-vaulted. Helpful notes are pinned to the door in English as well as French, sure evidence that a local British resident has been keeping an eye on the place. He wasn't hard to find. An angular figure in baggy corduroy trousers had to be the man I was looking for. He showed me the frescoes he had discovered behind the whitewashed walls of the church, mostly in the chancel; they seem to date from the late Gothic period, though some may be more recent. The hamlet itself has little to recommend it, and the nearby limestone quarry, while providing employment in this otherwise deeply rural corner, scarcely enhances the

Above **A stately eleventh-century church stands at the top of the busy market town of Ribérac.**

Left **Near Ribérac, the Dronne flows peacefully through the rich agricultural land of Périgord Blanc.**

landscape. Just over a kilometre away, off the road to Chapdeuil, stands the Château de Teinteillac, an engagingly shabby structure with a fortified square tower and Renaissance living quarters. Around the château are dovecots and farm buildings, and the courtyard is enclosed by a crenellated wall. The château and its outbuildings, unrestored and of scant architectural distinction, are nevertheless an excellent example of an unpretentious seigneurial home that doubles as a farm.

Chapdeuil itself is still dominated by the massive twelfth- or thirteenth-century keep of the moated château. The structure is capped with fifteenth-century machicolations and loopholes, and the living quarters of the château and its dovecot date from the same period. There are other attractive *manoirs* in the village, but they are overshadowed by the beautiful, yet slightly sinister, old château.

Those pressed for time should continue northwest to La Tour-Blanche, but an attractive loop can be made via Paussac-et-Saint-Vivien. Saint-Vivien has a modest little Romanesque church with a fine though over-restored west entrance. Visible to the south, perched on a wooded cliff, is the Château de Marouatte, a romantic pile surrounded by walls and watchtowers. It dates from the fifteenth century, but was excessively restored in the nineteenth century, with the addition of heavy-handed machicolations and exaggeratedly high roofs. The resulting skyline, while aesthetically questionable, has a definite panache. Just north of the village, off the road to Paussac, are two dolmens, though I was unable to find them. At the neighbouring village of Paussac, there's a very fine domed Romanesque church. The splendid ornamentation of the blind arcades along the south side is at odds with the fortifications, which were added in the fifteenth century. The capitals, both inside and on the exterior, are beautifully carved with birds and human faces.

This loop strays beyond Périgord Blanc into wilder landscapes, but towards La Tour-Blanche the farming country returns. The town takes its name, it soon becomes obvious, from the remains of the twelfth-century donjon rising from an artificial mound. The property of the French king in the fourteenth century, this château was also visited two centuries later by Henri IV and his wife Marguerite. During the fifteenth and sixteenth centuries the château belonged to the Bourdeilles family, and the writer Brantôme (see p. 67) was a regular visitor. The town itself contains some substantial if slightly sombre seventeenth- and eighteenth-century houses. At Cercles to the east there's a magnificent fortified church. The west façade, with its tall recessed arch rising to the height of the west tower, is reminiscent of that of Saint-Amand-de-Coly, the greatest of all Périgordin fortified churches (see p. 78). The finely moulded arches of the Gothic west door rest on beautifully carved capitals, deeply cut and finely detailed. Sadly, the church as a whole is badly neglected. Damp crawls up the interior walls, as in so many fine French churches, and the south transept seems on the verge of collapse.

35

Head northeast to the village of Léguillac-de-Cercles. The church, with its fifteenth-century fortifications and domed nave, is quite attractive, though much renewed. It's worth driving south towards Paussac through the Forêt de Saint-James for a look at the exceptionally large boulders, cumbersome and threatening, that lurch along the cliffs that line the road. Continue north to Vieux-Mareuil in the shallow valley of the Belle. This large village has an imposing church that may well date from the thirteenth century, though the style is unquestionably Romanesque. The fortifications date from the fourteenth century, and the crossing tower is a modern reconstruction. The fortified west front has a large entrance with six ornamented arches around the door. The interior has been much restored, but remains impressive, with its three domed bays, deeply recessed windows, and a fine barrel-vaulted chancel.

Further up the valley Mareuil-sur-Belle is dominated by its attractively irregular château. Mareuil was one of the four baronies of Périgord, but of the original château, where the troubadour Arnaud de Mareuil was born in 1150, nothing remains, for the English severely damaged the castle in the fourteenth century; the buildings seen today date from the fifteenth and sixteenth centuries. In the following century the property came into the hands of the Talleyrand family, but after decades of neglect it became little more than a ruinous farmyard, until in 1964 the Duke of Montebello acquired the château, undertook its restoration, and opened it to visitors.

The castle, which used to be moated, is entered over a bridge that leads through the first set of ramparts. A ramp leads to a second bridge, formerly a drawbridge, guarded by a splendid gatehouse with two flanking half-ruined towers. Despite this fierce medieval entry, most of the castle windows are Renaissance in style, with the distinctive exception of the chapel's Gothic window. The yellow-grey masonry is embellished with panels of lively tracery in low relief set like tablets above and below the windows. Inside the courtyard there is an exquisite crocketed doorway in the

---

The solid church at Mareuil screened by a wall of poplars.

late Gothic style known as flamboyant, with leaf- and flower-like ornament. The doorway leads into the remarkable chapel, a gem of flamboyant architecture, with lovely pointed vaulting and bosses. This inner courtyard also gives access to the living quarters, where the duke has installed a family museum.

The town church is of twelfth-century origin but has been much altered. There's a fine turreted square tower to the northwest, though the bell stage is modern. The church is entered through a Renaissance west doorway, delicately carved and flanked by canopied niches. The broad interior, despite some inventive tracery in the east windows, is unexciting, but contains a half-classical, half-baroque gilt altarpiece of the eighteenth century, and a pretty gilt canopied pulpit of 1650. A few kilometres south of Mareuil is the rewarding hillside hamlet of Saint-Pardoux-de-Mareuil, with its very fine twelfth-century church. The west façade is in the Saintonge style (see p. 19), reminding us that this part of the Dordogne borders the Charente. The vaulting was added in the sixteenth century and in the south chapel is a huge carved pendant boss. A kilometre or so beyond the hamlet stands the lovely Château de Beauregard, with its two square machicolated towers of the fourteenth century, and a seventeenth-century range at right angles to the main block. Also look out for the attractive dovecot that stands nearby.

Northwest from Mareuil on the Route Nationale you will come to the small town of La Rochebeaucourt on the border with the Charente. There's a large Cluniac church with a fine thirteenth-century rose window, and in the adjoining hamlet of Argentine is a Romanesque church built on a hillock and accessible only by foot. It's worth pausing here if you are travelling from the Dordogne to the city of Angoulême, but hardly worth a special journey. Instead, from Mareuil drive southwest to Cherval, where there is an exceptional church. With the pointed arches of the blind arcades and those spanning the nave, not to mention the row of four domes that vault the interior, this church doesn't conform to widely held notions of the features that usually characterize Romanesque architecture. Yet in its spirit this raw, rough-hewn building is entirely Romanesque, austere but eloquent, deeply impressive despite, or perhaps because of, its badly aligned masonry and primitive capitals.

The tourist with no shortage of time could head northwest from Cherval to Champagne-et-Fontaine and Vendoire, set among rolling open farmland. At Champagne there is a château of sixteenth-century origin that, despite excessive restoration, presents a lively appearance. Here, too, is a fortified Romanesque church, much rebuilt in the sixteenth century, that contains an unusually well-carved seventeenth-century altarpiece. The former priory at Fontaine is of little interest, but close to the village are some attractive old farms with dovecots. Vendoire is rather more rewarding. Its château has an elegant seventeenth-century façade with scrollwork dormers and a parapet, and a stone coat of arms with swags embellishes the main entrance. The church has a fine façade in the Saintonge style and capitals carved with leaves and mythical animals.

From Cherval continue southwest (or from Vendoire head south) to Saint-Martial-Viveyrol, a small village in pleasant rolling farmland. There's a massive fortified church here, with a powerful west belfry that doubles as a donjon; two bays of the nave are domed. The nearby village of Bouteilles-Saint-Sébastien also has a fortified Romanesque church, though here the defensive chambers rise over the lofty east end. Drive on to Lusignac, a most remarkable hillside village with fine views over the open farmland of Périgord Blanc. The castle, dating from the fourteenth century, is surrounded by a high wall punctuated by towers and fortified gatehouses that must once have enclosed an entire fortress complex. These magnificent fortifications have been much restored, but the appearance is most picturesque and a delightfully romantic contribution to a skyline that, in this part of the Dordogne, is rarely so dramatic. The church is not without interest either. A fortified Romanesque structure with a powerful machicolated west tower, it contains a small mutilated stone pietà of the sixteenth century and a well carved seventeenth-century wooden altarpiece.

Allemans lies south of Lusignac. The fortified domed church here has been wrecked by the addition of a hideous modern belfry porch. South of the church is a fine *manoir* of

---

The castle walls at Lusignac, punctuated by watch-towers, enclose an area almost as large as the rest of the village.

the fifteenth or sixteenth century, with a polygonal tower. Continue to Comberanche, where there is a Templars' church dating from the twelfth century, and from here cross the valley of the Dronne once more and make for Bourg-du-Bost. The twelfth-century church has a tall square crossing tower decorated, on the interior, with traces of medieval frescoes, including a Crucifixion. Note, too, the very pretty seventeenth-century gold and white altarpiece. The village churches of the Dordogne are crammed with examples of popular art, mostly in the form of rustic altarpieces. I confess I am not among those who admire these vigorous if primitive expressions of rural piety. However, the Périgord Blanc does seem to possess better examples of popular art than most other parts of the Dordogne, and this altarpiece is an attractive example.

It's a short drive from Bourg-du-Bost southwest to Saint-Antoine-Cumond, where it's worth glancing at the very fine entrance to the restored twelfth-century church before continuing to Saint-Privat-des-Prés, an agricultural village containing one of the most noble fortified churches in the Périgord. From the outside it's a boxy structure, with no tower or belfry to give the building a lift. Dark loopholes and crenellations peer out from under the eaves and only the tall blind arcades along the exterior walls relieve the austerity of the masonry. The west wall, which is pierced by a deeply recessed doorway beneath nine moulded arches, is about 3 metres thick. The interior is a splendid surprise, especially after the awesome but undeniably crude interior of Cherval. The arches that span the barrel-vaulted nave rest on richly carved capitals, and the church is aisled, a rarity in the Dordogne. But then Saint-Privat is not an ordinary parish church, since it was originally a Benedictine priory. The aisles are extremely narrow, like a corridor, and are spanned by lofty arches. Note, too, the powerful twelfth-century font and the wooden altarpieces in the east chapels.

To the west lies the small market town of Saint-Aulaye, set in the Dronne valley. Although founded as a bastide in 1288, it is not immediately recognizable as one, for it lacks the regular street layout found in the bastides of southern Périgord. The church has a lovely west façade, though later extensions to the north and south have robbed it of much of the rhythmic vitality provided by the two layers of blind arcades. There are exceptionally vigorous carved capitals within the eleventh-century chancel, depicting monstrous birds and animals and crouching men with outstretched hands within the mouths of lions. From the church there's a good view of the large Hôtel de Ville (town hall) built on the site of the former château.

A detour can be made at this point down the Dronne valley to La Roche Chalais, an unexciting market town, but one that offers a fine panoramic view from the terrace by the church. Just beyond La Roche Chalais is the village of Saint-Michel-de-Rivière, where the church has a remarkable façade in the Saintonge style; the capitals are all carved with foliage or mythical beasts, and above the doorway are the remains of some early medieval statuary, including a seated Christ in Majesty. Inside the church stands a massive twelfth-century font. However, only the most dedicated church enthusiast will want to make this long detour from Saint-Aulaye. Better to drive east to the attractive village of Festalemps, where there is yet another fortified church, and then continue eastwards to Vanxains, where the twelfth-century church has particularly fine capitals in the chancel. A few kilometres to the southeast is the hillside village of Siorac-de-Ribérac, set in countryside considerably more attractive than most of the terrain around Ribérac. Here too there is a fine church, with a domed crossing. Fortified, the church has a tall crossing tower and an uncompromisingly sheer west tower of the fourteenth century. The area south of here, stretching to the Isle valley in the south and as far west as the department border, is the forest of the Double. Not that it's a thick unrelieved forest, for there was extensive felling during the last century and clearings and ponds are scattered throughout this region of oak and pine. The Double has the lowest population density of any part of the Dordogne; in the past malaria deterred settlers and the clay soil discouraged arable farmers. A cheese-making Trappist monastery stands in the heart of the Double at Echourgnac, and Saint-André-de-Double is the only village of any size.

From Siorac drive east, then bear left towards Segonzac. Its impressive Romanesque church contains some crude capitals that date from the eleventh century. Just south of the village is the Château de la Marthonie, built in the fourteenth century and restored in the seventeenth, and approached through a courtyard flanked by square guard towers. The road south towards Saint-Aquilin passes close to the fifteenth-century Château de Belet, a charming ensemble of buildings, round towers, square towers, and a stout dovecot. Nearby there's a dolmen known as Peyrebrune – or so they say, for I followed the signs assiduously and yet failed to find it.

From Belet drive north to the Château de Fayolle, closed to the public but visible from the road a few kilometres south of Tocane-Saint-Apre. It was built in 1766 by the local architect Chauvin and is still the home of the Fayolle family. The Marquis de Fayolle who lived in the early nineteenth century was a noted agricultural reformer, an advocate of more scientific methods. The dignified classical façades of the château where he lived are topped with high roofs and chimneys that rise to the same height. Drive north across the Dronne valley to Montagrier, a pleasant hillside village from which there are fine views over Périgord Blanc. The Romanesque church (the nave and part of the tower are nineteenth-century, however) is set beside the cemetery, and the three-lobed plan of its apse, with its radiating chapels, is unique in Périgord.

North of Montagrier is the village of Grand-Brassac, where the Romanesque church is truly formidable. It was fortified in the thirteenth century, and the loopholes and crenellations and towers rising over the west end and the crossing give the boxy building more the appearance of a castle than a church. An interesting collection of sculpture, dating from the twelfth to sixteenth centuries, has been inserted over the north door. Although not of particularly high quality, the figures placed here, which include statues of saints, a Virgin and Child, and a seated figure of Christ, retain traces of their original polychrome decoration. In addition some fine bas-reliefs and heads are gathered here, some of far higher quality. The austerity of the outside is no preparation for the grace and purity of the interior. Tall pointed arches of grey and white stone separate the bays, three of which are domed. The barrel-vaulted choir was rebuilt in the sixteenth century, following severe damage

Sculpture from the twelfth to the sixteenth centuries adorns the doorway of the church at Grand-Brassac.

inflicted on the church by the Protestants, but in style it blends well with the older parts.

Just west of Grand-Brassac stands the splendid Château de Montardy (which the Michelin map, alone, calls Monlardit), surrounded by walls but visible through the gatehouse of 1666. The grey façade, with its few windows, thorough machicolations, dark turrets with projecting parapets and narrow dormers, is reminiscent of a Scottish castle. It dates from the fifteenth century and was restored in the nineteenth. From Montardy return south to the Dronne and the road back to Ribérac. I was often content to end my daily excursions here, since there is an excellent *Artisan Conservateur* in the main street, from whom I bought delicious pâtés which I would take back with me to the cottage where I was staying. Once the fire was lit I'd pour myself a glass of chilled Monbazillac to sip in between bites of pâté and bread. Then I might peer into my small tub of *confit* and extract a thigh of duck still slicked in its own white fat. I would scrape off this fat and sauté some potatoes in it while I warmed the morsels of duck or goose in the oven. Twenty minutes later my dinner, simple yet rich and satisfying, would be ready. By now a bottle of red Bergerac or Cahors would have had a chance to breathe and these sturdy wines would admirably complement the intense flavours of the *confit*. Then, nibbling on some cheese or a pastry, I'd watch *Dallas* dubbed in French, and go to bed.

Copses and Foundries: The Nontronnais

Nontron, as the name suggests, is the principal town of the Nontronnais, a region of farms and woods also known as Périgord Vert. This last name is not fanciful. The dampness of the climate and the granitic subsoil that keeps the earth moist and fecund result in a verdant region of pastures and copses. The Nontronnais is traversed by numerous rivers and streams, such as the Bandiat on which Nontron itself stands, waterways that once sustained the local economy. They were used less for transportation than as a source of energy for sawmills and forges. Those days have long been over, and the Nontronnais derives such prosperity as it has from more domesticated industries such as shoemaking. Agriculture, too, as elsewhere in the Dordogne, is an important activity.

Nontron itself is a dramatically sited town perched on a promontory and on neighbouring hillsides that rise steeply from the riverside to form ravines. The Roman fort that once stood here has vanished, but Roman remains dating from the first century exist at the nearby village of Nontronneau. Nontron's medieval château was razed during the Wars of Religion, and the present-day château is a structure of the eighteenth century and later. Some of the old ramparts are still standing, but the town has spread well beyond the old walls. The best way to view Nontron is to make for the large terrace with the war memorial laid out near the château. From here you can gaze up to the newer quarters dominated by the nineteenth-century church, or, more vertiginously, down to the half-timbered houses that speckle the roads along the river in the ravines far below.

Like Brantôme to the south, Nontron is an excellent base for exploring not only the Nontronnais but Périgord Blanc to the west. The town itself, it must be said, is less exciting than its situation. Nor could one claim that Périgord Vert is as rich in tourist attractions as the more celebrated regions around Sarlat or Martel. There are, to be sure, some fine churches, but the area imprints itself on the memory more because of the landscape than because of its monuments. The views over steep meadows and chestnut woods, lush and vigorous, are immensely satisfying. The area's neglect by most tourists may well induce more adventurous travellers to visit it. Perhaps I can best characterize the terrain by observing that it is one of those landscapes that looks almost as beautiful in the rain as in bright sunshine.

Leave Nontron by the Brantôme road. On the outskirts you will come to the busy village of Saint-Martial-de-Valette. The Romanesque church here has a splendid doorway surrounded by three arches featuring low-relief carvings of lions, serpents, and strange human figures. They are lively and well preserved, though it's not clear what the significance of their arrangement is. The interior is not of great interest, though there is a charming west gallery. The building is topped with a *clocher-mur* (which I shall translate literally as bell wall), a common feature among village churches in the Dordogne. These slender walls of masonry usually rise over the west end, though some are placed more centrally over the crossing, and they are pierced by as many as four bell openings.

Above **This fanciful water pump enlivens an otherwise blank wall at Nontron.**

a convert to Islam and ended his days as pasha of Algiers. The soldier and writer Brantôme (see p. 67) was a frequent visitor.

Some kilometres east of Champeaux is the agricultural hamlet of Saint-Front-sur-Nizonne. Its Romanesque church has a tower of a type commonly found in the Nontronnais. These are square towers with two layers of arcades over the junction of transepts and nave (known as crossing towers). In many cases the lower arcades are blind, while the higher arcades function as bell openings. There are finer examples of Nontronnais towers than this one, and the most worthwhile feature here is the west door, which has primitive but lively capitals depicting naked human figures, a siren, and a monster munching foliage. The horizontal mouldings just above the capitals are also carved, with birds, leaves, fleurs-de-lis, and lozenge designs. Although hardly a masterpiece of Périgordin architecture, this church

Below **An elegant fountain adds a stylish note to the severity of the church walls at Bussière-Badil.**

To the southwest lies the village of Champeaux, set in the valley of the Nizonne, another of the small rivers that bustle through Périgord Vert. Cliffs bristle to the north. There's an attractive Romanesque church with a broad crossing tower and an emphatic, though rather crude and weathered, ornamented west door. East of Champeaux, hidden in the woods, stands the much restored fifteenth-century Château de Puycheny, which, with its many towers and turrets, still forms a compact, attractive cluster of buildings. There is an even finer château west of the village: Bernardières. Built on a series of terraces of different heights overlooking the Nizonne, it is enclosed within ramparts; the lowest level, set on the valley floor, is partially moated. The castle towers date from the thirteenth and fourteenth centuries, and the living quarters from the seventeenth century. Founded in the twelfth century, Bernardières was besieged, though without success, by the French commander Bertrand du Guesclin in 1377. One of its owners, Antoine d'Authon, was

is a building of great stylistic purity, unsophisticated yet authentic and sure.

Drive eastwards, past Sceau-Saint-Angel, where there is yet another attractive Romanesque church, to a second village called Saint-Front. This one stands beside the Dronne, and is known as Saint-Front-la-Rivière. There is a lovely fifteenth-century château here built of pale grey stone, with attractively patterned tiles on the conical roof over the machicolated round tower. Just north of here is the little town of Saint-Pardoux-la-Rivière. The church is unexciting, though it does house a seventeenth-century polychrome statue of the Virgin and Child; the infant Jesus bears a remarkable resemblance to André Previn. Stroll into the town centre, keeping an eye out for the façade of the Hôtel des Voyageurs, which is enlivened by a sixteenth-century window with delightful carved projections depicting a jester and a bagpiper.

Continue north to Champs-Romain. The attraction here is not the village but a waterfall nearby known as the Saut du Chalard, reached by a footpath. The waterfall, formed where the Dronne cascades between the rugged slopes of its valley, is, while scarcely a Niagara, a reminder of the wildness concealed in the valleys of Périgord Vert. Drive on to Augignac, where there's a domed church and a ruined fifteenth-century *manoir*, and west to Saint-Estèphe. Here there is one of the small lakes known as *étangs*, and nearby a dirt road leads to the Roc Branlant, which is more impressive than it sounds, being a large squarish boulder balanced on a flat ledge by a rushing stream. Nearby is the Chapelet du Diable (the devil's rosary), a collection of boulders beneath which the rushing waters flow. The dirt road looks negotiable by car, but it isn't advisable. Better to park and walk. These natural wonders of the Nontronnais, though much touted, are, it has to be said, only remarkable in the context of the overall gentleness of the Dordogne landscape. In the Auvergne or Savoie they would go unremarked. Still, these relatively tame traces of natural ferocity are welcome contributions to the variety of the region.

Spring comes to a Dordogne farm: the wood supply has lasted all winter and sheep graze beneath the blossoms.

Before leaving Saint-Estèphe, take a glance at the modified twelfth-century church, attractively placed above a meadow and a pond. The main interest of the church lies in its furnishings. The pulpit and its canopy are splendidly carved and gilded and decorated with coloured panels of lesser quality. In the aisles are traces of frescoes, some heraldic, others of New Testament scenes. Although their quality is not high, they add a pleasing decorative note.

Continue north to Piégut, an unprepossessing little town set in a region of woods and small lakes. Its only attraction is the remarkably tall and slender round keep, set on a steep mound, all that remains of the château razed by Richard Lionheart in 1199. Just beyond Piégut is the village of Pluviers, where there's an attractive church of twelfth-century origin. One of the admirable later additions to the church is visible on the south side: a fine flamboyant window.

From here continue north to Champniers. The church reveals how close this part of the Dordogne is to the Limousin region. Built from granite, it is graced with an octagonal belfry, a typical feature of the Limousin Romanesque and common in these northern corners of the Dordogne. Close to the church stands the stark square twelfth-century keep of the former château; the crenellations are modern. Neighbouring Reilhac also has a twelfth-century church of granite. As in many hamlets of the region, the farmyard intrudes into the village. I had to tramp through the mud and step round the ducks to reach the broad south door, which is set under five wide arches. Enter the church and its tall nave lined with shallow blind arcades. A flight of steps leads up to the domed bay immediately preceding the chancel. Beneath the choir lurks a dark crypt, where there used to be a fountain, and perhaps still is, for it was much too dark to make out what was down there. The details of the interior are certainly crude, but the proportions are superb, and Reilhac is a good example of a parish church that is modest yet deeply impressive. There is a bonus in the form of no fewer than three fonts, one of which is a vast polylobed granite piece dating from the twelfth century.

From Reilhac drive westwards towards Busserolles, and continue to the small old town of Bussière-Badil. I was keen to visit the large and splendid church here and, finding it closed, applied to the nearest café. Helpful young men then dragged various old ladies away from their lunch tables, until eventually we found the guardian of the key. She politely informed me that the church was in fact open. I simply hadn't pushed hard enough. Having disrupted the life of the town for almost half an hour I felt embarrassed, but the good people of Bussière-Badil fortunately found it more amusing than irritating. The church was originally a Benedictine foundation, though it was altered at various later periods. Its style is mostly Limousin Romanesque, as its octagonal crossing tower establishes. Some machicolations remain over the chancel and nave, which were heightened by fortifications. You can gauge the original height of the church by the presence of carved projections that once marked the roof-line, which are, incidentally, of great variety. The finest carvings, however, are found on the west front, which shows the influence of the Saintonge style. The broad arches are beautifully carved with friezes of animals, leaves, and birds, while placed around the doorway are a number of twelfth-century statues of apostles; although headless, their postures are expressive and lively and the carving of the draperies is exceptional. The bas-reliefs placed lower down depicting such scenes as the Annunciation and the Nativity could well be pre-Romanesque.

The interior is equally fine. As at Saint-Privat-des-Près (see p. 39), the nave is flanked by narrow corridor aisles. All the capitals are splendidly carved, though many of them date from the sixteenth-century restoration. Some of the historiated capitals high up beneath the vaults are, sadly, hard to decipher without binoculars. Step beyond the domed crossing tower into the choir, which contains another series of magnificent capitals in deep relief, carvings of grandeur and complexity on the capitals supporting the arcading, and more modest grotesques and foliage above the columns on either side of the five windows. After the grandeur of Bussière-Badil, there's a change of mood at Varaignes to the southwest, a pleasant village set among woods and meadows, very typical of the Nontronnais. The château, now a museum of local culture, is in the middle of town and dates from the thirteenth century. The scale is domestic, despite the presence of two substantial towers. With its mullioned windows flanked by columns, the courtyard has a sixteenth-century appearance. In early

A staircase at Javerlhac employing a medieval version of recycling.

November a famous turkey market is held in Varaignes, and the birds are walked into town for 5 kilometres, a turkey trot of epic proportions.

On the other side of the Bandiat valley, a few kilometres southwest, lies La Chapelle-Saint-Robert. The foundry that used to support the village has gone, and been replaced in typical Nontronnais fashion by a slipper factory. This hillside village is the unlikely site of one of the noblest churches of the Dordogne. The great Benedictine priory was built in the twelfth century, but by the sixteenth century it was no longer functioning. The crossing tower of the church is typically Nontronnais with its tiers of arcading, and its proportions are especially fine. The west door is also flanked by arcades, and the doorway capitals depict elephants, a unique occurrence in the Dordogne. The interior draws the eye down the long nave, beneath the domed crossing, to the rounded apse. Here, too, there are fine capitals carved with beasts and foliage. The former priory, far too large for the needs of the village, is neglected and sadly bare of furnishings, but at least it has also remained unspoiled.

Javerlhac is situated in the Bandiat valley itself. In the village centre stands the stout château, overlooked by a large round machicolated tower and set within a small attractive park. Below the dormers of the living quarters carved panels have been inserted, while above the windows rise tall ornamented gables. Unusual features of the church, which is of twelfth-century origin, are its double nave and nineteenth-century domed chancel. In the southwest corner two mutilated fourteenth-century effigies lie beneath an arched recess.

South of the Bandiat valley lies Connezac, a hamlet set in lovely rolling hill country and dominated by its large seventeenth-century château. The living quarters are flanked by square towers, but there are no signs of fortifications, though a large fifteenth-century machicolated

The church at Javerlhac has two naves – and two elegant Gothic doorways.

tower does guard the ramparts that embrace the courtyard. A wing extends to the rear at right angles, and the spacious château is finely positioned on a large terrace. The neighbouring village of Beaussac is close to a clutch of Renaissance châteaux. One of them can be clearly seen on a clifftop a kilometre west of the village, a turreted range of buildings resembling a fortified farm more than a seigneurial residence. The cliffs themselves are riddled with caves and the buildings above certainly appear to be perilously positioned.

From Beaussac drive south to Saint-Sulpice-de-Mareuil, where the domed church has a very fine Romanesque doorway. The nearby sixteenth-century Château de la Faye is handsomely set in its own park. Lussas, a pretty village among woods typical of Périgord Vert, is about 10 kilometres to the northeast. Its gloomy church sports a richly moulded thirteenth-century south door, and a strange bas-relief depicting two animals (lions?) and a man's head. Just north of Lussas is the fine sixteenth-century Château de Beauvais. Two machicolated towers flank the living quarters, and the dormer windows, surmounted by triangular pediments and urns, are particularly attractive. There's an impressive dovecot nearby too.

Cross the Bandiat valley again and drive northeast to Saint-Martin-le-Pin. The twelfth-century church here has a typically Nontronnais tower, and a south door similar to the portal at Saint-Martial-de-Valette, ornamented with human figures and crude but very charming carvings of dragons with entwined tails. The interior has exceptionally beautiful proportions; the surfaces are all undecorated and so there is nothing to distract the eye and spirit. The apse has that rounded form the French call *cul-de-four*, best translated as oven-vaulted. This simple lovely church is an appropriate place at which to pause before returning to Nontron, since it encapsulates the modest but rich qualities of the Nontronnais countryside and the sturdy dignity of its churches. From Saint-Martin it is an easy drive back to Nontron.

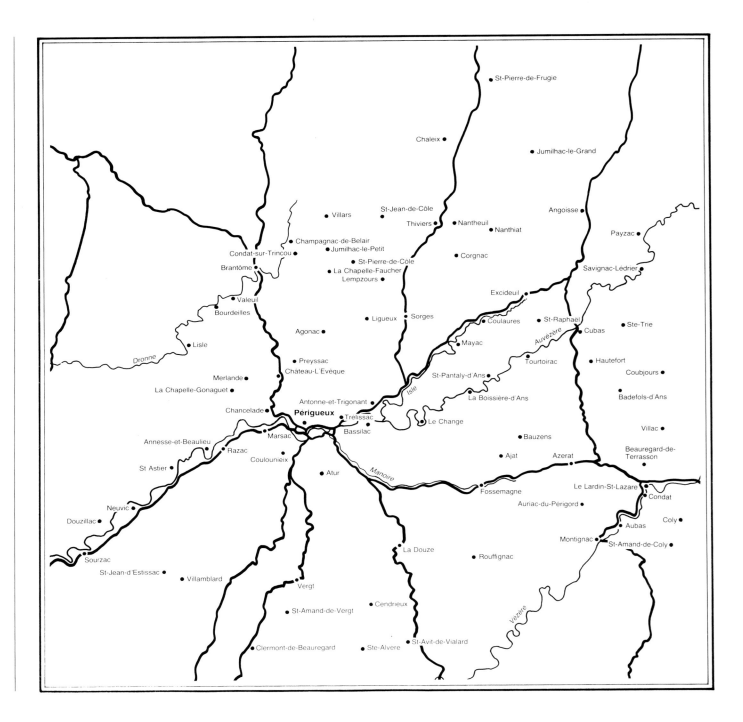

2
Around Périgueux

Périgueux – Chancelade – Merlande – Château-l'Evêque – Thiviers – Jumilhac-le-Grand – Saint-Jean-de-Côle – Puyguilhem – Brantôme – Bourdeilles – Château de Mont-Réal – Château de l'Herm – Ajat – Montignac – Saint-Amand-de-Coly – Hautefort – Tourtoirac

Gauls, Romans, and Monks: Périgueux

Périgueux was not always the principal city of the Dordogne. Bergerac, because of its site on the banks of the Dordogne river, was for centuries the virtual capital of Périgord. Nowadays Bergerac has the air of a provincial town, while Périgueux exudes the confidence and offers the refinements of a major city. It has been an important settlement since Roman times because of the fertility of the Isle valley and its position at the hub of a complex network of communications with other parts of France. The Gaulish tribe that gave the city its name, the Petrocorii, may have resented the Roman domination, but there's no doubt that the Romans transformed the settlement, which they named Vesunna, into an important and prosperous city, as the remaining monuments confirm.

Nowadays Périgueux is clustered round the prominent cathedral of Saint-Front, but in Roman times and the Middle Ages the city was focused on La Cité, the area now dominated by its other great church, Saint-Étienne. The urban area around Saint-Front, called Puy Saint-Front, sprang up after the pilgrimages to the tomb of St Front (later sacked by Protestants during the Wars of Religion) converted the little religious centre into a commercial one. Once Puy Saint-Front had won the protection of the French king, it rapidly superseded La Cité in economic importance. In the thirteenth century the rival settlements accepted that their survival against hostile forces would be more assured if

they presented a united front, and in 1251 they amalgamated. During the Hundred Years War, Périgueux adopted the French cause, even after the Treaty of Brétigny brought it under English sovereignty. The flourishing city suffered during the Wars of Religion, when it was captured by the Huguenots. Their destruction of two bays of Saint-Étienne speeded the decline of La Cité, and in 1669 its loss of rank was made official when the more prominently sited Saint-Front was promoted to cathedral status.

Modern-day Périgueux, with its excellent tourist facilities and splendid shops, is a pleasure to visit. Its sophistication and evident prosperity save it from the provincialism that constricts many other French towns of comparable size, while at the same time the city has remained compact and harmonious. It is easily explored on foot, and its 2000-year history has left an architectural legacy of the greatest diversity and interest. That legacy, moreover, is not merely a succession of great monuments. Many medieval houses and shops, indeed entire streets, are still standing and have been sensitively restored. The authorities have avoided the dangers of over-reverent restoration that can lead to fossilization; the old houses are preserved, but they are also lived in and used, and old Périgueux bustles with much the same vitality that it must have exuded during the few moments of the Middle Ages that weren't made miserable by war and disease.

Begin a visit to Périgueux near the town centre at the

Above **Not gravestones but millstones, gathered in from long defunct mills that centuries ago sustained the economy of the northern Dordogne.**

Left **The Rue du Calvaire in the old quarter of Périgueux, restored but not fossilized.**

century, the Arena became a refuge for the citizens of Vesunna, and that defensive function continued into the Middle Ages when it was used as a fortress. Towards the end of the Hundred Years War, the amphitheatre was dismantled and many of its stones reused to construct other buildings.

Just beyond the Arena stands the Porte Normande, one of the old gates of Vesunna; it dates from the third or early fourth centuries. Embedded in the short brutish section of town wall that adjoins it is an astonishing collection of recycled masonry; tombstones, cornices, fluted columns and other Roman remains piled together in what may well have been a hurried attempt to defend the city. The untidy patchwork now resembles an impromptu lapidary museum crammed into the smallest possible space. Pass through the Porte Normande and you will see the ruins of the Château Barrière. This château, with its twelfth-century keep and elegant doorway and Renaissance windows, was gutted by the Protestants in 1575, and now stands forlorn in a small park where you will also find a few more vestiges of the town wall. Follow the signs for the Tour de Vésone. As you cross the bridge over the railway, glance behind you at what appears to be a most unremarkable building until you notice that its walls are built from huge chunks of stone, probably plundered from the Arena. Shortly before you reach the tower, you'll see on the right an excavated Roman villa complete with baths, central heating, and frescoes.

The immense tower, 24 metres high and 17 metres in diameter, was, like the rather smaller tower attached to the Manoir de la Rigale at Villetoureix (see p. 33), once a Roman temple. Built of fairly small stones, its openings are faced with brick. No one knows whether the tower was originally roofed or whether it has always been open to the skies. It has no more grace or beauty than a gas storage tank, but its sheer size and bulk are awesome, and even after centuries of decay and plunder it remains impressive.

Walk up the Rue Romaine past more scraps of Roman wall to the former cathedral of Saint-Étienne. Despite demotion and destruction, it is still a powerful and moving building, though little enhanced by its transformation into an island stranded between streams of heavy traffic. Originally the church, which dates from the eleventh century, had four bays and a tower, but after the Huguenots had finished with

Syndicat d'Initiative, where free maps and up-to-date information are available. Walk first to the Arena, a ten-minute stroll from the town centre. Little remains of the first-century amphitheatre that once stood here, and the site has been converted into an attractive park and playground. In its heyday the amphitheatre accommodated 20,000 spectators, a reliable indication of the importance of Roman Vesunna. Some of the tunnels remain, and in their encrusted condition they bear a slight though entirely accidental resemblance to some of the caves and grottoes for which the Dordogne is celebrated. During the invasions of the third

it only two bays remained, one of which needed to be rebuilt. The one original dome is both the oldest and the largest in the Dordogne. As you enter the church and gaze at the vast and lofty space within, reflect on the ferocity of the combat that could destroy half of so mighty a building. Like many of the great churches of the Dordogne, Saint-Étienne is impressive not because of the richness of its ornament or furnishings, but because of its proportions. The height and breadth of its domes lift the space within so that it exudes serenity and grandeur. On the north wall an exquisitely decorated arch that once sheltered a bishop's tomb now soars over the font; excellent though the carving is, it seems incongruous in this huge still church that is otherwise so free of purely ornamental distractions. The majesty of Saint-Étienne is so complete that it is not even spoilt by the presence of a vast and gloomy baroque altarpiece, filling the entire south wall of the west bay.

From Saint-Étienne stands the convent school of Sainte-Marthe. Battle your way to the courtyard past the squads of nuns, who do look as if they suspect you of being about to abduct one of their charges. Here you'll find the Chapelle Saint-Jean, all that remains of the Bishop's Palace. It was during the Protestants' siege of the palace that Saint-Étienne was so terribly damaged. As architecture the chapel is worlds away from the former cathedral that overshadows it. Built in 1521, it is a showcase of Renaissance carving, and the single bay of the interior is encrusted with lavish niches and canopies, shallow rectangular columns, friezes and coats of arms, and roofed with splendid pointed vaulting and ornate bosses. Although the Dordogne is peppered with domestic building of this period, Renaissance church architecture is less common, and the episcopal chapel shows it at its exuberant best.

From Saint-Étienne take the Rue de la Cité to the Tour Mataguerre. There were once twenty-eight towers guarding the walls of Puy Saint-Front, and this tower is the only one still standing. It dates from 1477, though a tower stood on this spot for many earlier centuries. Bear left past the tower to the Rue des Farges. The houses numbered 4 to 6 are the

Maison des Dames de la Foi, a very rare example of twelfth-century domestic architecture and, not surprisingly, the oldest house in Périgueux. Here the French commander du Guesclin had his lodgings in the mid fourteenth century. Although much modified by the nuns who later occupied the house, the ornamented rounded arches are still clearly visible. At the end of the street is the excellent military museum (only open during the afternoon). Turn left into the Rue Aubergerie till you come to the turrets of the Hôtel D'Abzac de Ladouze, a fine fifteenth-century town house. At the foot of the street you'll see on the left the excessively restored Hôtel de Sallegourde. Backtrack a few metres and walk along Rue Saint-Roch, which is packed with ancient houses.

Follow the signs to Saint-Front. You'll emerge into a square; turn left, then right down the Rue de l'Hôtel de Ville. Bear right into the Place du Coderc, where the citizens used to keep their pigs and where a weekday market is held today, till you reach the corner of Rue de la Sagesse. In the courtyard of No. 1 is a beautiful square stone staircase of the mid sixteenth century. Its balusters and columns are inventive and varied, and the ceilings of the house are decorated with a splendid range of ornament. Note the depiction of a topless Venus laying down her arms, an indication that the house was first built for occupation by newly-weds. I can only hope that the bride was better looking than this Venus and that her breasts were correctly located. Rue de la Sagesse leads to a small square lined with old houses. On the right you'll see the Italianate Maison du Pâtissier of 1518 with its fortified porch. Turn right, then right again into the celebrated Rue Limogeanne, where at No. 12 you'll find a superb doorway beneath a coat of arms. No. 3, the Maison Estignard, also has a winsomely carved Renaissance doorway from the time of François I, whose reign (he died in 1547) brought true prosperity to the city for the first time since the Pax Romana. Indeed, the whole façade, with its moulded mullions and transoms, its lofty dormers, its shallow columns embellished with further ornament, constitutes a remarkable example of the Renaissance townhouse at its most lavish. The adjoining house, the Maison Lapeyre at No. 1, is equally striking. The Rue Limogeanne is perhaps the finest single street in Périgueux, and is also crammed with superb food shops.

The Place St Louis in the heart of the historic old town of Périgueux.

Backtrack a few metres and turn right into the Rue de la Miséricorde. At No. 2, the Hôtel Saint-Astier, you'll find another sixteenth-century stone staircase only slightly less exuberant than the staircase at No. 1, Rue de la Sagesse. Continue down the street. Just before the corner, turn right through an archway into a large, charmingly restored courtyard. At the corner itself, glance to the left for a view of the mesmerizingly hideous late nineteenth-century Masonic Lodge before crossing into the Rue de la Constitution. No. 3, the sixteenth-century Hôtel de Cremoux, has an attractive flamboyant doorway. A few metres further along enter the courtyard of the Logis Saint-Front (also called the Maison Gamenson), with its sixteenth-century polygonal staircase tower and seventeenth-century well with an oddly shaped cupola. Badly over-restored, the Logis is less graceful than many of its neighbours.

Bear right to the Place Daumesnil. This square, alongside the cathedral of Saint-Front, is named after one of

A delightful ornamented fountain in a quiet square in Périgueux.

Napoleon's most loyal generals, who was born here. Walk down towards the river and onto the bridge for a good view of the old houses along the quai. Furthest on the right is the Maison Lambert, with its rather pretentious Renaissance balustrade and loggia. Next to it is the formidable fifteenth-century Maison des Consuls, more a château than a house. On the corner stands the rather dull sixteenth-century Maison de Lur, and to the left of the bridge is the Vieux Moulin, a modest wooden house that appears to perch precariously (though it is well supported on stone corbels and wooden posts) on a small section of the town wall. The Vieux Moulin used to overhang the river. Now it overhangs the main road to Bordeaux. Return across this main road and walk a few metres back up the Avenue Daumesnil before turning right or left. This will bring you, according to the direction you choose, to either the Rue Port de Graule or the Rue Sainte-Marthe, which, free of expensive shops and restaurants, convey perhaps more accurately than the splendours of Rue Limogeanne how the ordinary streets of old Périgueux must have looked – and smelt.

For some time now you will have been skirting around the unmistakable bulk of the cathedral of Saint-Front. It is now time to confront it. I remarked earlier on the ugliness of the Masonic Lodge, but it is a thing of beauty compared to the icy geometry of Saint-Front. There once was, no doubt, a great church here, a huge domed edifice that must have been Western Europe's answer to Hagia Sophia in Istanbul. Then in the nineteenth century a vandal called Abadie got his hands on Saint-Front and 'restored' it. (He also 'restored' the cathedral at Angoulême, with equally appalling results.) It's as if he'd built a plaster model of Saint-Front, correct in all dimensions, then inflated it to full size. Abadie's cathedral has as much life to it as a morgue. The smoothness of the masonry sounds the alarm, and a first glance at the interior confirms one's worst suspicions. Yes, the proportions may still be as they were, and the sheer vastness of the space, the domes still floating at an astonishing height, the vistas of the

Right **The fanciful domes and cones that Abadie added to the cathedral of Saint-Front at Périgueux. Restoration or vandalism?**

immense building opening up as one peers through the open towers – yes, towers, not piers – on which the central dome rests – all this is still mightily impressive. What has vanished entirely is the texture of old stone, the feeling, so fundamental in the most modest of Romanesque churches, that it was built by human hands and with human care.

There was a chapel on this site back in the sixth century, but this has vanished. Some remains of the eleventh-century church are, however, incorporated into the twelfth-century design we see today. Saint-Front is laid out in the form of a Greek cross. The east end is lengthened into an oven-vaulted apse which houses a vast seventeenth-century wooden altarpiece that came from the abbey at Ligueux. It's splendid in its way – barnacled with carvings of the Assumption and angels, and with twisted columns and urns and ornamental scrolls – and it usefully obscures some of Abadie's fanciful friezes and capitals. For Abadie was not content to rebuild; he invented ornament on the capitals and, worst of all, over the roofs. Those seventeen silly turrets with conical roofs that give Saint-Front its exotic skyline are all the work of Abadie. Only at the west end, beneath the immense 64-metre-high belfry, can we peer up at some relatively untouched parts of the original structure and get an inkling of how Saint-Front looked before Abadie killed it stone dead.

It used to be possible to visit the roofs and the tombs of fifth- to eighth-century Frankish kings in the cloisters, but they are being restored and no one is willing to predict when the work will be completed and these areas reopened.

The Musée du Périgord is the best museum in the Dordogne. From the cathedral take any street across the old town until you come to the Allées de Tourny, one of those large shady squares without which no French provincial city is complete. The museum faces onto it. In addition to collections of primitive art, fossils and shells, Egyptian mummies and Greek jars, you can see the fruits of the excavations of ancient Vesunna and other Roman sites nearby: fine mosaic pavements, frescoes, vases, inscriptions, busts, and gravestones. Most of the upper floor is devoted to prehistory: a substantial collection of Palaeolithic and Neolithic remains, mostly weapons and tools, and engraved stones. The captions are written with a light touch. Above the hunched skeleton of the important Chancelade Man a sign in copperplate script laments his decease 15,000 years ago. A drawing shows Stone Age men prowling the pavements close to the museum, and points out that, while these Palaeolithic men were taking a stroll, 'they mislaid their tools', which, sure enough, are on display. On leaving the museum, you can take an agreeable stroll up the Cours Tourny to the Place Montaigne and along the boulevard into nineteenth-century Périgueux, with its solid bank buildings and spacious shops. None of it is particularly distinguished as architecture, but it confirms that Périgueux is a civilized and habitable city.

Périgueux is also a splendid base for excursions and here I shall describe one that will fill a spare morning or afternoon and will take you to some of the most rewarding sites in the region. Take the main road to Angoulême till you reach the sprawling village of Chancelade. On the outskirts stands the abbey and, a few metres away, the delightful chapel of Saint-Jean. Of the abbey complex, only the church, begun in 1129, and a handful of abbatial buildings survive. In the early Middle Ages this was an important religious centre, and its temporal power was considerable too. But, like so many other foundations, it suffered greatly during the Hundred Years War. Centuries later, the Huguenots damaged it so severely that the church had to be rebuilt. A glance at the south side shows how extensive the rebuilding was. Its lower half, with round-headed windows and blind arcades, is clearly Romanesque, while the Gothic-style upper portions are seventeenth-century.

The symmetry of the charming blind arcades on the lavish west front has been wrecked by the intrusion of the abbatial buildings into this corner of the church. However, the doorway itself is intact, its pointed arches incised with dogtooth and other ornament. Two flights of steps lead from the entrance into the aisleless nave. The blind arcades of the exterior are repeated inside, and above the Gothic windows elegant ribs rise from corbels to vault the nave. The effect is

---

The lower portion of the abbey of Chancelade is Romanesque, the upper portion seventeenth-century, yet the two styles blend perfectly.

light and cheerful. The crossing is domed, but ruined by the presence of a dreadful modern canopy over the altar that looks as if it began life in a DIY shop. The fine vaults of the choir were erected when the church was rebuilt. Impressive panelled choir stalls line the walls and two powerful and dignified fourteenth-century frescoes, depicting St Christopher and St Thomas Becket, adorn the south side. In the south transept there is, of all things, a tiny Russian Orthodox chapel and a small prettily painted organ that is probably eighteenth-century.

The garden south of the church used to be the monks' cemetery. Adjoining the church to the west are the former abbatial dwellings added in the seventeenth and eighteenth centuries. These house an excellent museum of religious art, open during the summer, and from here you can also gain access to the abbey grounds and outbuildings. The greatest of the museum's treasures is a painting formerly attributed to Georges de la Tour. The chapel of Saint-Jean, built on a rock close to the church, was consecrated in 1147. Its fine west doorway resembles the abbey's. It's a rare delight to find two Romanesque churches not only cheek by jowl, but with design features that are clearly interrelated.

A winding drive northwest through the forest leads to La Chapelle-Gonaguet, where there stands a fortified twelfth-century church with admirable carved capitals. A massive but fairly routine seventeenth-century carved wooden altarpiece fills the height of the chancel. There's a more important monument to the northeast at Merlande, deep in the Feytaud forest, reached along a poorly marked road. Although just a few kilometres from Périgueux, Merlande feels remote and utterly tranquil. Its past was anything but peaceful, however. Founded in 1142, the priory was partly destroyed by the English in 1170, pillaged by the Huguenots, and sacked during the Revolution. It's astonishing that anything is left at all, even more so because in the nineteenth century the church was scheduled for demolition and the belfry had been taken down before the order was rescinded. The church was fortified in the sixteenth century (with limited success, it appears) and a corbelled watchtower projects from the chancel. Walk down the nave – one bay retains its original dome – past the massive Romanesque font to the low chancel arch, where voracious lions are depicted on the capitals. Steps lead up into the low-roofed chancel which is flanked by very fine blind arcades that rest on a stone bench. The capitals here, too, showing foliage and fantastical beasts, are of high quality, with inventively carved projections supporting the arches. Of the priory dwellings only one heavily restored sixteenth-century building remains.

Examine your map carefully before going on, for although Château-l'Evêque is only a few kilometres away, the roads across the forest are anything but direct. Château-l'Evêque (Castle of the Bishop), as the name suggests, used to be the country residence of the bishops of Périgueux. Their imposing château, now a hotel surrounded by high walls and set within a small park, still dominates the little town and this whole stretch of the Beauronne valley. It was built in the fourteenth century by Bishop Adhémar de Neuville, though the building was much altered in the sixteenth century; the mouldings around the Renaissance windows are of particularly good quality. Although the town church is a nineteenth-century structure, it does incorporate part of the château's chapel, where St Vincent de Paul was ordained in 1600. A very fast road will take you back to Périgueux.

Truffles and Castles: North of Périgueux

From the centre of Périgueux the main road to Angoulême conducts the roaring traffic past the city's two great churches and out through the industrial suburbs. Just after Château-l'Evêque turn right for Preyssac. There's an exceptional view of Bishop Adhémar's château from this road as you leave the valley. At Preyssac there's an imposing twelfth-century church with a large square fortified belfry. It looks like a dress rehearsal for the fortified church at Agonac, which one passes just before entering the little town. In fact, the church at Agonac, at least its nave, was built before Preyssac, in the eleventh century. This nave, three bays long, is a severe, rough-hewn structure with

---

Despite the ravages of medieval warfare, the Huguenots, the Revolution, and, ironically, a demolition order, the lovely priory of Merlande still stands in the woods outside Périgueux.

Above **A Renaissance-style drinking fountain enlivens a medieval wall at Thiviers.**

Left **Poplars parade like soldiers along the edges of a field ploughed after the harvest.**

thick, badly aligned piers; the masonry is broken only by small lancets and Gothic wall recesses. The bay immediately preceding the chancel and the choir itself are domed. Rising massively from the crossing is the fortified sixteenth-century tower. Continue into the village and make your way to the château, which crowns it. The ruins of the twelfth-century keep are barely visible behind the castle walls, and the seventeenth-century living quarters dominate the skyline. From the top of the village there are good views over the fields and woods that spread out on all sides, typical Dordogne countryside where walnuts are grown and truffles hunted. Opposite the grassy ramp that leads to the château an alley threads between shabby old houses to a fortified gateway, a remnant of the medieval fortifications.

Ligueux to the northeast is the site of a twelfth-century Benedictine convent. Unfortunately it is very difficult to visit the domed church, which dates from the 1180s and is enclosed together with the abbess's lodgings, a handsome seventeenth-century mansion. The entire property is owned by a Parisian family who only occasionally occupy it. It's irritating that the public are denied access to an important church in this way. Still, the principal buildings are clearly visible from the village. The abbess's lodgings indicate why, before the Revolution, the ordinary people resented the clergy as deeply as the nobility; the mansion, the magnificent seventeenth-century gateway separating village from church, and the extensive wall that surrounds the convent's domain suggest an ecclesiastical landholding as ostentatious and extensive as any nobleman's estate.

At Sorges, directly east of Ligueux, there is a charming château, the Manoir de Jaillac, and a much restored twelfth-century church. The fine Renaissance west doorway is flanked by shallow rectangular columns and carved medallions adorn the lintel. Inside the church are traces of heraldic frescoes, and carvings, mostly of heads and animals and clearly not in situ, have been inserted around the domed crossing. The church, though interesting, is not the principal reason for visiting Sorges, for the little town claims to be the truffle capital of the Dordogne. Since 1982 there has been a museum here devoted to the fungus, the Ecomusée de la Truffe – and an excellent little museum it is. Informative visual displays explain the botanical status of the truffle, its gastronomic uses, and methods of cultivating the stunted truffle oaks. Even more interesting, a special trail has been laid out south of the town that winds through plantations in various stages of growth. If you are going to be around Sorges in winter during the truffle-hunting season, inquire at a Syndicat d'Initiative about the expeditions organized by the museum that allow visitors to participate in an actual hunt with a truffle farmer and his pig. And for the latest news on *trufficulture*, tune in to Radio La Truffe, broadcast to the world from Sorges itself.

If Sorges is the truffle capital of the Dordogne, then the hilltop town of Thiviers to the north is its *foie gras* capital. During the winter months, beginning in late November, the Saturday morning markets held in the square in front of the church specialize in the sale of these bloated livers. When I visited the market, there were dozens of these delicacies on sale, but few takers. A glance at the prices of whole livers explained why. The church at Thiviers appears large but not especially interesting; the belfry is modern and the domed nave was replaced in 1515 by pointed vaults. However, it is well worth a visit. Although the crossing and chancel are also vaulted, the ribs spring from much earlier Romanesque piers that have remarkable late eleventh-century capitals. Those beneath the crossing are of exceptionally high quality, patterned with palm-leaf designs and depicting monsters swallowing men, lions and horses, as well as Christ and Mary Magdalene. Behind the church, piled against the steep slope, stands the stuccoed Renaissance château of Vaucocour, which has been quite horribly restored. Near the church are a few half-timbered overhanging houses, but modern-day Thiviers is for the most part an unalluring little town. The cluster of buildings around the hilltop must have been far more dramatic before the ramparts were dismantled in 1575.

East of Thiviers is the village of Nantheuil with its château and attractive fortified Romanesque priory. In the north aisle stands an elaborate seventeenth-century gilt altarpiece constructed under Franciscan auspices; it is crowded with statues and portrays scenes from the life of the Virgin. From Nantheuil make your way across country southwards to Corgnac in the Isle valley. A saw-mill still operates close to the river, which is crossed by a fine medieval bridge with cut-waters. North of the village stands the powerful Château de Laxion. It was probably built in the late sixteenth century, during the Wars of Religion, which would explain its ferociously fortified appearance. Although there once was a drawbridge in front of the main entrance tower, there is no evidence that Laxion was ever moated. The buildings are ranged around a central courtyard, and at each corner stands a massive round tower. Until recently Laxion was in deplorable condition – three of the towers had lost their roofs – but it is now being restored. Some of its picturesque characteristics, such as the undulating roof tiles, are of course a symptom of the decay below the surface; a joy to the eye must mean a headache for the owner. I was shown round by one of the young men helping to restore it. After taking me into the attics, where I could see the complexity and rough beauty of the vast timber beams, we crawled out onto the sentry walks that circle the towers, not an experience I recommend to anyone with no head for heights. When the restorations are completed, apartments will be let to visitors and the château should take on a new lease of life.

Laxion, for all its raw splendour, has a grim feel to it, so it's a relief to head north again to the charming hamlet of Nanthiat. The military character of the towers of the château has been modified to impose a more domestic atmosphere on the building: some of the machicolations have been replaced by an elegant ornamented window. The unpretentious living quarters were added in the seventeenth and eighteenth centuries. Opposite the château stand a modest church of Romanesque origin and a seventeenth-century stone Calvary.

From Nanthiat it's a delightful drive up the mostly wooded Isle valley to Jumilhac-le-Grand. The village itself is far from *grand*, but its magnificent château certainly is. Built on a rocky outcrop overlooking the Isle valley, it is one of the most imposing of all the castles of the Dordogne. Of the fortress that stood here in the twelfth century, nothing survives. The hefty grey central block we see today has a fourteenth-century core but was substantially altered in the late sixteenth century, when the property was acquired by a wealthy ironmaster, Antoine Chapelle. The two broad side wings that terminate in square towers were added in the seventeenth century, employing a similar stone to that used in the tall irregular main block, so that the later wings blend beautifully with the schist of the medieval castle. Jumilhac is justly famed for the fantastical roofscape Chapelle added. Above the machicolated sentry walks and the slate roofs rises a panoply of turrets, lanterns, dormers, pepperpot roofs and chimneys, all capped with a dazzling display of varied lead ornaments, depicting birds, human figures and angels.

Considering the hugeness of the château, the interior is comparatively modest, though the staircases and halls of the seventeenth-century wings are on a more spacious scale. The most famous room, known as 'La Fileuse' (the spinner), is decorated with naive frescoes painted, legend has it, by an unfaithful wife who was confined here. Far more sumptuous is the salon in one of the side wings, partly modelled on a room at Versailles and richly furnished. After a chequered history, which saw the castle pass through many hands, it was bought in 1954 by Count Odil de Jumilhac, and part of the château is open to the public.

The former castle chapel is now the parish church, and it's a curious building. Its octagonal crossing tower reminds us that we are on the edges of the Limousin. The choir is fourteenth-century, and its damp-stained walls are painted with large architectural motifs. Furnishings, in the form of choir stalls, an altarpiece, and statuary, some of quite high quality, fill the choir. The effect is grandiose but shabby, scarcely worthy of the splendid castle the chapel adjoins. One would imagine that the château would overwhelm the village entirely, but it has been incorporated into it with a charm that does nothing to lessen its grandeur. The fourth side of the château is filled with an arcade low enough to allow a good view of the courtyard from the upper part of the large village square, which slopes up the hillside. Thus the château itself becomes one side of the village *place*. Beyond the square, an avenue of trees in effect forms a small park. In this way castle and village supplement each other perfectly.

The unhurried traveller could do worse than drive north through wild and beautiful valleys to Saint-Pierre-de-Frugie, close to the Limousin border. The church here has a charming wooden roof with carved bosses, not at all what one expects to find in the Dordogne, and nearby stands the sixteenth-century château, with its machicolated towers and ruined donjon. Or drive west from Jumilhac to the village of Chaleix, which also has a sixteenth-century château and an ancient forge, founded in Gallo-Roman times and now a country mansion. The more direct route, however, returns to Thiviers and goes on west to Saint-Jean-de-Côle. This impeccably maintained village deserves its fame on two counts: it has buildings of exceptional quality and interest, and the village itself has retained a charm that can have altered little over the centuries. Its narrow streets are crammed with half-timbered houses, roofed with the mossy red-brown tiles for which the village is famous. The best view of this roofscape can be had from the narrow medieval bridge that crosses the Côle.

The main square is lined by the remarkable church, the old covered market place (unfortunately attached to one of the apsidal chapels of the church, thus obscuring it) and the Château de la Marthonie. An Augustinian abbey was founded here in the late eleventh century by Renaud de Thiviers, Bishop of Périgueux, though the church was not built until the following century; the belfry is seventeenth-century. The abbey had a chequered history, and was abandoned for much of the fifteenth century. Eventually monastic life was resumed, but finally came to an end in 1904. The peculiar layout of the sandstone church is unique in the Dordogne, and is determined by the fact that the nave was never completed. Inside the church, one appears to be standing in a broad chancel area, since a pentagonal apse and two apsidal chapels radiate from the central space. This space was once domed with a vault that matched in size the domes of Saint-Étienne in Périgueux, but despite repeated rebuilding, the dome kept collapsing. Because of the vastness of this central space, the church seems to have no focus; the eye is drawn hither and thither rather than down a nave to the chancel. The main apse, though stacked with

The best view of the cloisters and roofs of the lovely little town of Saint-Jean-de-Côle is from this bridge.

fine seventeenth-century panelling and stalls, appears no more important than any other part of the church. In a south chapel reposes the effigy of a seventeenth-century bishop, while close to the chancel is a lumpish polychrome Virgin and Child dated 1611. Only part of the sixteenth-century cloister remains, but seen from the river bank (it's no longer accessible from the church) it's an attractive sight with latticed windows rising over the stonework of the tracery. The best feature of the church exterior is the array of projections and capitals depicting biblical and legendary scenes that support the blind arcades around the radiating chapels. It's easy to admire this church, its noble exterior and its splendid carvings, but it's not one that dwells in my affections. One is too aware of its failures: its failure to achieve completion, and the failure of its magnificent dome to stay in place.

From the main square both principal wings of the Château de la Marthonie are visible (open to the public). The keep is fourteenth-century, but the main living quarters were built over a century later by the wealthy Marthonie family. The château, particularly its windows, has an attractively random quality, but a more orderly element is introduced by the seventeenth-century wing built over stylish open arcades. With its camping site, crafts museum, hotels, and restaurants, Saint-Jean-de-Côle offers excellent facilities for visitors without destroying the charm and beauty that make it worth visiting in the first place.

Near Villars, to the west of Saint-Jean, stands another château built by the Marthonies. The great Château de Puyguilhem is one of the outstanding Renaissance houses of the Dordogne. Its special quality is that it still expresses the pride and personalities of those who built it. Mondot de la Marthonie, who began Puyguilhem in the early sixteenth century but died in 1517, was first president of the parliament of Bordeaux and Paris. The work was continued by his son Geoffroi, who completed it in 1530. Like most châteaux in the Dordogne, Puyguilhem is stoutly fortified, but this is yet another example of that anachronistic adherence to a style already thoroughly old-fashioned. Puyguilhem was built as a country house, not as a castle. Set on a gentle hillside, it grandly occupies a small park planted with old lime trees. Like so many other great houses, it lost the majority of its furnishings during the Revolution;

Exuberant Renaissance carving adorns much of the Château de Puyguilhem, including this pair of false windows over the tower.

although it has been restored and restocked with seventeenth- and eighteenth-century French furniture and tapestries, the uninhabited interior, which may be visited, is somewhat lifeless. Not so the exterior.

It's a complex composition, and the living quarters are flanked on one side by a fat round staircase tower with an ornamental frieze above the fortifications, and on the other by a square staircase tower, over which there's a parapet with dummy dormer windows. The dormers all along the roofs are especially fine, zestfully adorned with friezes and medallions and carved columns, and capped by elaborate superstructures. The chimneys are equally ornate. Plaques carved with rosettes and inscriptions give the date the round tower was completed, and initials that may be those of the château's builders. Inside, the staircases have beautifully decorated ceilings; realistic carvings of foliage and animals, including the salamander (the symbol of François I, and a common sight among the mansions of Périgueux too), enliven the stairwells. Some rooms retain their splendid Renaissance fireplaces; the finest of them all has panels depicting the Labours of Hercules. Climb up to the parapet above the square tower – from here your eye can wander freely over the roofs around you and over the surrounding countryside.

Although not visible from the roofs of Puyguilhem, just over a kilometre west of Villars are the ruins of the abbey of Boschaud, a Cistercian foundation of 1154 situated close to one of the pilgrimage routes to Compostela in Spain. The ruins are well preserved, and the complex chancel is fairly intact, as are the domed crossing and transepts. The Cistercians, reacting against the ostentation of Cluniac monks, eschewed all decoration, but their abbeys, and Boschaud is no exception, are invariably harmonious and beautiful. Cistercian austerity also required that their abbeys be built far from civilization, and Boschaud is typical in occupying a remote wooded site. Its isolation may explain why so much of the abbey is still standing, for it was already in ruins by the fifteenth century, and a hundred years ago was being used as part of a farm! South of the church are the remains of the cloister, and various rooms with fireplaces and moulded windows.

Four kilometres north of Villars are the Grottes de Villars, which were only discovered in 1953. Some Périgordin caves are worth visiting for their bizarre rock formations, others for their prehistoric paintings. Villars has both. There are galleries with bright white stalactites and other translucent concretions, and chambers decorated with paintings of the Upper Palaeolithic period that are disappointing only in comparison with some others to be found in the Dordogne. With so many attractions clustered around Villars, it's a shame that Villars itself should be of so little interest. There's a sixteenth- or early seventeenth-century church with a solid Renaissance-style west entrance, but it's a severe cold composition.

From Villars head south towards Jumilhac-le-Petit. From the hilltop chapel there's a splendid view of the Périgord Vert. The Romanesque chapel's an attractive building, with carved heads decorating the cornice that surrounds the apse; a colony of doves inhabits the roof. Clearly visible from the hill is a remarkable fortified farm; the elaboration of its towers and turrets shows that it was no ordinary farm, but, like the chapel, once the property of the powerful Templars. The road continues to La Chapelle-Faucher. On a cliff overlooking the River Côle looms the fine fifteenth-century château, which is partially gutted. Securely positioned behind two sets of ramparts and a massive gatehouse, it is best viewed from the opposite bank of the river. Between immense crenellated round towers sprawl the living quarters, with their hectic superstructure of turrets, machicolations, and pinnacled dormers. The village church is imposing too. The blind arcades on its exterior rise almost to the full height of the church. The domed crossing rests on fine capitals depicting humans and animals, all of a primitive design and shallow cut.

Not far from La Chapelle-Faucher are a few villages of considerable interest, such as Saint-Pierre-de-Côle, where the over-restored Romanesque church has an impressive west front. Two kilometres beyond Saint-Pierre you can see the ruins of the fifteenth-century Château de Bruzac; the gaping medieval towers loom like spectres out of the woods. South of Saint-Pierre is the excellent domed church at Lempzours. Northwest of La Chapelle are the little towns of Condat-sur-Trincou and Champagnac-de-Belair. The powerful fortified Romanesque church at Condat is built over the remains of a Gallo-Roman cemetery, while north of the church are remnants of the ramparts that once circled this hilltop village. South of Condat is the Dolmen de Pierrelevade. The small resort town of Champagnac-de-Belair has a large sixteenth-century church with an extravagant rose window and a richly flamboyant south door; on the north side a passageway has been formed beneath the flying buttresses. Champagnac also has one of the best restaurants in the Dordogne, the Moulin du Roc, a good indication that we are now within the orbit of Brantôme, the gastronomic centre of Périgord. In 1985 the Moulin achieved brief international fame when it was rumoured that John McEnroe had ordered vast quantities of its celebrated *foie gras* to be flown to the United States for his wedding party.

Brantôme, a gem of a town, is set on an island formed by a brief division of the River Dronne. Ideally, the visitor

should alternate the pleasures of sightseeing with those of the table, for there are four or five restaurants in or near Brantôme that make it a mecca for gourmets. Even though most of the town is crammed onto the little island, the most interesting buildings are on the mainland. Here, backed up against the hollowed-out cliffs that border the Dronne, a great abbey was founded in the early Middle Ages. Some credit Charlemagne with its foundation in 769, but that is not certain. No matter, for of this early structure nothing remains. Norman troops pillaged the abbey, and in 1075 it was entirely rebuilt. The oldest part of the abbey still standing is the extraordinary belfry. You can see it more easily from the island than from the abbey, for the tower, detached from the church, is built over a rock that juts out from the cliff face. This belfry is not just the oldest in the Dordogne, but one of the oldest in France. The complex eleventh-century structure has five ever smaller stages, many adorned with rough arcades, that climb up towards a pyramidal roof. This orderly upward progression is interrupted, but also urged on, by the huge steep gables on all sides – a most extraordinary composition. It certainly isn't beautiful or refined, but its scale and power speak volumes about the nature and fervour of religious faith, and of local pride a thousand years ago.

The abbey church has been rebuilt so many times that it's hard to assign a date to it. The domes that once vaulted the structure were replaced in the fourteenth century; and extensive restorations took place in the eighteenth and nineteenth centuries. Our friend Abadie, the vandal of Périgueux, got to work on Brantôme too, but with less disastrous consequences. It was he who rebuilt the fourteenth-century pointed vaults. The overall style of the church is Gothic, but an examination of its splendid capitals shows its Romanesque origins. Entering the west door you'll pass a large Romanesque capital that has been recycled as a font. Above it is a thirteenth-century bas-relief depicting the Massacre of the Innocents, and a scene showing the souls of the Innocents making their way heavenwards. In the

---

The River Dronne encircles Brantôme, with its mighty abbey and remarkable eleventh-century belfry.

baptistery you will find, appropriately enough, a fourteenth-century bas-relief of the Baptism of Christ, his nakedness cunningly concealed by an obliging angel.

West of the church are the few remaining arcades of the fifteenth-century cloister, which leads into the chapter-house, a square room with ribs rising, fountain-like, from a central pier. Beyond the cloister begins the long handsome block of mostly eighteenth-century abbatial buildings. The door opposite the church entrance leads onto a splendidly virile seventeenth-century stone staircase that climbs to the lengthy former monks' dormitory, now used for exhibitions. The top of the staircase, incidentally, offers the closest view of the awesome belfry. The abbatial buildings now serve as municipal offices and also house a museum devoted to the work of the local painter, Fernand Desmoulin. Walk into the courtyard, which is blocked at the rear by the cliffs. Caves have been hollowed out under the cliffs, and long ago they were inhabited. (On the road to Bourdeilles which skirts these same cliffs, you can see caves fronted with façades of houses that are still occupied.) A spring courses through some of the caves, providing water for a fountain as well as laundry facilities for the monks. In the cave nearest the church a large Crucifixion and Last Judgment have been carved into the rockface. These late sixteenth-century carvings are impressive from a distance, but closer inspection reveals a disappointing level of craftsmanship.

These urban monks seem to have had little in common with those of Boschaud; they evidently put no premium on austerity. The best indication of this lies just beyond the abbatial buildings. Walk past the bust of Brantôme's most famous abbot, Pierre de Bourdeilles, who is also helpfully known as Brantôme, to the round tower that once formed part of the town fortifications. Opposite it you'll see a delightful Renaissance pavilion built by an abbot in the 1530s. Cross the charming fourteenth-century elbow bridge to the gardens and you'll find two elegant summer-houses, where the monks could sit in the shade and contemplate the beauty of their surroundings. After seeing dozens of fortified churches, keeps and ramparts throughout northern Périgord, it is positively touching to come upon these signs of ease and relaxation in a land where neither could have been common. A walk round the gardens also shows how

The bust of Brantôme – soldier, cleric, historian, gossip-monger – at the town from which he took his name.

deftly the islanders make use of the divided Dronne. Many of the old houses, some of them galleried, have gardens that creep down to the water's edge.

Yet the island town itself is something of a disappointment after the splendours of the abbey. The main road from Périgueux to Angoulême blasts right through the middle of town, and visitors must dodge between articulated trucks travelling at alarming speeds through the narrow streets. I rented a house on this main street and had daily first-hand experience of this. At night the town was more tranquil, and I would spend peaceful evenings in front of the log fire, paying occasional visits to the toad who lived in the outhouse. Rue Joussen, however, off the Rue Gambetta, is mercifully free of heavy traffic and full of fine old houses. The street leads to another footbridge over a particularly lovely stretch of the Dronne. Do not leave Brantôme without making a short foray out on the Thiviers road to see the

dolmen. The Dordogne is richly endowed with these prehistoric sites, but few are as accessible, or as impressive, as this one.

Brantôme and its abbey enjoy a worldly, pleasure-loving atmosphere that I fancifully perceive as a legacy of the town's most famous abbot, Pierre de Bourdeilles. He was born in 1540 into a noble family and appointed abbot in 1555. Pierre was magnificently ill-equipped for the office. Not only was he a mere fifteen years old, but he showed few traces of piety. He didn't linger long in his splendid abbey, but scoured Europe in pursuit of his two principal obsessions: war and women. In one of his most famous exploits he accompanied Mary Queen of Scots to Leith in 1561. During this period the Wars of Religion were devastating the Dordogne and Pierre was naturally on the Catholic side. When the Protestant leader, Coligny, approached Brantôme in 1569 with the clear intention of obliterating the abbey, it was Pierre, with his reputation as a chivalric warrior, who helped persuade Coligny to spare the town. This was no mean achievement, especially since the very fact that a warrior and libertine such as Pierre could hold high ecclesiastical office since boyhood was a prominent example of the abuses that Protestants were attempting to end. A fall from a horse left Pierre a bed-ridden cripple and persuaded him to retire permanently to his abbey. The accident may have put a stop to his physical exploits in bed and battle, but it released energies of a different order. Pierre took up the pen and became a historian and memoirist; his taste for gossip and his acerbic style produced volumes still read today for their often scurrilous portrait of his times. His recollections may bear little relation to the truth, but they are unquestionably readable. In the days before *Deep Throat* was enjoyed by millions, Brantôme's *Les Dames Galantes* used to pass as mildly pornographic. He died in 1614.

The town of Bourdeilles, where Brantôme was born, lies a few kilometres down the Dronne valley, and it's an exceptionally pretty drive, past overhanging cliffs with caves below and small châteaux above. On the other side of the river is the village of Valeuil, with its fortified Romanesque church. Bourdeilles is a splendid little town, completely dominated by a magnificent château, appropriate to one of the four baronies of Périgord. There has been a castle on this site since the eleventh century, though the buildings we see today are of a later date. With its immense octagonal keep towering over what is in any case an imposing mass of ramparts and buildings, Bourdeilles presents a stunning profile from whichever direction one approaches it. The walls enclose two châteaux, quite separate, that sprawl along the cliffs that overlook the rushing Dronne.

The older of the two dates from the thirteenth century and was built by Gérard de Maumont. It fell into English hands in 1369 but was then recaptured by the French. The castle (which is open to the public) is approached through a number of gates guarding the three sets of ramparts and beneath machicolated walls patrolled by sentry walks. Eventually you reach the courtyard in front of the early fourteenth-century keep. This courtyard is in a ruinous state, but still visible are the stone window seats constructed like inglenooks on either side of recessed arrow slits. Climb the steps into the immense hall of the keep, once warmed by two Renaissance fireplaces. Here, too, there are window seats, and they show how massive the castle walls are: in some places they are almost 3 metres thick. Alongside the spiral staircase that leads up to the tower is an octagonal chamber with beautiful vaulting, a design repeated on the floors above. The long climb to the top is well worth it for the spectacular view. Looking down you can see the fine Gothic bridge that straddles the Dronne, the charming seventeenth-century fortified mill on a small prow-shaped island near the weir, and the spacious formal gardens laid out between the different sections of the castle.

The second château at Bourdeilles is a Renaissance building that was hurriedly erected by Jacquette de Montbron, wife of André de Bourdeilles, the brother of Pierre. She had invited Catherine de Medici to call at Bourdeilles and was determined to accommodate the queen and her court in style. Although Jacquette evidently went to a great deal of trouble, Catherine never turned up, to the fury of her hostess, who left the building incomplete. Catherine's loss is our gain, for the rectangular three-storey mansion is of great interest. Its exterior is fairly plain, though embellished in places with shallow rectangular columns and delicate friezes, and it's topped with a battlemented parapet. The original contents are no longer in place, but the château has been turned into a museum specializing in French and Spanish sixteenth- and seventeenth-century furniture. Unfortunately the guided tour moves too briskly past this splendid collection of chests, cabinets, religious statues, tapestries, ornately decorated beds, lovely tapestry chairs and rarities such as a sixteenth-century salt mill made of stone, a magnificent sixteenth-century Entombment from Burgundy, and a fine effigy of Jean de Chabannes. One original room has survived, and it's worth touring the mansion to see this alone. Called the Gold Room, its ceiling was sumptuously and cheerfully painted by Ambroise Le Noble in the 1560s. The walnut floor is original too, as are the frescoes; on one wall hangs a superbly preserved Fontainebleau tapestry depicting François I and his falconers.

From the castle you can spend a pleasant hour strolling down to the river and up to the church, which is of twelfth-century origin, though so heavily restored that anyone could be forgiven for ascribing it to the last century. Bourdeilles is full of attractive *manoirs* that would be worthy of closer inspection if they weren't so grandly overshadowed by the splendours of the château.

From Bourdeilles you can either return across country to Périgueux, or continue down the Dronne valley to Lisle. Although it is well equipped with tourist facilities, I would not put Lisle high on my list of favourite Dordogne resort towns. The town has a good church that dates from the late twelfth century, with excellent carved capitals in the nave, and a covered market place with stone columns. The drive back to Périgueux from Lisle passes through attractive wooded countryside.

Into the Heartland: South and East of Périgueux

This route explores the Isle valley before crossing the Barade forest and the attractive hill country to its north. From Périgueux drive south to Atur, a sprawling village set in open countryside. There's a long Romanesque church here with a domed crossing, but the main attraction of Atur is that it is one of three places in the Dordogne where you can see a 'lantern of the dead', one of those strange funerary monuments the precise use of which remains obscure. The one at Atur, which stands in the former graveyard, is

Below Two for the price of one: fourteenth-century keep and sixteenth-century château within the mighty walls of Bourdeilles.

Right The fortified church of Saint-Astier looms over this riverside town in the Isle valley.

slender and has four rectangular openings at the top and a small conical roof. It has entered French literature by featuring in the final sentence of Eugène Le Roy's famous novel *Jacquou le Croquant*: 'Like the lantern of the departed in the cemetery of Atur, I remain alone in the night and I wait for death.'

From Atur proceed northwest to Coulounieix, with its curious twelfth-century house (La Maladrerie) and the ruined sixteenth-century Château de la Rolphie. Continue to Marsac on the banks of the Isle and drive downstream to Razac, where across the river lies the hamlet of Annesse-et-Beaulieu. Its church is of twelfth-century origin, though in the sixteenth century fine rib-vaulting was added to the nave. The crossing and chancel are filled with excellent seventeenth-century woodwork. Note, too, the unusual sixteenth-century wall safe in the pentagonal apse. Saint-Astier, further down the valley, is both an agricultural centre and the site of cement and shoemaking factories. Its church dates from the eleventh century, though its outward appearance, especially the massive west belfry, shows the extent of the mid fifteenth-century alterations. The south aisle is fortified, though most of the thirteenth-century machicolations beneath the sentry walk have been renewed. The fortifications didn't prevent the English from capturing the church in 1339, and it suffered further during the Wars of Religion. Above the west door of the aisle, which is decorated with wavy, flame-like lines in flamboyant style, are six large statues of apostles, four of which are still in a fine state of preservation. They clearly predate the aisle itself, and the distinguished art historian Jean Secret believes they are pre-Romanesque. The interior of the church is gloomy, since many of the nave windows have been blocked. The choir gleams with the handsome seventeenth-century stalls and misericords made from walnut wood. To visit the oldest part of the church, the eleventh-century crypt, you must obtain a key from the Syndicat d'Initiative, which conveniently faces the south side of the church in a street full of half-timbered houses. The Isle valley between Périgueux and Coutras, so suitable for the development of light industry, has attracted all the least appealing towns of the Dordogne – Mussidan and Montpon are especially grim – but Saint-Astier is amiable and dignified, and the streets around the church are worth exploring. Just outside the town is the powerful Château de Puy Ferrat, which dates from the fifteenth century and stands within a small park.

Neuvic is another shoemaking town a few kilometres downstream. Its Romanesque church has been ruined by later alterations, but the early sixteenth-century château is worth looking at. Although the façades are generously provided with machicolations and turrets, these gestures towards fortification seem half-hearted. The windows are unusually plain – how rare it is to see undecorated dormers in the Dordogne! Built by Annet de Fayolle, the château is now used as a school.

Leave the Isle for the side valley of the Vern to inspect the dramatic Château de Grignols. Perched on a rock, it dominates the little valley, though it is distinctly less impressive from close quarters. Constructed in the twelfth century, and much added to subsequently, Grignols belonged to the Talleyrand family. Assaulted by the Protestants during the Wars of Religion, it also played a part in the *croquants'* uprising in the early seventeenth century. Our own century has been unkind to this splendid landmark. The battlemented corner tower has been rebuilt in a toy-town style using smooth white masonry that conspicuously fails to blend with the weathered yellow limestone of the rest of Grignols. Two sets of ramparts encircle the moated castle, and the outer ones, also crassly restored, rise straight from the rock.

Return to Neuvic and continue down the valley. Shortly before Douzillac you'll pass the powerful Château de Mauriac. There has been a castle on this splendid riverside site since the twelfth century, though the present building, flanked by hefty machicolated towers, dates from the sixteenth. Douzillac itself is attractively situated on a hillside from which there are panoramic views of the Isle valley. Further down the valley, on the opposite bank, is the village of Sourzac, picturesque beneath rough cliffs, an unusual feature in this valley. Its essentially fifteenth-century church has a powerful west bell wall, and ruinous masonry attached to the wall indicates that there used to be a twelfth-century church here. Opposite the church a pretty cascade lopes down the cliff face.

From Sourzac head south to another side valley, that of the Crempse, which is dominated at this point by the

Pierrot, safe behind the massive walls of a farmhouse, laments the coming of autumn.

Château de Mont-Réal. The mostly Renaissance château is surrounded by ramparts that date from the eleventh century. The main living quarters are not especially attractive, but the early sixteenth-century chapel with its irregular towers and stone statues is charming. Inside repose the tombs and effigies of François de Pontbriant and his wife. It was François' descendant, Claude de Pontbriant, who, accompanying Cartier on his second visit to Canada, named a settlement Montréal. The chapel also contains the holy thorn carried by the unfortunate Sir John Talbot at the battle of Castillon (see p. 21). Much good it did him. Beyond the chapel stand some splendid high-roofed outbuildings.

Cross the Crempse valley and drive east through lovely wooded hills to Saint-Jean-d'Estissac. This is not a famous village, but to me it encapsulates the appeal of the Dordogne. It has, of course, a Romanesque church, admittedly not a very distinguished one, behind which stands a handsome seventeenth-century *gentilhommière*, with a square dovecot attached to it. Just south of the village, overlooking the road to Saint-Hilaire, is an even lovelier house, the Manoir de la Ponsie, set on a broad terrace. Here, in and around one small village, is that blending of gentle countryside, farms, a church, and the houses of the gentry which is so characteristic of the Dordogne, a landscape that's settled and stable and in which each structure, be it modest or grandiose, plays its part. Just beyond Saint-Jean-d'Estissac lies Villamblard, where a distillery makes some of the liqueurs that are a speciality of the Dordogne. It's a town that frequently changed hands during the Hundred Years War and the Wars of Religion, though the damage done to the ruined Château Barrière is the result of a relatively recent accident. The gaping walls of the fifteenth-century building reveal Renaissance fireplaces and windows. From these sad ruins the broad main street leads up to the Hôtel de Ville (town hall).

Now drive southeast, crossing the Crempse again, and make your way to Clermont-de-Beauregard. As the road climbs up to the village you will see across the valley the splendid Château de la Gaubertie, proudly standing on a long terrace. Although heavily restored earlier this century, La Gaubertie retains its blend of medieval and Renaissance styles, with watchtowers and machicolations and corbels from the former period, and elegant windows from the later. Particularly lovely are the tall steep roofs over the sentry walks and the high slender chimneys emerging from them. Clermont itself is a bizarre place. Next to the nineteenth-century church stands the ruin of a very tall corner tower, its spiral staircase visible behind windows and gaping doors. On top of this late medieval tower has been placed a statue of the Virgin Mary, appropriately known as Notre Dame de la Tour. Close by stands a small château, relatively unspoiled, with massive towers and steep roofs.

To the east and north of here spreads a large area of woods and meadows with the town of Vergt at its centre. This is surely one of the duller stretches of the Dordogne. Vergt itself is a bastide town composed of a series of rectangles, some filled with houses, others left as open squares. Its dull hotels cater more to commercial travellers than to tourists, and this area is one of the very few in the Dordogne where it's hard to find good cooking. The one reason for stopping in Vergt is to glance at the church, which contains modern furnishings and ornaments of a high standard. Vergt, then, is no tourist centre, but an agricultural town specializing in strawberries, and as you cross this area you will frequently see sloping fields filled with rows of cloches sheltering the fragile plants. Unusually, not even the village churches have much to offer, and most of them date from the nineteenth century. Nor are there many great castles or houses in the region. South of Saint-Amand-de-Vergt, however, stands the splendid fifteenth-century Château de Saint-Maurice, a copybook Périgordin château, complete with round and square towers, machicolations, Renaissance windows, tiled roofs – and the less common feature of a swimming pool. Behind the château a charming little Romanesque chapel overlooks the cemetery. One village with vestiges of character is Sainte-Alvère, about 15 kilometres east of Clermont. Little is left of the medieval castle that once stood here; it was destroyed by Lakanal during the Revolution, though by driving to the massive gateway at the top of the town, you can still view the remaining fortifications. The mediocre seventeenth-century church is typical of the uninspired ecclesiastical architecture in this region. If you still yearn to see another fortified Romanesque church, you will find one north of Sainte-Alvère at Cendrieux. East of Sainte-Alvère is the hamlet of Saint-Avit-de-Vialard, where the simple Romanesque church has been restored with exceptional dignity and warmth.

Whichever route you choose, you should emerge onto the Route Nationale east of Cendrieux and make your way to La Douze (sometimes referred to as Ladouze). It's best to park in the village, as you must obtain the church key from Claude's grocery. The good lady who runs the shop may eye you suspiciously and demand of you, as she did of me, 'Pour quoi faire?', but a little perseverance pays off. The Gothic church stands on a hillock just north of the village and its massive belfry is made even broader by its angle buttresses. Steps lead from the west door down into the vaulted nave. In a north chapel part of a lavish but crudely carved Roman column now serves as the font. Attached to a south pier is the sixteenth-century stone pulpit, with amateurish fluted columns, garlands, cherubs, and a representation of St Peter. In the elegant chancel is a stone altar, evidently by the same artist; it is of higher quality than the pulpit, though it does lack finesse. On either side of a bas-relief of the Crucifixion kneel the figures of Pierre d'Abzac, Seigneur of La Douze, and his wife Jeanne de Bourdeilles. A later Pierre d'Abzac had the misfortune to be accused of murder and, despite his protestations of innocence, was eventually executed. With his death the Abzac family ceased to inhabit the castle at La Douze, which crumbled away. Today nothing is left to remind us of the lords of La Douze except the memorials in the powerful church.

Taking the road to Les Eyzies, look out for signs to the Grotte de Rouffignac to the left. Rouffignac is one of the most spectacular of the underground caverns of the Dordogne, not least because its length requires visitors to ride a small electric train. It's a dramatic little journey, since only the lights of the train and the torch of the guide illuminate the darkness. The tunnels at Rouffignac, gouged out by water erosion, are on two levels, and the lower, which is closed to the public, is 10 kilometres in length. In prehistoric times there were two principal groups of inhabitants in these caves: bears, whose favourite spots for hibernation can still be seen, and Magdalenian man. Rouffignac has more to offer than the genuine excitement of moving through these long tunnels deep under the earth, for the walls and roofs were lavishly decorated by their early inhabitants. You can clearly make out designs of horses, rhinoceroses, and mammoths; some were engraved, others painted with a mixture of magnesium dioxide and clay. The astonishing thing about Rouffignac is that it is not, like so many other painted caves in the region, a fairly recent discovery. These tunnels have been visited for centuries, but only in 1956 were the cave paintings identified as late Magdalenian work by Professor Nougier, and even today some experts question their authenticity. The local people, however, must have known of the ancient paintings, for they left graffiti scrawled over the prehistoric work. Fortunately, this early nineteenth-century vandalism has only partially obscured the remarkable designs, the finest of which are a magnificent frieze of mammoths and a portrait of two stags in combat.

The village of Rouffignac lies to the north. It is that rarity in the Dordogne, a modern village. The Germans shot or deported the villagers and razed the old town in March 1944 as a reprisal for Resistance activities, and it was later rebuilt in a traditional style. Only the church, one of the best flamboyant buildings in the Dordogne, was spared. Below the ugly west belfry a porch shelters a splendid though much mutilated doorway of 1530. On what remains of the finely carved pillars and lintel are faded representations of sirens, and the doorway has a carved festoon of flowers that seems quite secular in spirit. The aisled interior is equally exuberant, the cylindrical piers being gripped on all sides by twisted attached columns.

Continue north into the forest of the Barade and make for the Château de l'Herm (open to visitors). The forest may disappoint those expecting vast tracts of unbroken woodland. Before the Revolution, though, the forest was both wild and dangerous, and L'Herm recalls those perilous times. Built in 1512 by Jean III de Calvimont, it was the scene of violence when Jean's son, Jean IV, was killed there, and when Jean's granddaughter Marguerite was assassinated on the orders of her husband, François d'Aubusson, who found murder more convenient than divorce in those religious times. Other unsavoury deeds are alleged to have taken place within its sombre walls, and Eugène Le Roy set much of *Jacquou le Croquant* in the Barade forest, and installed the villainous character Comte de Nansac at L'Herm itself. The ruined château still makes a sinister impression on the visitor. You approach it through a copse and cross the moat to an octagonal tower with a magnificent floridly decorated doorway topped with pinnacles. Other towers, thick and round, are attached to the main rectangular block. The main living quarters are Renaissance in style. Inside, the floors have disappeared, exposing layer upon layer of Renaissance fireplaces and doorways. Weeds and shrubs sprout from walls and windows, giving the château a desolate and neglected appearance.

From L'Herm drive north through the Barade to Fossemagne, with its twelfth- to fourteenth-century church, then head north to the former Templar village of Ajat, where the church and château stand side by side on a slope. The fortified choir of the church is particularly lovely, a broad oven-vaulted structure with blind arcades that is roofed with *lauzes*. The adjacent château dates from the fourteenth and sixteenth centuries, and its two distinct blocks present confusing but diverting façades depending on which direction you look at them from. The half-timbered gallery

is positively quaint, a welcome touch amid so much forbidding masonry.

North of Ajat lies the hamlet of Bauzens. There was once a priory here, attached to the abbey at Tourtoirac to the north, but only the church and a dovecot survive. The twelfth-century church is very beautiful, yet little known. On the upper level of the west façade are three arcades with plain capitals. Below, a single arch shelters the door and rests on exquisitely cut capitals depicting tendrils emerging from the mouths of beasts. Most of the nave is now roofless, and the tiny population of Bauzens can fit comfortably into the single remaining bay and the domed chancel. The east wall is dominated by a crude but powerful painted Crucifixion. A lovely dovecot stands in a field near the church, and both these structures are roofed with *lauzes*. Well off the beaten track, Bauzens is a profoundly rural spot, the only sounds the twittering of birds picking over the fields and the buzz of insects.

The wedding is long over but the churchyard is still adorned with cheerful paper decorations.

Drive north to the valley of the Auvézère, a lovely little river that begins as a mountain stream that we shall meet again among its high gorges (see p. 84). Many villages in this area have the suffix 'd'Ans', a Flemish word that came to the Dordogne when a medieval seigneur of Hautefort, who owned these lands, married off his daughter to a Flemish nobleman from Ans. At La Boissière-d'Ans there's a Romanesque church and a château, and nearby the eighteenth-century house of the ironmaster who owned the local forge, where he manufactured cannonballs. Along the river bank at Saint-Pantaly-d'Ans stand the romantic ruins of the fifteenth-century Château de Marqueyssac, another Hautefort property. Its towers still thrust into the sky, but most of the former living quarters are obscured by rampant weeds and creepers. The ruins have been imaginatively put to use as a rubbish dump. From the Auvézère valley you can drive north to Mayac, which boasts a church with a fine twelfth-century doorway and an unusual eighteenth-century château with a double staircase that sweeps up to the principal floor.

A simpler route is to continue down the winding Auvézère valley to Le Change, a delightful town of tightly packed houses and narrow streets. Just before the town you'll see on your right the twelfth-century chapel of Saint-Michel-d'Auberoche on a cliff near the ruined Château d'Auberoche, which was dismantled during the Hundred Years War. The little building is barrel-vaulted and its chancel was once decorated with Gothic frescoes; sadly they have all but disappeared. At Le Change the twelfth-century church is of scant interest, but, with two châteaux close by, it contributes to a charming urban group. Château de la Sandre has a fourteenth-century machicolated tower, and La Faurie a round tower from the sixteenth-century; both mansions have fifteenth-century living quarters. West of the church a lane leads to a wooden bridge over the river from which there are fine views of an old mill and of the rest of Le Change.

Near Antonne-et-Trigonant, a few kilometres before the looping Isle is met by the looping Auvézère, you can see the grey bulky form of the Château des Bories (open to the public). After the romantically random architectural concretions of such châteaux as Ajat, Les Bories seems oppressively rectangular, though the corners of the main building are accented by machicolated towers with conical roofs. Built at the end of the fifteenth century for Jeanne de Hautefort, it was not constructed as a forbidding fortress but as a country mansion, although its design shows little evidence of imagination or delight. The interior is notable for a fine staircase and for a vaulted kitchen with an immense fireplace. This section of the Isle valley was much favoured by the nobility for their châteaux, and close to Les Bories are a number of other grandiose buildings: the fifteenth-century Château de Trigonant, the charming fifteenth-century walled Château de Caussade perched behind the village, and, between the two rivers, the eighteenth-century Château d'Escoire. At Bassilac, 2 kilometres or so to the south, is the sixteenth-century Château de Rognac and, close by, a seventeenth-century mill. The road back to Périgueux passes through the suburb of Trélissac. Its nineteenth-century château was built by the family of Pierre Magne, the notable minister who under Napoleon III brought direct benefits to his native Dordogne; it is now a branch of the city hospital. The main road leads back to Périgueux.

Medieval Terror, Classical Splendour: North of Montignac

Montignac, long a thriving agricultural centre, has more recently developed some light industry as well as facilities for the hordes of tourists who come here to visit Lascaux (see p. 119). A bridge spans the Vézère and from the south bank there is a good view of the ruined castle of the counts of Périgord, dating from the twelfth century but destroyed in the fourteenth, and of the terraces of houses rising up the hillsides. To the left is the fine seventeenth-century Hôtel de Bouilhac, with its terraces and balconies and many dormers. Some of the medieval houses along the north bank have charming wooden balconies. For a close view walk down the Quai Merilhou, from where you'll also be able to see the substantial old houses on the opposite bank. Cross the bridge, turn left down the Rue Daumesnil and left again into the narrow Rue de la Pegérie. This lane, lined with medieval

The Quai Merilhou at Montignac.

half-timbered houses, brings you to the thirteenth-century priory church with its *lauze*-covered roof and west belfry. Next door you'll find the Syndicat d'Initiative, the small local museum, and a second museum commemorating the novelist Eugène Le Roy.

From Montignac drive east to the Château de la Grande-Filolie, where, as so frequently in the Dordogne, a Renaissance mansion of the seventeenth century has been added to an older medieval wing. The château, with its chapel and farm buildings, must once have formed a complete community, virtually a village in itself. The buildings, which vary in style and height and self-importance, are united by their roofs of *lauzes*. Northeast of La Grande-Filolie lies Saint-Amand-de-Coly. Here stands the greatest fortified church in the Dordogne, an early twelfth-century building that achieves this supremacy both because of the rigour of its defences and because of the remarkable beauty of its interior. Even without its great abbey church, Saint-Amand would have much to recommend it, not least the beauty of its setting among lovely wooded hills. It's hard to realize that this gentle spot was the source of the gravest threats to life and property in the Middle Ages. In the heyday of the Augustinian abbey, hundreds of monks as well as villagers sought protection here.

This sense of danger is evident the moment you approach the church, for it is still surrounded by high walls. Yet these walls seem almost insignificant compared to the immense fortified west front. Above the early thirteenth-century entrance is an immense round-headed window surrounded by many moulded arches; this entire west front is gripped by a vast fourteenth-century wall of masonry, 4 metres thick, that defends the porch below. If you think of this west front as a donjon, which it really is, then in height and thickness it equals, and probably exceeds, the proportions of any other castle keep in the Dordogne. Other fortifications guard the nave and transepts, which are pierced by only the most perfunctory of windows. The chancel is slightly less intimidating than the rest of the church: it is flanked by the apsidal chapels of the transepts and has three Romanesque windows beneath a small circular window (known as an oculus). As you stand hemmed in between the mossy church walls and the tall rough-hewn walls of the outer fortifications, you may wonder, as I did,

why the builders placed the church against a hillside which might, it's reasonable to suppose, make it vulnerable from above. Certainly, the complex system of defences did not keep the abbey immune from attack. By the end of the Hundred Years War, only a single monk continued to inhabit the abbey. Years of monastic revival were interrupted again by the arrival of the Huguenots in 1575. Yet again the monks returned, but the Revolution put an end to religious life at Saint-Amand.

Steps lead from the west door up to the uneven flagstones of the main body of the church, essentially a tall two-bay nave without aisles. Beyond the spacious domed crossing, more steps lead to the severe but elegant chancel. Here three recessed windows survey the church with calm intensity, while above them the oculus illuminates the chancel vaults. The transepts are barrel-vaulted and have tall blind arcades that rise to a gallery halfway up the walls. From this corbelled gallery, in both transepts and chancel, doors lead to passages behind piers; some of the piers are hollow and contain staircases that climb to defensive chambers above. Saint-Amand is mostly free of ornament and relies for its effect on a purity of line and elegance of proportion rarely found in fortified churches.

A few kilometres to the north lies the valley of the little River Coly. The village of Coly itself is set on a hillside and many of its houses are luxuriantly bearded with ivy. A grassy track climbs to the top of the village, past some rampart walls with round watchtowers, to a little château. Its almost vertical hipped roof covered with *lauzes* is charming and eccentric, and in strong contrast to the mighty abbey at Saint-Amand that once owned it. North of Coly the little river runs into the Vézère at Condat, once an outpost of the Knights Hospitaller. Around the church are ranged the former buildings of the Knights and of the Templars, dominated by a fifteenth-century machicolated tower. Nearby are other *manoirs* of great charm and in the background rushes the often turbulent Vézère. The church is Romanesque but of little interest. Just north of Condat is

Massive proportions and walls 4 metres thick make Saint-Amand-de-Coly the mightiest fortified church in the Dordogne.

Above **At Condat-sur-Vézère the millstream still thunders beneath the bell-wall of the Romanesque church.**

the small industrial town of Le Lardin-Saint-Lazare. Its large paper mill is important for the economy of the region but hardly contributes to its beauty. Behind the town rise the steep roofs of the fine seventeenth-century Château de Peyraux; fifteenth-century round towers with pepperpot roofs shield the principal wing. Just beyond Peyraux lies Beauregard-de-Terrasson. As its name implies, there are fine views over the hills and woods towards Hautefort. By the time you reach Villac a few kilometres to the north, you will be in very different country. Gone are the golden-hued houses of the Vézère valley. The houses here, and the church, are built of a red sandstone the colour of dried blood. The effect is startling and sombre. Two walls, pierced to provide an open porch, project west from the façade of the mostly twelfth-century church, and at the top they are joined by a wooden structure and roofed to form a belfry – a curious design.

As you continue north towards Badefols-d'Ans and beyond you will see more houses and farms built from red sandstone. It is surprising how much the colour of the stone affects the atmosphere of the landscape. In late afternoon sunshine the stone glows with wonderful warmth, but on a grey winter day the russet blocks seem dour and grim. Near Hautefort are a number of villages with the suffix d'Ans (see p. 76), an indication that they once belonged to the Lord of Hautefort. Badefols too is within his former domains. The château at Badefols belonged for centuries to the Born family. The oldest part is the fourteenth-century keep, with its machicolations and sentry walk, while the main block and the adjoining square tower were built in the following century. If the château presents a stylistically uniform appearance, compact and solid, this is largely due to the major restoration work undertaken after the Germans attempted, with only partial success, to raze the building in 1945. The church is of considerable interest and curiously

Below **Not a sleeping owl, but a weathered gatepost at Condat-sur-Vézère.**

laid out. The mutilated seventeenth-century south door opens into the vaulted side chapels. Because the nave is wider than the crossing arch, narrow passages have been thrust through from the nave into the transepts. There is attractive blind arcading in the chancel and transepts, and the capitals are of good quality.

I have a special fondness for this corner of the Dordogne, far from the major tourist areas of the Périgord Noir and Les Eyzies. This northeast corner of the department is deeply rural: meadows sweep down the hillsides and between them are thick oak woods and ancient farmhouses. It is a landscape to explore almost at random, chancing upon lovely views and modest villages such as Coubjours (there's a fine sixteenth-century pietà in the church), and eating or staying at the many unpretentious but welcoming auberges in the area. However, the high point of any trip to this region must be a visit to the Château de Hautefort. Its bold stately silhouette is visible from all sides and is quite distinct from that of any other château in the Dordogne. More a palace than a mansion, the symmetrical grandeur and opulence of Hautefort seem more appropriate to the Loire valley.

The celebrated troubadour, Bertrand de Born, fought his brother Constantine for possession of the medieval castle that stood here, Bertrand with the backing of Henry II's heir, Henri Court Mantel, Constantine with the support of Richard I of England. As Bertrand had persuaded Henri Court Mantel to rebel against his father (see p. 163), when his son was killed Henry II besieged Bertrand at the medieval château of Hautefort. The castle was totally destroyed, Bertrand surrendered and was sentenced to death; but he composed a *planh* (plaint) for the dead heir that so moved the king that his life was spared. Bertrand subsequently retired to the Cistercian monastery of Le Dalon. He composed more than love songs, for many of his most celebrated lyrics are in praise of the military virtues, while others are effective political propaganda. Dante was unimpressed by Bertrand's ardour and gallantry, and consigned him to one of the deeper circles of Hell for inciting Henri Court Mantel to rebel against his father. The name Hautefort only came into the family in the fourteenth century when Martha de Born married Hélie de Gontaut, who took the name Hautefort. The family was granted a marquisate in 1614, and Marie, daughter of the first marquis, was much esteemed both in

literary circles and by King Louis XIII, though she had the fortitude and good sense to decline to become mistress to this rather boring monarch. After many changes of ownership, the château came into the possession of the Baron de Bastard, whose widow still lives there. (It is open to the public.)

The architects of the present structure are the local man, Nicolas Rambourg, and the Parisian, Jacques Maigret; though little known, they evidently produced a masterpiece. From afar Hautefort can be seen sprawled across its great terraces, its heavy round towers, capped with lantern turrets, rising above the seventeenth-century wings. Below the terraces crouches the little town of Hautefort, utterly dominated by the palace that imperiously looks down, not so much onto it as over it. To enter the château, walk under a bridge that links the gardens to the vast terrace alongside the gatehouse, skirting the edge of the great park, which contains beautiful woodlands and shrubberies crossed by 15 kilometres of paths. The château itself is so broad that it is easy to underestimate its considerable height. Note the sheer size of the windows, each tier taller than the one below, rising to the slate-covered roofs. A drawbridge gives access to the fourteenth-century gatehouse, the sole remnant of medieval Hautefort. Everything else dates from the seventeenth century or later. From the enormous basements, which contain kitchens and servants' quarters and run the length of the building, steps lead up to the main courtyard, the *cour d'honneur*. The principal block rises above a grand arcade, while at right angles to it are the wings and towers. On the fourth side the courtyard is open, and there are superb views from the balustrade.

It is astonishing that the principal wing still exists, for in 1968 one of Madame de Bastard's guests disposed of a cigarette too carelessly, and so began a fire that, a few hours later, had reduced most of the château to a roofless shell. With the help of the Monuments Historiques, and the châtelaine's determination not to abandon her home, Hautefort has been superbly restored. Exact copies were made of beautiful doorcases and floors, but even so much was lost, including the magnificent carved chimneypieces. The chapel, which fills one of the wings and towers, was spared, and it still proclaims the pride of the Hauteforts. The family crest (sheep shears) appears repeatedly in the stone

Left **The mighty terraces at Hautefort, the château undiminished in its grandeur despite the ravages of a recent fire.**

Above **The village of Hautefort cringes beneath the walls of its stupendous château.**

floor and elsewhere; the fine furnishings date from the sixteenth and seventeenth centuries. Leading off from the main arcade is the grand staircase, the *escalier d'honneur*; this too was virtually destroyed by the fire and has been meticulously reconstructed. Rooms at either end of the arcade are furnished with items saved from the conflagration: seventeenth- and eighteenth-century beds and cabinets, and old Flemish and Aubusson tapestries. If you missed the Eugène Le Roy museum at Montignac, you are now given another chance, for in 1836 the novelist was born here, where his father was a steward, and a room honours Le Roy and his work. Finally, you will be taken up to the dome of the other tower. Above you rises a miracle of carpentry: dozens of huge chestnut beams curve up from the floor to meet near the top of the dome. Admiring this forest of stout beams, one can also appreciate how so substantial a building as Hautefort could have gone up in flames as rapidly as it did.

Before leaving Hautefort, descend into the town and take a look at the old hospital, built in the form of a Greek cross and contemporary in style as well as date with the château. The crossing is now the parish church, while the wings are used for exhibitions and other secular purposes.

Tourists pressed for time could continue northwest from Hautefort to Excideuil, but those with more leisure should continue their exploration of this lovely corner of the Dordogne by travelling up the Auvézère valley to Cubas. The church here, a former priory chapel, is set right beside the river. It's a much altered twelfth-century building, with an exceptionally well preserved set of carved heads ringing the three-sided apse. In the churchyard stands a slender thirteenth-century 'lantern of the dead', similar to the one at Atur (see p. 69). This lantern has four rectangular openings at the top, and a cross above the small conical roof. On a plateau to the east lies the village of Sainte-Trie. Inside its tall Romanesque church reposes a thirteenth-century stone effigy of an abbess, a rare survival in a parish church. Not far from the village are the ruins of the Cistercian abbey of Le Dalon.

Continue north to return to the Auvézère, and follow the winding road up the increasingly steep valley to the village of Savignac-Lédrier perched high above the gorges. The small restored Romanesque church is of slight architectural interest, though it does contain a medieval Madonna and a dark and dignified wooden altarpiece. However, one travels to this far corner to admire scenery more than architecture, for the gorges are spectacular. Across the Auvézère from Savignac is the splendidly situated sixteenth-century Château de la Forge, with its round towers and asymmetrical Renaissance windows. The village was once famous for its foundry, which was active from the early fifteenth century and only ceased operations in 1930. The seventeenth-century building that housed the foundry still stands close to the river. North of Savignac the road climbs high above the gorges to Payzac. Its large twelfth-century church is dominated by a massive square crossing tower. A large late Gothic west doorway leads into the restored yet remarkably pure interior. Contrasting with this austerity is the pulpit, a colossal baroque extravaganza, adorned with panels and the usual cherubim. (There's another notable pulpit in the church of the agricultural town of Angoisse to the northwest, as well as a jolly statue of a saint dated 1632.)

The small fruit-growing town of Excideuil stands southwest of here. On the edge of the old town is the castle, rising from a rocky hillock. Behind the forbidding rampart walls stand the early medieval keeps, which are variously dated from the eleventh century to the fourteenth, depending on which authority you believe. What seems most probable is that the two keeps were built in the eleventh and twelfth centuries by the viscounts of Limoges, but rebuilt in the fourteenth after the French commander, du Guesclin, recaptured the castle from the English. The property is not open to the public, but you can walk through the gateway to the turreted early seventeenth-century gatehouse with its worn coats of arms (the château once belonged to the Talleyrand family). Walk into the courtyard for a good view of the machicolated and crenellated keeps and the Renaissance wings. Unexpectedly, the two constituents of the château, the military and the elegantly domestic, blend well. The town itself climbs the broad slopes of a hill, and near the top stands the much restored Benedictine priory. Its flamboyant south

Medieval keep and Renaissance living quarters stand side by side at the château of Excideuil.

At a typical Dordogne farm household chores supplement the architectural detail.

door is exuberantly decorated with pinnacles and ogee arches and panelled arcading. Inside, apparently, is a Romanesque statue, a sixteenth-century pietà, and a fine seventeenth-century altarpiece and painting, but I have never found the church open. West of the church are some charming Renaissance houses, and No. 4, Rue Saint-Antoine, still retains its Gothic windows. The market square is also overlooked by some attractive houses.

Follow the River Loue downstream until you come to its confluence with the Isle. At this strategic point lies the attractive village of Coulaures, bypassed by most fast-moving travellers, but well worth a visit. By the bridge leading into the village notice the square seventeenth-century chapel of Notre-Dame-du-Pont, with its small belfry and hexagonal cupola perched on a high steep roof. The parish church lies just beyond it, over-restored but retaining a stylish Romanesque doorway flanked by ancient decorated coffin lids. The crossing tower and rounded apse

are fortified; within are traces of Gothic frescoes and well carved capitals. Opposite the church stands the Château de Conti, a nineteenth-century building adjoined by fifteenth-century towers. A far more splendid château lies 3 kilometres south of the village in the hills. The living quarters of La Cousse, a long high-roofed block with two flanking wings, are eighteenth-century, but the sturdy round tower dates from the fourteenth. The grounds are screened by high iron railings and an ornamental gateway.

From Coulaures either drive directly southeast to Tourtoirac or make a detour to Saint-Raphaël to the east, for there are exceptional views to be enjoyed from this spot. Within the much altered former Benedictine priory stands the stone tomb of St Rémy, who must have been a dwarf, and above it a small crude polychrome statue of the seated saint. The apse contains exceptional twelfth-century capitals. The market town of Tourtoirac in the Auvézère valley is, however, even more rewarding, for it is the site of a large Benedictine abbey. Enter the abbey grounds by the gate just east of the church. Bear right and you'll see the small twelfth-century hall that was once a chapel and is now a storeroom, and next to it a bread oven deep enough to bake dozens of loaves at a time. The east end of the church is truncated, for the apse destroyed during the Revolution was never replaced; consequently the square crossing tower rises straight up from the east, with semicircular transepts on either side. The interior of these transepts is in deplorable condition, but it is still possible to admire the tall domed vault under the belfry and, with greater difficulty, the capitals and corbels on the twelfth-century wall arcades. A door leads into the nave, largely rebuilt in the last century and now the parish church. Return to the garden and bear left this time, to the door marked 'Salle Capitulaire'. Inside there is a chapter-house decorated with carved capitals, including some of men tearing each other's beards. Nearby are the remains of the old cloister.

A plaque on a house near the church informs us that this is where Antoine Orélie de Tounens died. Who? Born in Périgord in 1825, this young lawyer set off for Chile to free the Indians from Spanish rule. He had little success, and was twice thrown out. Nevertheless he persisted to the point of proclaiming himself king of the Indians. None of his subjects, not to mention the Chilean government, were too convinced by his claim, however, and he was deported. A third expedition, this time to Patagonia, also came to nothing and King Orélie-Antoine I ended his days in Tourtoirac, where he died in 1878 and is buried in the cemetery.

From Tourtoirac drive back towards Hautefort and then 15 kilometres south to the Brive-Périgueux road. Bear right and you will soon come to the Château de Rastignac. It will look familiar, I dare say, but its resemblance to the White House in Washington is coincidental. It was built in the 1810s by the local architect Mathieu Blanchard, who designed the feature that it shares with the White House: a central semicircular row of columns looking out over a balustraded terrace. In a region of medieval and Renaissance châteaux it comes as a surprise to find this dignified Palladian mansion aristocratically surveying the country-side. Once again the occupying German army set a great building to the torch and this time succeeded in burning it down. Fortunately it has been skilfully rebuilt.

The nearby village of Azerat, with its lovely old houses and a Gothic chapel that centuries ago was the goal of a pilgrimage, is worth a visit before driving south to the Nauze valley and the ramshackle but attractive village of Auriac-du-Périgord. Its formidable Romanesque church possesses a most charming feature: a covered and balustraded stone bridge that links the upper nave with the presbytery. North of the village, and visible from it, perches the compact Château de la Faye high on a cliffside. The ruined keep dates from the twelfth century, while the square towers are fourteenth-century and the living quarters sixteenth-century. Nearby stands the fifteenth-century chapel of Saint-Rémy, a pretty vaulted building that attracted pilgrimages once word spread that the statue of the saint kept here had miraculous healing properties.

Return south to Montignac via Aubas, where the carved capitals in the church date from the eleventh century. The nearby seventeenth-century Château de Sauveboeuf was once owned by the Mirabeau family.

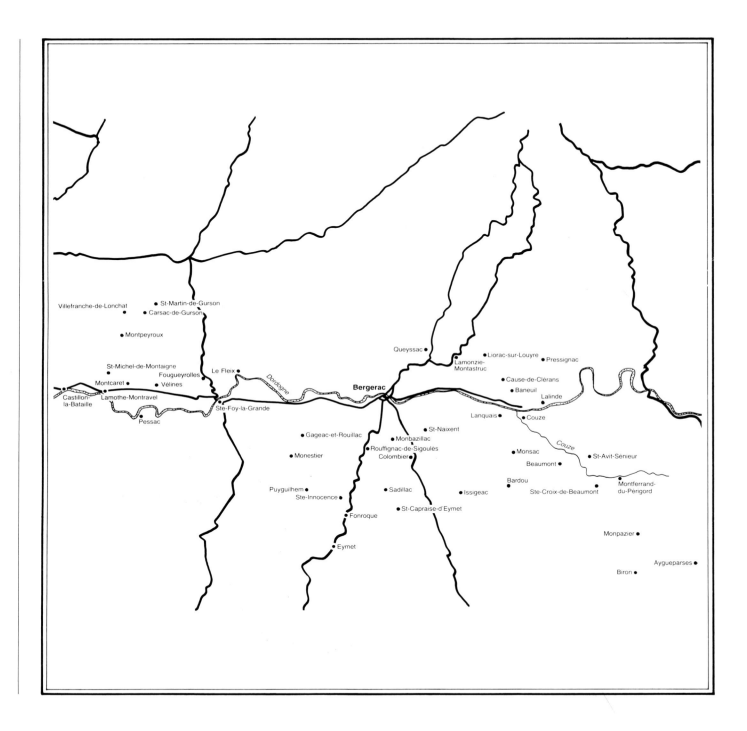

3
Around Bergerac

Bergerac — Monbazillac — Eymet — Montcaret —
Saint-Michel-de-Montaigne — Issigeac — Beaumont
— Monpazier — Biron — Saint-Avit-Sénieur —
Lanquais

Wine and Wisdom: West of Bergerac

Bergerac no longer shines with the importance it radiated some centuries ago when it was the leading city of the Dordogne, thanks to its connections with the wine and salt trades and its strategic position on the Dordogne river. Nevertheless, Bergerac is no backwater and it remains a thriving town. To this day commerce rather than tourism keeps it bustling, and this requires the visitor to seek out the city's attractions; they are not lavished on us. In addition to its unpretentious charms, Bergerac, with its decent hotels and restaurants, is an excellent base for exploring the southern Dordogne.

Start close to the river, on the north bank where the old city is located. The Quai Salvette is a popular spot with fishermen, and a marker on the corner of the quai and the Rue du Port shows the water levels reached when the river was in flood. As recently as the 1950s the waters rose high over the banks, though they never approached the disastrous levels that prevailed in the eighteenth century. From this spot the tiny Rue Salvine leads to the tranquil Place du Feu. Bear right along the Rue de l'Ancien Port past some well-restored half-timbered houses to the Maison Peyrarede, which contains the tobacco museum and the municipal museum. Any anxieties about links between tobacco and serious illness are sublimely ignored as the tobacco museum, the only such museum in France, chronicles the development of one of the Dordogne's leading

agricultural activities. Since 1927 Bergerac has also been the home of the Institut Expérimental du Tabac. The museum exhibits prints and snuffboxes that show how exuberantly early smokers regarded their addiction: some boxes are shaped like shoes or men's heads, while others, in ivory or enamel, are adorned with paintings of naked women. Less licence is shown in the actual production of the weed. Harvests are strictly regulated, and the large leaves are suspended on frames and dried in sheds (*séchoirs*) for two months before being pressed and packed. The second museum, housed within the same group of old buildings, dutifully traces the history of Bergerac and its area from prehistoric days to Gallo-Roman and medieval times. Old prints show how the city looked before its ramparts and moat were demolished on the orders of Richelieu in 1629. As a Protestant stronghold, Bergerac found itself in economic difficulties after 1685, when the Revocation of the Edict of Nantes prompted the emigration of half its citizens to the Low Countries and other Protestant havens.

On leaving the museums return down the Rue de l'Ancien Port till you see on your left the Protestant church of the Récollets and the delectable square between the Rue du Grand Moulin and the Rue de la Mirpe. Here you'll find a rather uninspired statue of Rostand's flamboyant creation, Cyrano de Bergerac. Another monument to Cyrano can be found in the Place de la République, where the cinema is also named after him, as is the best restaurant in town. Cyrano's

Cyrano de Bergerac may be a fictional character, but that hasn't stopped the city fathers from erecting a statue in his honour.

nose has proved a useful peg on which to hang the prestige of the town, although it filled the hero of Rostand's play with shame. Bergerac's appropriation of Rostand's colourful creation is understandable, though it has not the slightest historical foundation, for Cyrano was based on one Savinien de Cyrano, whose family was rooted in an entirely different Bergerac near Paris. Next to the Récollets you'll find a gate marked Maison du Vin. This leads to some medieval cloisters that are largely constructed of wood. In the far corner gapes a monastic bread oven. The buildings opening out onto the cloister house offices connected with the local wine trade, and a roofed stairway leads down from the cloisters to the wine cellars, which are still used for tastings though not for storage.

From the Rue de la Mirpe follow the signs for the Musée de l'Art Sacré and continue up a flight of steps into the heart of the old town and past the ungainly church of Saint-Jacques, an ancient foundation repeatedly restored and as glum inside as it is unattractive outside. Beyond the church you will come to the Grand' Rue, a pedestrian precinct full of shops that leads to the Place Gambetta and Abadie's church of Notre-Dame, an ugly nineteenth-century structure. It contains in its transepts two sixteenth-century Italian paintings (much admired by those who, unlike myself, have been able to make them out through the dim light) and an immense Aubusson tapestry depicting Bergerac's coat of arms. This part of the city is at its liveliest on Wednesdays and Saturdays, when the pavements and squares are crammed with market stalls.

Driving south out of Bergerac, you immediately see spread out before you along the broad river plain the vineyards of Monbazillac, first planted at least a thousand years ago; in the distance rise the slopes around the château where the best vineyards are situated. Monbazillac itself is a dull little village grouped around a grassy square, but nearby stands the grand château built by Charles d'Aydie in 1550. Like Puyguilhem and Les Bories, it was built in a style that was already anachronistic. The moats and towers were not entirely without purpose, since the history of the Dordogne encouraged its inhabitants to fear the worst, but nevertheless these châteaux were evidently built with pleasure as much as defence in mind. Monbazillac, with its pepperpot roofs and double tier of dormers, looks imposing from all angles, and the countryside returns the compliment by offering a magnificent panorama from the terrace behind the château. The prominence of wine in the local economy is made clear by the fact that since 1960 the château has been the property of the local cooperative, and in an outbuilding you can taste and buy the recent vintages, which are of a far higher quality than most cooperative-made wine. Inside the château you can inspect displays of local crafts – not twee pottery, but the implements used by such artisans as fishermen, wheelwrights and shoemakers. Other rooms elucidate the role of Protestantism in the region – for

What could be more French than these rows of poplars outside Bergerac?

Below The ungainly church of Saint-Jacques at Bergerac is in the heart of the bustling old town.

Right The fortifications of the lovely Château de Monbazillac were ornamental even when they were built in 1550.

Monbazillac, like Bergerac, was devoutly Huguenot – and display exhibits relating to the wine trade.

For an even better view of the vineyards, return to the village and follow the signs to the fifteenth-century Moulin de Malfourat, a disused mill, now lacking its sails, where the tourist is aided by a *table d'orientation*. From here continue south to Rouffignac-de-Sigoulès, though anyone with a keen interest in church architecture might want to make an eastward detour to Saint-Naixent (alternatively spelt Saint-Néxans), set among vineyards and low wooded hills. Its Romanesque church has an exuberant west front, decorated with ornamented arches and crude carvings, and topped with a bell wall in a vaguely Spanish style. At Rouffignac the Romanesque church is relatively plain, but is nonetheless a well-restored building of considerable dignity.

Just south of Rouffignac stands the splendid Château de Bridoire, built on an outcrop above a small valley. Despite, or possibly because of extensive restoration, this is one of the most romantic of all Périgordin châteaux, its pepperpot towers and steep roofs rising above the trees among which it is set. High walls, some built onto the rock, make it difficult to obtain a close view of the building, which is not open to the public. The courtyard is overlooked by the main living quarters, which are flanked by fifteenth-century machico-lated towers. There's a good view of the building from the rear, with its great expanses of grey stone and acres of brown-tiled roofs broken by gabled dormers and turrets. From this side, the castle walls plummet down to the brisk stream below.

From Bridoire there is a direct road south to Eymet, but you may prefer to make a detour past the villages of Sadillac and Saint-Capraise-d'Eymet. The church at Sadillac has been crudely stuccoed but it is a fine domed building that contains carved capitals of high quality. Adjoining the church is a dilapidated sixteenth-century *manoir*. The exterior of the church at Saint-Capraise is equally uninspired, and the interesting features are all found inside. There's an impressive tall domed crossing, and some excellent carved capitals, including one of the Last Supper which crowds round three sides of the northeast crossing pier. The furnishings are worth a close look too. The simple chairs, dated 1856, were apparently made by Eugénie, wife of Napoleon III, though no one at Saint-Capraise seemed to

Above **The pepperpot towers of Bridoire loom suddenly over the lush landscape of southern Périgord.**

have any idea why she went to so much trouble. It's more likely that the chairs were a donation by the Empress. The church also contains parts of an elaborate eighteenth-century altar and confessional in a debased Baroque style, and a badly painted seventeenth-century pulpit.

Eymet, a small market town on the Dropt river specializing in fruit preserves and vegetables, was founded as a French bastide by Alphonse de Poitiers. The construction of bastides permitted kings and overlords, whether French or English, to establish a foothold in areas such as the Dordogne, and also further south. Between 1250 and 1350, about 140 were founded. Families prepared to build, inhabit and defend them were granted certain

A sturdy dovecot retreating into the undergrowth near Bridoire.

Above **A vision of delights to come through an open window at Eymet.**

Left **The ruins of the fourteenth-century château at Eymet now house the local museum.**

There would be a covered market place in the square, though the church would be located in a nearby street. Patterns of building were rigid and standardized. Alleys divided the blocks to provide access to the rear of houses, and each house was divided from its neighbours by a very narrow passage called an *androne*, which served as a fire-break. Because of their regularity, bastides are not conventionally beautiful or picturesque; but they have a dignity and convey a sense of social organization that we do not normally associate with the war-torn medieval era. The Hundred Years War proved that bastides were no more impregnable than great fortress châteaux, but not even a century of siege and warfare could obliterate them from the landscape, and many still preserve their highly developed medieval quality.

Eymet displays this quality well, and its central square is probably the finest after Monpazier (see p. 105). Although many of the houses around the square, and the broad pointed arches on which they rest, are of stone, there are also some charming half-timbered houses on stout wooden supports. The rest of the town, though complete with its rectangular blocks and alleys, is not especially attractive and new façades give a bland tired appearance to many old houses. An unusual feature of Eymet is the presence of a château within its walls. Built in the fourteenth century, its ruins stand close to the neo-Gothic church. A round watch turret still perches on the castle walls, and the square keep is smothered in ivy. Pass under the fortified gateway into the courtyard where you'll find the small local museum, which is open during the summer.

From Eymet drive north to Fonroque, a small English bastide with a fortified church, and continue north to Sainte-Innocence, where the fifteenth-century church has a magnificent pinnacled and richly decorated west entrance in flamboyant style. Nearby is the hilltop village of Puyguilhem, which should not be confused with the great Renaissance château of that name (see p. 64). A great castle once stood here too, and at Puyguilhem the first cannon shots of the Hundred Years War were fired. Only the grey walls and the thirteenth-century gatehouse are still standing. Due north from here you will come to the incomplete English bastide of Monestier and the village of Gageac-et-Rouillac. The château here belonged to the family

privileges relating to trade, jurisdiction over the surrounding countryside, and in some cases freedom from military service; moreover the fortifications gave them greater protection than they would have enjoyed in their villages or farms. All bastides, whether English or French, share common features. The first, and most basic, is the grid plan, by which the town was divided into rectangular blocks. The early bastides, established for economic more than military reasons, were not fortified, but public pressure soon led to most bastides being ringed with walls and towers. Most bastides have lost their ramparts – Domme is an exception (see p. 152) – but they all preserve their original layout. In the centre of the town there would be a large square surrounded by houses built over open arcades, which provided shelter and space for traders to set up their stalls.

Left **This farmyard is near Fonroque, but it's a scene visible in countless rural villages in the southern Dordogne.**

Below left **Not all châteaux are ferocious castles. This one at Gageac-et-Rouillac is a country mansion – but fortified just in case.**

of the Protestant warrior, Geoffroi de Vivans, whose name recurs frequently in this region. It is entered across a dry moat and under a fortified gatehouse flanked by tall battlemented walls. On either side of the main block are fourteenth-century square towers topped by sentry walks. Although the sixteenth- and seventeenth-century living quarters are more recent than the medieval towers, the grey stone and weathered brown roof tiles give the ensemble grandeur and unity. The locked church at Gageac is said to contain an attractive pulpit and eighteenth-century statues of good quality.

Although Sainte-Foy-la-Grande lies technically in the department of the Gironde, anyone visiting these western reaches of the Dordogne river can hardly help passing through the little town, which is of considerable interest. An early bastide, it was, like Eymet, founded by Alphonse de Poitiers. Although it retains the standard grid plan, it has seen many alterations over the years. The main square still has some of its arcades, though most of the houses and arches are fairly recent. Nor is there a market place in the middle of the square, which instead is dominated by a dignified town hall. The large Gothic church has often been rebuilt. The original thirteenth-century Templars church was destroyed during the Wars of Religion in 1561, for Sainte-Foy was a staunchly Protestant town, and the present building dates from the mid seventeenth century. The fine tower and spire were added in 1871. The spacious aisled interior is darkened by good though over-elaborate stained glass, and the seventeenth-century pulpit is worth seeing. From the church walk east along the Rue de la République. Here, and on the Rue des Frères Reclus, which runs south from the same point, are some old houses, though few are especially noteworthy. Nos 94 and 96, Rue de la République, are decorated with carved wooden posts, and on Rue Louis Pasteur, a block south of the square, there's a fine medieval stone house with carved heads around the windows. On the north side of the town the river flows past a broad quai. Until well into the nineteenth century, Sainte-Foy was an overnight stop for the boatmen who used to make regular journeys down to Libourne from as far upstream as Souillac.

Take the same route, though by road rather than water, to the village of Pessac. This, too, is in the Gironde, but it does possess a church quite unlike any other in the region, for its eleventh-century bell wall is built of brick and decorated with three rotundas in a quasi-Byzantine style. Pessac also has a château with pepperpot roofs overlooking the river. North of Pessac lies the very important Gallo-Roman site of Montcaret. All round the church are major excavations, which can be visited, as can the small museum behind the church. In the first century a villa stood here but it was destroyed again in the following century. Some fine mosaic pavements have survived, their panels ornamented with designs of fish. The builders of the church re-employed some fourth-century Roman capitals, presumably taken from the ruins of the villa. The square tower, with its pre-Romanesque bas-reliefs depicting Adam and Eve, dates from the eleventh century. The combination of one of the best-preserved Gallo-Roman sites in the Dordogne and an early Romanesque church make Montcaret one of the most fascinating villages along this stretch of the river.

I mentioned that the first shots of the Hundred Years War were fired at Puyguilhem, and at Lamothe-Montravel, just west of Montcaret, you can find the spot where on 17 July 1453 the last shots rang out. The little wine town is close to the battlefield of Castillon, and halfway between Lamothe and Castillon itself stands the monument to the octogenarian English soldier, Sir John Talbot, who perished in the battle. In Lamothe-Montravel itself, attached to the town hall, are two towers, all that remains of a fifteenth-century château once owned by the archbishops of Bordeaux. Castillon-la-Bataille is a spaciously laid out little town on the banks of the Dordogne. The neo-classical town hall is an attractive building, as is the eighteenth-century church, and Castillon's streets and tree-lined *allées* have considerable charm.

It's tempting to stray beyond this westernmost point of the Dordogne, especially with the great wine estates of Saint-Émilion and Pomerol only a few kilometres away. I myself gave way to this oenophilic lure. There's no reason why you shouldn't do the same, but this book won't aid you and instead I shall direct you northeast from Castillon to Saint-Michel-de-Montaigne. In 1533 the great essayist Michel Eyquem de Montaigne was born at the château here, a property he inherited in 1568. Montaigne fulfilled public duties at court and also in Bordeaux, of which he was mayor for a time, but the world remembers him as a writer of rare eloquence and learning, his work a perfect expression of the tolerance, openness to inquiry, and love of humanity itself that characterized the finest flowering of the Renaissance. Though he lived through the Wars of Religion, he adopted a neutral position (in part because, while he himself was a

The ancient château of Saint-Michel-de-Montaigne burnt to the ground in the nineteenth century, to be replaced by a new château in lively neo-Gothic style.

Catholic, two of his brothers were Protestant) and maintained contact with leaders of the opposed sides, though his attempts to effect a reconciliation between the warring factions failed. Despite his disappointment, his humour and wisdom kept bitterness and disillusionment at bay. The life of the mind would continue despite everything.

The château where he was born (and died in 1592) was destroyed by fire in 1885, and it was rebuilt in an unashamedly nineteenth-century style. Fortunately the tower to which Montaigne retreated to think and write his essays survived the fire and may be visited. The estate is approached down an avenue of pines that leads directly to the tower. A wall connects it to a second tower, where his wife had her quarters, and a walkway along the top of the wall links the two structures. No doubt they met each other halfway. On the ground floor of the tower is a small chapel decorated with frescoes in a vaguely classical style. A hole communicating with an upper chamber enabled Montaigne to hear Mass without descending to the chapel. On the second floor is his bedroom; and on the floor above is the famous library, which once contained a thousand volumes, none of which survives. What can still be seen is the remarkable ceiling, with the rafters liberally painted and inscribed with Montaigne's favourite Latin and Greek maxims. Although the main block of the château is closed to the public, you can stroll onto the terraces and enjoy the fine view of the Lidoire valley, a view Montaigne described as 'a far-extending, rich and unresisted prospect'.

You should not leave the village of Saint-Michel without looking at the twelfth-century church, both because Montaigne's heart is buried in the chancel and because it is attractive in itself. From Saint-Michel drive north, crossing the Lidoire river, to Montpeyroux, a hilltop village with exceptionally fine views over the rolling hills. The rounded chancel of its twelfth-century church is sumptuous and beautiful. The blind arcading is meticulously ornamented, and the carved capitals, and almost one hundred carved heads along the cornice, are of high quality. The west front is in the Saintonge style, though the dome rising over the bay immediately preceding the chancel reminds us that we are still in the Dordogne. The mostly eighteenth-century Château de Mathecoulon stands next to the church, and across the lane from the mansion you'll see a park filled with magnificent old trees.

Four kilometres north from Montpeyroux is the small English bastide of Villefranche-de-Lonchat. The town has lost most of the features that would have made it recognizable as a bastide, though it still has a main square where you'll find a small regional museum and the slender fourteenth-century chapel of Sainte-Anne. The main church is outside the town on the road to Libourne. A Gothic structure, it contains interesting furnishings, including a twelfth-century font. From the east side of this wine-growing town there's a good view of the ruins of the Château de Gurson (or Gurçon) which, perched on top of a hill, dominate the surrounding countryside. You will get a closer view of the ruins when you continue east to Carsac-de-Gurson. The original castle was destroyed in 1254 and the property given in 1277 to Jean de Grailly, the steward of Edward I and Henry III and founder of many bastides. The castle was rebuilt in the fourteenth century but suffered badly during the Hundred Years War and had to be rebuilt again in the eighteenth. Montaigne paid regular visits to this neighbouring château and wrote his essay on the education of children for the Lady of Gurson. Surrounded by vineyards, Gurson is now a peaceful place, as is the hillside village of Carsac, where the twelfth-century church has a lavish façade in the Saintonge style. There's an even more fanciful west front on the large Romanesque church at nearby Saint-Martin-de-Gurson; the capitals on either side of the door are vivaciously carved with birds and animals. The effect is certainly lively, though rather crowded. A square crossing tower rises over the church, which is domed. The chancel was fortified in the fifteenth century.

Make your way back towards the valley of the Dordogne and the small wine- and fruit-growing town of Vélines. The church, of twelfth-century origin but with many later alterations, has a powerful east tower and an attractive stone pulpit dated 1733 built into the north wall. From Vélines begin the return journey to Bergerac through vineyard country, via Fougueyrolles, which offers fine views over the countryside and a fifteenth-century church, and then Le Fleix, a former Gallo-Roman settlement where numerous artifacts from the period have been unearthed. What remains of the sixteenth-century château is now the

A steep-pitched roof gives unexpected grandeur to this house near the church at Issigeac.

Protestant church. From Le Fleix (its name derives from the Latin *flexus*, referring to the bend of the river) it's an easy drive east to Bergerac.

Bastide Country: East of Bergerac

In this region there are some of the best-known bastides of the Dordogne as well as some splendid châteaux. Much of the countryside has a more southerly aspect than most of the Dordogne, and on the whole it's an expansive, gentle region. Leave Bergerac by the Agen road, skirt the Monbazillac hills, then briefly leave the Route Nationale to climb the vine-clad slopes to the hamlet of Colombier. The view is lovely, as is the church with its elaborate though weathered flamboyant west door, which the elderly but gracious old lady from the farm opposite will open for you. Inside, twisted columns against the nave wall support rough stone

vaults, a sixteenth-century addition to the original Romanesque building. The earlier style is represented by the plain but beautiful early thirteenth-century chancel. Near Colombier stands the badly restored Château de la Jaubertie, which Henry IV gave to his mistress Gabrielle d'Estrées late in the sixteenth century.

Return to the main road and continue southeast towards the delightful town of Issigeac. You will pass through a patchwork of farms that grow cereals and fruit, mostly flat country that reminds me as much of the Midi as of Périgord. There are a few typically Périgordin farmhouses, with their turrets and galleries, but equally many southern-style farms, with long low ranges set around courtyards. When the summer sun beats down on the mostly treeless landscape, one could easily imagine oneself somewhere near Toulouse or Moissac rather than close to the Dordogne valley. When you reach Issigeac, head for the main square, which is dominated by the large church built by Armand de Gontaut-Biron, Bishop of Sarlat (see p. 134). Work was begun in 1495 and completed in the 1520s. Stepped angle buttresses provide a broad base for the west belfry porch, which narrows to two octagonal stages at the top, and there are flying buttresses on the north side of the church. Facing the church is the late seventeenth-century Bishop's Palace, now the town hall, founded by a later bishop of Sarlat, François de Salignac. The long façade is terminated at both ends by square towers to which, unusually, slender round brick turrets are attached.

Issigeac is packed with small streets and alleys. No other small town in southern Périgord has quite this atmosphere. The half-timbered houses jutting out over the lanes remind me of Normandy, while the gardens flourishing well into December confirm that the Midi is not far away. And in bastide country it is quite refreshing to be in a town where curves are permitted and the eccentricities of vernacular architecture can flourish.

To the east, the hamlet of Bardou is set, like Issigeac, among expansive farmland. The grey stone church has a dignified twelfth-century entrance, but the principal attraction of Bardou is its palm-shaded château and park, just outside the village. Alongside the main seventeenth-century living quarters is a fifteenth-century corbelled square tower; the two styles blend because the same grey

101

At Issigeac even modest houses gain an element of grandeur when broad steps sweep up to the entrances.

stone and brown tiles are used throughout. Sadly, this elegant château is not open to the public. North of Bardou is the attractive village of Monsac; here broad farmlands blend with more characteristic mixed woodland. Most of the houses are built of lovely golden stone and roofed with old brown tiles. The church is nineteenth-century, though an ancient doorway is incorporated into it, and nearby stands a tall fifteenth-century *manoir* with a ruined round tower attached to it.

Winding roads lead northeast to the Château de Bannes, dramatically perched on a rock and glowering over the Couze valley. Like so many Renaissance châteaux, Bannes stands on the site of an earlier castle. The present château was erected for Armand de Gontaut-Biron, Bishop of Sarlat and builder of the church at Issigeac. Richly asymmetrical, its pepperpot towers cling to the main block of the château, which is approached across a drawbridge. Pinnacled

dormers break the roofline, and from each angle the château's appearance keeps changing, presenting new views, different juxtapositions of wall, window and turret. Unfortunately this magnificent château, apparently as grand on the inside as from the outside, is also closed to the public.

South of Bannes lies the English bastide of Beaumont, founded in 1272 by Lucas de Thanay. Since its original features, the fortifications and arcades, only survive in fragmentary form, its overall appearance is comparatively modern. West of the square a lane leads to the thirteenth-century Porte de Luzier, the only surviving gateway; originally there were sixteen. To see the remaining ramparts, walk out through the gate. What gives Beaumont special interest is its formidably fortified late thirteenth-century church. There are two towers at each end of it, all fortified. Loopholes peer from the defensive chambers at the top and the southwest tower is also machicolated. These stern fortifications contrast with the elegant rose window and balustrade of the façade. The west porch, with its finely carved frieze and canopied niches, is a decidedly refined piece of work. The gloomy interior, however, is as thrilling as a bar of milk chocolate, and what is memorable at Beaumont is the complexity and thoroughness of its defensive system. There is even an internal well to provide water during a long siege.

Three kilometres south of Beaumont is one of the Dordogne's finest and most accessible dolmens, the Dolmen de Blanc, which is both rough-hewn and fragile, like a house of cards, only made of slabs of rock. In the Middle Ages this prehistoric monument became a Christian site, when a girl lost in a storm prayed for help and these massive stones conveniently arranged themselves around her. There is a direct road from Beaumont to Monpazier, but a brief detour can be made to the interesting village of Sainte-Croix-de-Beaumont. The fortified Romanesque church, a Benedictine foundation, is remarkably unspoiled, and the capitals inside include a crude representation of Adam and Eve. Next to the

The Château de Bannes, as perfect a castle as you'll find in the Dordogne.

church is an old priory, half-ruined, that still has some elegant Gothic windows. The château dates from the seventeenth and eighteenth centuries.

Of all the bastides of the Dordogne, Monpazier is the best preserved. In 1284 Edward I instructed Jean de Grailly to found the bastide, and it was jointly administered by the king and by the lord of nearby Biron. Set on a flat hilltop above the Dropt, Monpazier was repeatedly besieged during the Hundred Years War and the Wars of Religion. It was also the scene of one of the *croquants'* uprisings, and in 1637 one of their leaders was executed in the main square. The old gateways at either end of the principal streets, the Rue Notre-Dame and the Rue Saint-Jacques, are still standing, as is the covered market place, rebuilt in the sixteenth century but still with the old vessels used for measuring goods. The main square is a delight, with its arcades and its old houses with their lovely Gothic and Renaissance windows. It only takes a few minutes to walk the length of the Rue Notre-Dame, a stroll that allows you to enjoy all the features of a bastide: its pleasing and orderly geometry, its straight streets and alleys, the narrow passages between the houses, the market square and arcades. The church of 1290 has been much renewed; the choir is fifteenth-century and the striking Renaissance west door, sadly vandalized during the Revolution, dates from the sixteenth. The Revolution also made its contribution, for pompous slogans were inscribed on the west front lauding *le peuple français*. The interior reveals a broad hall church, vaulted, with numerous side chapels and good fourteenth-century misericords.

The road to Biron passes the Château de Saint-Germain, a small fifteenth-century building flanked by towers, its site more exciting than its architecture. Biron, as the premier barony of Périgord, possesses one of the largest and most fascinating châteaux of the region, an awesome sight from whichever angle one approaches it. The hilltop castle is like an anthology of building styles, so frequently has it been rebuilt and added to. Because of its strategic importance, Biron was much fought over during the Middle Ages. Simon

Medieval arcades ring the square around the magnificent market at Monpazier.

de Montfort captured it on his rampage north after decimating the heretics known as Albigensians (who interpreted the Bible allegorically and rejected the flesh and material creation as evil), and the English occupied and partially destroyed the castle in the fifteenth century. From the eleventh century Biron was in the continuous possession of the Gontaut family, which produced some of the most colourful figures who strut across the stage of French history. Most celebrated of all was Charles de Gontaut-Biron, a favourite of Henri IV, who conferred countless honours on him: he was created a Marshal of France and Governor of Burgundy. These marks of favour didn't deter Charles from plotting repeatedly against his king, and his stubborn refusal even to apologise when caught planning an invasion of France in conjunction with the Duke of Savoy — even though the king had already pardoned him once for an equally treacherous plot — left Henri with no choice but to order his execution, and Charles lost his head in the Bastille in 1602. It was not until 120 years later that the barony of Périgord was restored to the Gontauts. Another Gontaut also lost his head, to the guillotine. The last Marquis de Biron, an inveterate gambler, grew so impoverished that he had to sell the château. Biron is now in the care of the state, which is fortunately undertaking long-term restoration work. Although the château appears to be built on a rock, it sits on an ordinary hilltop and is consequently prone to landslides, which makes maintenance all the more arduous.

Biron is more than a castle situated in a village, for the village only existed to serve the castle. This dependence is still noticeable today, since many of the houses are built within the outer walls. The small village square is overlooked by the lofty sixteenth-century castle chapel with its elegant balustrade. Although village and castle were interdependent, a strict division was maintained between the two, as the chapel's structure makes clear. The upper portion, entered from the castle courtyard, served the château, while the lower portion, entered from the village square, was a parish church. There was no direct communication between the two tiers.

The castle gate gives access to a grassy courtyard flanked by terraces, the stern twelfth-century keep, a fifteenth-century watchtower with modern machicolations and a Renaissance dormer, a sixteenth-century loggia, the sentry

walk along the walls, various outbuildings, and the chapel. When I first visited Biron, I found the entire castle unguarded, even by the usual fee-collecting custodian at the gate. So I gave myself a tour for half an hour until I was eventually spotted and apprehended by the custodian. She was irate, but I had been enjoying my lone conquest of Biron. By way of penance she gave me her longest and most exhaustive tour. Begin, as I did, at the chapel, which is entered through a resplendent flamboyant doorway decorated with elaborate tracery and ornamental friezes. At the east end, beneath pointed vaults, are the early sixteenth-century tombs of two of the Gontauts. Although mutilated during the Revolution, the tombs remain some of the finest examples of Renaissance carving in the Dordogne. The tomb chests are ornamented with friezes of grinning skulls and bas-reliefs depicting New Testament scenes. On top of the chests repose the effigies of Pons de Gontaut-Biron, who built the chapel, and his brother Armand, Bishop of Sarlat, who left so considerable an architectural legacy at Issigeac and Bannes. Until 1912 the chapel also contained a marvellous early sixteenth-century Entombment, but it was sold by the last gambling marquis, and is now at the Cloisters in New York. Two other examples of carving are worth notice: the exquisite reliquary frame in the chancel wall, and the effigy of a Gontaut discovered during excavations at the abbey of Cadouin (see p. 127) and returned to Biron.

On leaving the chapel, cross the courtyard, take the staircase up into a crenellated tower and walk through a vaulted fifteenth-century corridor into the upper courtyard. To the right is the old kitchen, which still contains a massive metal bowl in which the laundry was boiled – but only twice a year! On the far side of the courtyard is an eighteenth-century arcade under a broad arch; it offers panoramic views over the gently rolling woodlands and fields of southern Périgord and the Agenais. A door framed by a fifteenth-century ogee arch gives access to various chambers now undergoing restoration. The Renaissance windows overlooking the courtyard from this wing are especially fine. The wing opposite has immense reception rooms on two floors lit by tall eighteenth-century windows. Beneath them are the splendid eighteenth-century kitchens, among the largest in France.

To the traveller with a passion for Romanesque churches I recommend a detour to the east to see the isolated little church at Aygueparses. It has been restored, but well restored. Its most striking feature is a sheer thirteenth-century fortified west tower, but the church is remarkable as much for its simplicity and eloquence, for the way it fits into the landscape, as for its architectural features. It is in this kind of context that rustic art sheds its clumsiness, and the playful polychrome altarpiece seems entirely appropriate to the unassuming spirit of the place. From here or from Biron return to Monpazier and continue north to Montferrand-du-Périgord. This village overlooks the River Couze, the same pretty valley guarded by the château at Bannes. The village square is half filled by a sixteenth-century covered market supported on thick round limestone columns; a nineteenth-century church superseded the fine early Romanesque church still standing in the cemetery. Walk towards the top of the village – you'll pass a charming galleried house with a fine Renaissance window – up to the grassy terrace on which the well-restored medieval château stands. It's a tall oblong mass, without towers or external decoration, relieved only by a number of Gothic windows. Surrounding it are ramparts that date from the fourteenth century with a ruined corner tower. Apparently the precious relic of the holy cloth, kept for centuries at Cadouin, was hidden here during the Wars of Religion.

Continue northwest to the remarkable fortified church at Saint-Avit-Sénieur. The massive building dates from the eleventh century, though it was 500 years earlier that an abbey was founded here in memory of St Avitus, a sixth-century soldier who became a hermit. Some of the fortifications, such as the sentry walks above the nave, are a nineteenth-century invention, but even without these additions Saint-Avit would be a formidable structure of compelling ugliness. An immense southwest belfry of the late twelfth century rises to a great height, while next to it is a porch topped with fourteenth-century crenellations. To the northwest rises a much damaged second Romanesque belfry and a sentry walk connects the two towers. The interior is awesomely cavernous, great arches spanning the

A pastoral view of a much fought over castle, the Château de Biron.

breadth of the aisleless church framed by its thick eleventh-century walls, and moulded ribs vaulting the huge expanse. The great puzzle at Saint-Avit is whether these vaults are original. It seems unlikely. The mouldings are too sophisticated to match the supposed completion date of about 1150. Possibly the bays were domed, but architectural historians feel this too is unlikely. No one knows for sure. Saint-Avit is bare of decoration, though an eleventh-century stone lion stands in the nave, as does a font scooped out of a crudely carved capital. Some vestiges of the Augustinian monastery, which was razed by Protestants in 1576, are being excavated south of the church, and remnants of the eleventh-century cloisters and other monastic buildings are still visible.

From Saint-Avit drive northwest to Lalinde. The slender rectangle of the town spreads along the river bank, so that it isn't immediately apparent that Lalinde is a bastide, an English foundation of approximately 1270. Its citizens have made the most of such features as it possesses, and there are pretty gardens and terraces bordering the river. The town church is a large neo-Gothic structure, but on cliffs opposite stands the plain little Romanesque chapel of Saint-Front, from which there is an excellent view of the town. With its camping site and numerous hotels, Lalinde is a convenient base for exploring this stretch of the river and the many châteaux nearby. Continue westwards along the south bank to the busy little town of Couze. Papermaking has been the principal industry here since the fifteenth century, and mushroom-growing is another important local activity. The church with the spire is modern, but almost opposite it you'll spot the Romanesque church with its bell wall and funerary niches. The interior is less rewarding, since a false ceiling and partitions have been added to provide offices for the adjacent papermill that long ago acquired the redundant church.

Just west of Couze is the pleasant village of Lanquais, with its atrociously restored Romanesque church. However, on a nearby hillside stands the bulky château (open to the public). Of the fifteenth-century structure only a massive corbelled round tower remains, and, behind it, facing the courtyard, an octagonal staircase tower with a charming Renaissance door. The rest of the château was built in about 1570 in a cluttered and restless Renaissance style, though

At the Château de Lanquais, medieval towers do their best to blend in with the sixteenth-century wings.

reputedly designed by architects who also built part of the Louvre. Stone embellishments such as pediments and massive stone blocks separated by deep joints march up the façades, their verticality at odds with the horizontal flow of the building. The dormers, though, are invigoratingly excessive: ornamental scrolls frame the windows, over which urns stand on pedestals. In some cases these pedestals flank a fluted and scalloped niche which in turn is topped with a cornice upon which stand two more pedestals on either side of a complex rotunda! It would make a splendid cake. The interior of the château, with its monumental Renaissance chimneypieces and painted ceilings, is richly furnished in the Louis XIII style.

From Lanquais return to Couze and cross the Dordogne. Above the river, at Baneuil, you will find a Romanesque church with a powerful fortified crossing tower. The eleventh-century chancel is domed. South of the church is the fifteenth-century château, a low oblong block nudged by older buildings: the ruins of a twelfth-century keep and a round tower. Another ruined keep from the same period can be seen at the scattered village of Cause-de-Clérans just north of here. The old keep is still lofty and domineering, reflecting the power of the feudal lords who ruled over these lands. There are some fine solid houses nearby, but the village church is a kilometre away along the road to Pressignac. There's a powerful belfry over the crossing, and a dome over the bay preceding the chancel resting on strikingly carved capitals. From various points in this spread-out commune you can enjoy pleasant views over low wooded hills and fields. The drive north from here crosses the forest of Liorac, now a nature reserve. Liorac-sur-Louyre is dominated by a tall fortified Romanesque church with a sheer west belfry, and west of the village is a sight to bring joy to any gastronome, a pheasant farm.

Further west the little River Louyre joins the equally modest Caudau at Lamonzie-Montastruc. Here there's a large but uninteresting church and a château that dates from the thirteenth century, though the buildings visible today are mostly seventeenth-century, except for the two fifteenth-century towers with pepperpot roofs. Despite the dramatic siting of the buildings, this has always struck me as a depressing château compared to most of the castles in this area. From Lamonzie a fast road returns to Bergerac, or you can make a brief detour north to visit the wine- and strawberry-growing village of Queyssac. The church, with its excellent capitals, has a sixteenth-century nave, but the domed bay before the chancel dates from the late eleventh century; the pentagonal apse is striking too. In a nearby field stands a handsome sixteenth-century dovecot with open arcades beneath it. From Queyssac it's a short drive back to Bergerac.

No community is without its war memorial, such as this imposing example at Lamonzie-Montastruc.

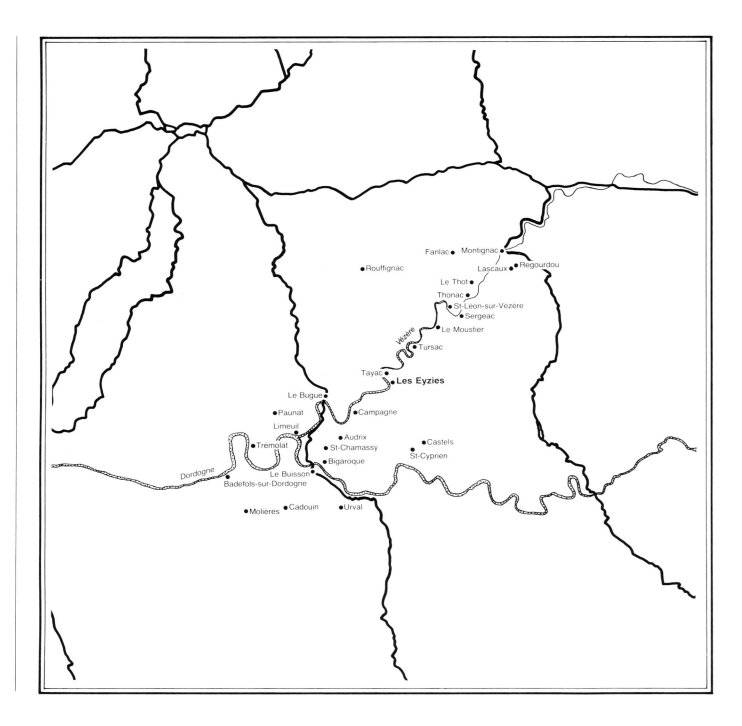

Fanlac • • Montignac

• Rouffignac

Lascaux • • Regourdou

Le Thot •

Thonac •

St-Léon-sur-Vézère

• Sergeac

Le Moustier

Vézère

• Tursac

Tayac • • **Les Eyzies**

Le Bugue •

• Paunat • Campagne

Limeuil

• Audrix

• Trémolat • St-Chamassy • Castels

Bigaroque • St-Cyprien

Dordogne

Le Buisson •

Badefols-sur-Dordogne

• Molières • Cadouin • Urval

4
The Cradle of Prehistory

Les Eyzies – Prehistoric Sites – Saint-Léon-sur-Vézère – Lascaux – Limeuil – Trémolat – Cadouin – Proumeyssac

Meet Your Ancestors: Les Eyzies

The reputation of Les Eyzies as the capital of prehistory is fully justified, for nowhere else in the world is there such a density of sites. The nineteenth-century traveller, Edward Harrison Barker, in *Two Summers in Guyenne*, described the area as 'a paradise of exceptional richness to the scientific bone and flint grubber on account of the very marked predilection shown for it by the men of the Stone Age'. Not all the sites contain cave paintings, but all are of archaeological interest. Some are simple caves or shelters (*abris*), such as the remarkable Abri du Poisson near the Gorge d'Enfer, which contains a single engraved image of a large fish. There are also the sites (*gisements*) which consist of layers of debris that reveal different epochs of habitation. The presence of so many natural limestone caverns in the Vézère valley clearly attracted Palaeolithic tribes, as did the climate of the area and the abundance of game. What distinguishes the region further is the fact that, even after tens of thousands of years, the images that the people of the Palaeolithic were moved to paint and engrave on cavern walls remain fresh and evocative. The atmospheric peculiarities of these caves, often set hundreds of metres into the cliff face and accessible only by long tunnels, have helped to preserve these earliest of all works of art, though sadly many were allowed to deteriorate through thoughtless exposure to changes of temperature and other intrusive factors that resulted in mould and bacterial damage.

Precise dating of sites or works of art is far from easy and information of this kind must be treated with some scepticism. Most of the sites, and their decoration, that you will see date from the Upper Palaeolithic era, which spans a period from 40,000 to 10,000 years ago. Some older objects displayed in the museum at Les Eyzies date from the end of the Middle Palaeolithic era, a period known as Mousterian after the neighbouring site of Le Moustier. Two of the subdivisions of the Upper Palaeolithic are also named after local sites: the four principal subdivisions are Perigordian, Aurignacian, Solutrian, and Magdalenian, Magdalenian being the most recent. It was with the Perigordian period that Neanderthal man was unmistakably replaced by the more recognizably human *homo sapiens*. Tools and jewellery dating from this time are frequently found in the Dordogne. The artistic legacy from this period almost 40,000 years ago is equally remarkable; it includes the exaggeratedly feminine figurines employed in fertility cults known as Venuses, and some of the paintings at Lascaux and Font-de-Gaume. The majority of paintings and engravings that we see at these and other caves are from the Magdalenian period, when cave painting reached a new level of sophistication and the colouring and design became more complex and refined. The artists used a variety of pigments, made from manganese compounds or ochre, and burins were used to fashion the engravings incised in the rock. No one can be entirely sure why the quality and quantity of prehistoric art declined

Above **Paul Dardé's unflattering portrayal of our ancestor Cro-Magnon man outside the museum of prehistory at Les Eyzies.**

Left **In many villages the churchyards are tended as carefully as the gardens of private houses.**

after the Magdalenian period, but it seems probable that changes in the climate caused the population to disperse. What remains certain is that only during the relatively recent Neolithic era did anything that we can honestly think of as art make a reappearance.

The scientific exploration and analysis of prehistoric sites in the Dordogne didn't get fully under way until the 1860s, when a major discovery was made at Les Eyzies: the skeletons of Cro-Magnon man and his family. Analysis established that these Palaeolithic men were, in physical appearance, far from the stereotype cartoon characters associated with Neanderthal man: hunched, squat bruisers wielding clubs. The Cro-Magnon people were, some of

them, over 2 metres tall. On the terrace outside the museum of prehistory at Les Eyzies is a statue by Paul Dardé that supposedly represents Cro-Magnon man. This ape-like hulk is surely a slur on these ancestors of ours and it's sad that so hideous a statue should be the first sight to greet visitors at this unforgettable museum. Over the next century other major discoveries followed. Experts were summoned to examine and authenticate the finds, and the names of anthropologists such as Denis Peyrony and Abbé Breuil recur repeatedly at the sites they explored and documented.

Scholars still dispute the significance of the designs found in the caves. In many cases the works of art were created far from the outer caverns where *homo sapiens* actually lived. As at Rouffignac, a long and surely terrifying journey was required to reach the often low and tortuous passageways in which the images of animals were painted or engraved. Abbé Breuil, among others, inferred from this that the works of art had a magical role and significance, probably related to hunting and hence to the survival of the race. Representations of the human form are extremely rare; the Magdalenians were clearly not interested in portraiture for its own sake. Images were frequently painted over, another indication that they were not intended merely to serve as likenesses, nor to please as decorations, but to invoke the spirits who were responsible for the provision of enough game to satisfy our ancestors' hunger. Other scholars question this theory on the grounds that the reindeer, widely hunted in the Dordogne during Palaeolithic times, is rarely represented. Breuil's theory may not answer all the questions posed by the presence of these early works of art, but it seems as likely an explanation as any. The Palaeolithic people themselves left no explanations, just these awesome indications that our ancestors showed no lack of sophistication, tenacity and skill. If all art is an attempt to come to terms with our personal and collective experience, then our ancestors had as strongly developed a sense of art as we like to think we possess today. That their art almost certainly served an ideology – magical rituals related to hunting – does not lessen its integrity or value, any more than medieval art only speaks to those who accept the dogmas of the Church it served.

The obvious base for exploring the prehistoric sites is Les Eyzies itself, where you will find some of the best hotels and restaurants in the Dordogne. The town itself is far from lovely and visitors who prefer more charming and tranquil surroundings should stay at Campagne (see p. 124) or Saint-Léon-sur-Vézère (see p. 117), where the accommodation is more modest but the environment more ingratiating. An essential introduction to the region is a visit to the Musée National de Préhistoire, which occupies the remaining portions of the fifteenth-century château built into the cliffs of Les Eyzies by the barons of Beynac. The museum holds large collections of tools and arrowheads; entire rooms are filled with examples of Upper Palaeolithic art, and some pieces, such as the powerful carvings of vulvas from La Ferrassie, which date from the Mousterian Age. There are fine collections of weapons, many of them decorated, and of human figures; other rooms contain human and animal remains. Adjoining Les Eyzies is the hamlet of Tayac, where you will find a formidable fortified church. The west front rises sheer from the ground; only the entrance, with its broad arches, intricate capitals and sculpture over the door, is decorated. A second tower, crenellated, rises from the east end. The interior is dominated by plain arcades that lack any mouldings or capitals. There is neither crossing nor transepts, and nave and chancel are divided only by a short flight of steps. The church at Tayac is as much a fortress as a place of worship.

From Les Eyzies follow the signs for Périgueux. You will soon come to Le Grand Roc, a cliff overlooking the Vézère that contains a network of caves filled with all manner of bizarre rock formations. Discovered in 1924, the caves contain, in addition to stalactites and stalagmites, gravity-defying formations called *excentriques*. The tunnel-like caves are very low, never more than 2 metres high, and burrow beneath 20 metres of limestone; consequently the humidity is extremely high, about 95 per cent. It's thought that the caves were formed by erosion about 60 million years ago. To identify some of the more peculiar formations, speleologists have given them names, such as the Chrysanthemum, Rabbit's Ear and Serpent's Nest, some of them rather far-fetched. In some cases stalactites have landed on clay supports that have now vanished, leaving the formations seemingly suspended in mid-air. Other stalactites are so closely bunched that they resemble drapery. For obvious reasons the tunnels are artificially lit, and the

translucence of the limestone, as well as the red of the ferrous deposits, produces an eerie glow that some find oppressive. Le Grand Roc is not recommended to anyone suffering from claustrophobia. Flanking this cliff is the narrow valley known as the Gorge d'Enfer (Gorge of Hell), now a nature reserve specializing in the animals that would have inhabited the region in prehistoric times.

Right alongside the Gorge is the entrance to the Abri du Poisson. This small cave was discovered in 1892, though the remarkable bas-relief on the roof was only found in 1912. The carving of a salmon is just over 1 metre long; by the head of the fish is a carved outline of another animal, possibly a bison. These carvings are particularly precious because of their antiquity; they date from the Perigordian period and are about 25,000 years old. To see the Abri you must apply to the guardian of the Gisement de Laugerie Haute just up the road, one of two nearby excavations (the other is the Laugerie Basse). There are about sixty of these *gisements* within the commune of Les Eyzies. The untrained eye viewing them will only discern orderly piles of debris, but to the archaeologist these sites provide crucial evidence about different epochs of more or less continuous habitation that range over about 20,000 years. Since its discovery in 1863, scholars have been able to use the evidence found at Laugerie Haute, which includes two skeletons as well as lamps and carved bones and other utensils, to date other finds with increasing accuracy.

A short distance further along this same road is the cave known as Carpe-Diem, a 200-metre-long tunnel packed with stalactites and stalagmites. Unless you wish to visit the magnificent caves at Rouffignac to the north (see p. 74), you should now return to Les Eyzies. South of the town lies the cave of La Mouthe. Discovered in 1895, this deep passage contains a number of prehistoric engravings and paintings. Since La Mouthe has been closed to the public since the early 1980s there is little point in offering a detailed description. From Les Eyzies take the Sarlat road to visit two of the finest caves of all: Font-de-Gaume and Combarelles. They are

---

Autumn in the Dordogne means walnuts, so fresh you can crack them open in the palm of your hand.

deservedly popular and it is wise to arrive well before opening time to buy tickets or book ahead for later in the day. The number of visitors admitted is strictly limited and many find themselves turned away.

The existence of Font-de-Gaume has been known for centuries, but it was not until 1901 that Peyrony discovered the paintings within. The tunnel leading into the cave is narrow, dark and twisting, and after about 100 metres emerges into narrow but lofty passages, as if squeezed between cliffs. It is here that most of the 200 paintings are to be found. The Monuments Historiques, who administer these two sites, have lit the cave minimally, and the result is suitably atmospheric; curiously, the subdued light makes it easier to make out the paintings. The caves are not large but the paintings, which date from the Perigordian and Magdalenian periods, are of outstanding quality. You won't easily forget the magnificent frieze of bisons drawn in a style not dissimilar to that of Lascaux. Particularly fascinating are the paintings of horses that use the contours of the cave wall to outline the animal's tail and flanks.

Continue along the Sarlat road to Les Combarelles, which was discovered in 1901 by Breuil and others at the end of a long tunnel. The legacy of Combarelles is stupendous: several hundred paintings in all, including most realistic horses, mammoths, a rather schematized human head, an equally schematized female form that lacks both head and arms (one of forty-nine human figures at this site), antlered deer, a donkey's head, a rhinoceros, and a lion. Not all the outlines are easy to make out, for many have been superimposed on others and the result is initially confusing, though the guides are skilled at elucidating the individual drawings. The variety of fauna depicted reminds us how different the climate was here tens of thousands of years ago. The floor of the tunnel containing the paintings has been lowered and so the roof is now almost a metre higher than it was in prehistoric times. The artists must have had to crawl down the passages on their hands and knees to execute their work; the actual painting would have required them to stoop or even lie flat on the ground. Surely only a religious motivation, however widely we define it, can have persuaded Magdalenian men to endure such self-inflicted discomfort?

Return once more to Les Eyzies and take the Montignac

The terraces of La Roque Saint-Christophe built into a cliff overlooking the Vézère were originally inhabited by Palaeolithic peoples and were last occupied by Huguenots in the sixteenth century.

road to Tursac, where there's a stern oblong Romanesque church with a high nave and defensive chambers above the domes of the vault. Soon after Tursac cross the Vézère and bear left towards the *gisement* that gave its name to one of the Upper Palaeolithic ages, La Madeleine. The road ends at the Château de la Goudelie and you must continue on foot for the last kilometre. These cave dwellings give us a fine idea of where and how the Magdalenians lived, though to see most of the objects uncovered here (including tools, weapons and bone ornaments) you must go to the museum at Les Eyzies. Rejoin the Montignac road and continue to La Roque Saint-Christophe, one of the most enjoyable of all the valley sites. For about 800 metres terraces have been gouged into the overhanging cliff. Before the road was built, the site must have been more dramatic than it is now; with the building of the road, the river was moved and the cliffs now overhang the roadway and the meadow that flourishes where the river used to flow. There is evidence that these terraces, which were connected by ladders and stairways and provide over 3 kilometres of passages, have been inhabited since the Mousterian age. The cliff was not only lived in by Palaeolithic peoples; it became a fortress in the tenth century when Viking raids were threatening the area, and during the Hundred Years War it was a bastion against the English, who occupied it for fifteen years in the early fifteenth century. The Huguenots made use of La Roque from 1580 until 1588, when Henri III ordered their expulsion and the destruction of the fortress. Shorn of vegetation and almost inaccessible, La Roque was just about impregnable, though it was vulnerable to siege.

The terraces are approached across a narrow bridge. Nearby are sentry posts from which stones and boiling oil could be hurled on unwelcome visitors. Further defence was provided by an early warning system, by which signals were sounded from lookout post to lookout post up the valley from Le Bugue in three minutes, allowing the cliff dwellers to prepare for possible attack. The inhabitants constructed chambers within the caves, and you can still see the ancient drainage channels, wall safes and hollows where roof beams were inserted. The chambers were quite sophisticated, with walls made of wattle and daub. From the roof hang small loops of rock, which were formed by rubbing rods against the rock until a small passage was driven through it, and from these loops ropes were threaded for tethering animals or hanging lamps. About 1500 of these loops still exist, indicating the number of people that must have occupied La Roque during its heyday. A slaughter-house and curing chamber stand side by side, and at the far end of the largest terrace, which is 700 metres long, is an area once used as a church. A final reason for visiting La Roque is to enjoy the splendid view.

Just across the river from La Roque is the village of Le Moustier. You can visit the *abri* (shelter) where excavations in 1908 led to an entire Middle Palaeolithic age being named after the spot. As at the Laugeries, you can clearly see the different layers of prehistoric habitation. Continue up-river to the splendid village of Saint-Léon-sur-Vézère. It fits snugly into a loop of the river and on a small terrace by the water stands one of the most perfect of Romanesque churches, a former Benedictine priory. An airy two-stage belfry rises over the crossing, but it's the east end of the *lauze*-covered church, with its rounded apse and flanking chapels, that is its most beautiful feature. The peaceful interior is a surprise, austere and harmonious. The domed crossing is supported on massive piers, and the chancel is ornamented with blind arcades that rest on stylized capitals and fragments of fourteenth-century frescoes. Note, too, the mutilated but beautiful sixteenth-century stone Virgin and Child and, on the west wall, a rough stone carving of a knight on horseback.

Most of the houses in Saint-Léon are built from lovely golden stone and it's a pleasure to stroll through the lanes of this well-tended village. You can't easily overlook the two

Architectural perfection: the Romanesque church at Saint-Léon-sur-Vézère, with its rounded apses and beautiful crossing tower.

splendid châteaux. The Château de Clérans dates from the fifteenth and sixteenth centuries, a fine complex mass of yellow masonry bristling with gables and corner turrets, loopholes and machicolations. Equally impressive is the Manoir de la Salle, built alongside a rugged fourteenth-century keep, with its *lauze*-covered roof rising over the battlements. A short walk out of the village brings you to the cemetery, which is graced with a square fourteenth-century chapel, also roofed with *lauzes*. From Saint-Léon drive up the valley to Thonac, where there is a relatively plain Romanesque church.

In the foothills behind Thonac there are two worthwhile sites. One is the Tour de Vermondie, a leaning tower in which, we are expected to believe, a lovesick prince so missed his girl that the tower, in sympathy, leaned low so that the two could kiss. Not far away is the prehistory centre at Le Thot, where photographic displays, plaster casts and film shows offer visitors an excellent introduction to the subject. The centre complements the museum at Les Eyzies, and its function is more directly educational. Attached to the complex is a park stocked with animals that commonly feature in prehistoric art, so it's possible to combine painless learning with a visit to a zoo. North of Le Thot is the lovely village of Fanlac, rather off the beaten track and often bypassed by tourists. Its setting on the edge of the Barade forest ensures Fanlac a mention in *Jacquou le Croquant* (see p. 75). As a group of buildings, Fanlac is impressive. The church is unremarkable, but around it stand many unspoiled *manoirs* and a seventeenth-century lobed cross carved with a Crucifixion; behind it is the village well. With its golden houses and peaceful setting, Fanlac is an idyllic spot; but by the church is a reminder that the village is not unacquainted with savagery, for a memorial commemorates a couple in their seventies who were shot and burnt by the Germans in March 1944.

From Fanlac drive east past Montignac to the most celebrated of all prehistoric sites in France, the cave at

A perfect Dordogne landscape near Saint-Léon-sur-Vézère: gentle hills, trees and meadows, and a snug *lauze*-covered Romanesque church.

Lascaux. The story of its discovery is well known, but worth repeating. In September 1940 some local lads were out rabbitting on the hillside with their dog, Robot, when the animal suddenly disappeared down a hole in the ground. When the boys followed, they found Robot, and themselves, in a cave which, their torch revealed, was lavishly painted. The American writer, Guy Davenport, has written a fine short story, 'Robot', about this discovery, and he describes what the boys found as follows:

'Everywhere they looked there were animals. The vaulted ceiling was painted, the crinkled walls lime-white and pale sulphur were painted with horses and cows, with high-antlered elk and animals they did not know. Between the animals were red dots and geometric designs. . . . Handsome plump horses trotted one after the other, their tails arched like a cat's. . . . They found long-necked reindeer, majestic bulls, lowing cows, great humped bison, mountain goats, plaited signs of quadrate lines, arrows, feathers, lozenges, circles, combs. All the animals were in files and herds, flowing in long strides down some run of time through the silence of the mountain's hollow.'

Abbé Breuil happened to be in the area, and soon confirmed that their discovery was of major importance. In 1948, the site was opened to the public, and the boys who'd discovered Lascaux, now young men, acted as guides to the treasures to which Robot had led them. Unfortunately, less was known in those days about the fragility of prehistoric paintings. About 2000 visitors a day used to pass through Lascaux. Moreover, the construction of a large staircase into the cave destroyed the stability of the atmosphere that had preserved the paintings for over 17,000 years in a state of such freshness. They became affected by *la maladie verte*, the green sickness, caused by fluctuating temperatures, the breathing of visitors, excessive carbon dioxide in the air, and by a second ailment, *la maladie blanche*, caused by other factors such as damp. In 1963 the cave was closed and the *maladies* have been to some extent cured. Although, to prevent any recurrence, Lascaux remains closed to the public, a facsimile of the original cave, called Lascaux II, has been built into the hillside a few hundred metres down the slope. Purists may raise an eyebrow at this, but visitors have nothing to fear. Dispassionate observers confirm that the fake is brilliantly made, so that even the contours of the walls match the original.

I do not propose to catalogue the marvels of Lascaux. The guides are excellent and allow visitors to examine the paintings at some leisure. The characteristics of the Lascaux paintings, while hardly unique among the cave paintings of the Dordogne, exist in greater proliferation and concentration here than elsewhere. First, there is the range of colours: yellow, ochre, black, brown, red and white are the most common. Second, there is great complexity of interaction between the animals depicted; they do not stand alone, but are shown in groups and in confrontation with each other. There are also some remarkable early attempts at perspective. These are mostly apparent in the paintings of horns, which attempt both frontal views and profiles. All the animals that tramp along the cave walls – there is but one spindly human figure at Lascaux – were likely to have been hunted by the Magdalenian people who painted them: ibex, oxen, bulls, cows, deer, horses. Our ancestors' respect for them is evident from the immense dignity and power that soar from these great friezes. The frequent depiction of pregnant animals suggests a likely connection with fertility rites. And could there be the earliest instance of humour in the image of an upside-down horse, painted around a corner of the cave so that it is impossible to see the whole image at one glance? Perhaps that's too fanciful, as is the theory reported by Freda White that it represents a way of killing horses by driving them off cliffs, but there's certainly no lack of sophistication at Lascaux. Even though the paintings must have lost some of their original splendour, it is extraordinary how well they have been preserved over the millennia. A film of calcite deposits had coated the walls of the original cave, keeping the paintings in remarkably fresh condition, a freshness accurately reproduced in the facsimile caves accessible to visitors.

On leaving, walk up the hill past the entrance to the original cave, and continue to Regourdou, where a 70,000-year-old skeleton of a Neanderthal man was found. There's a small museum at the site.

From Lascaux drive back down the Vézère along the road that follows the east bank and leads you past two highly picturesque châteaux. The first castle, Losse, is best viewed from this side of the river, though to visit the castle (which contains splendid furnishings and tapestries) you must cross the river at Thonac. The château was built in 1576 by Jean de Losse, and like Belcayre was built on a commanding and delightful site directly over the Vézère. As Freda White reminds us in her *Three Rivers of France*:

'Losse has a famous echo. Every visitor will be told how the Seigneur of Belcayre, finding himself in a tight place, went to his neighbour to borrow money. Losse, a canny man, cried to the echo: "Is Monsieur de Belcayre a good payer?" "Moussur de Belcayre ei teu buon pagaire?" "Gaire! Gaire!" "Watch out!" answered his echo, and poor Belcayre did not get his loan.'

Next you will come to the fifteenth-century château of Belcayre (Belcaire on Michelin maps), set on an outcrop over the Vézère. Turrets and machicolations and pinnacles give the building a charmingly irregular appearance, though much of what we see is the result of extensive later restorations.

At Sergeac, just over a kilometre downstream from Belcayre, you will find a great Romanesque church, but very different in style and atmosphere from that at Saint-Léon on the opposite bank. The latter is graceful, dignified and perfectly proportioned; the towering Templars' church at Sergeac is harsh, massive and blunt. The interior is dominated by the massive crossing arches; the east window is deeply recessed and resembles an arrow slit more than a source of light. The ornament, whether the stylized capitals or the zigzags on the ancient font, is rough, almost barbaric. Walk along the short main street and glance into the courtyard by the letter box for a glimpse of the thirteenth-century machicolated tower, all that remains of the Templar commandery. The entrance to the village is watched over by a fine sixteenth-century Calvary, and in the opposite direction you will find the prehistoric site of Castel-Merle. Many important finds have been made in the caves here, and some of them can be viewed at the small site museum.

From Sergeac a lovely road crosses the hills to Les Eyzies.

The delightful Château de Belcayre is built on an outcrop directly above the River Vézère.

Below The riverside terraces at the Château de Losse, one of the most romantic spots in the Dordogne.

Right A slightly melancholy park surrounds the much restored Château de Campagne near Saint-Cyprien.

The Dordogne Valley: South of Les Eyzies

From Les Eyzies drive south towards Saint-Cyprien. Shortly before reaching Saint-Cyprien, a sign on the left points to Fages. Rutted lanes lead to the château, which was a Catholic stronghold during the Wars of Religion. During World War II the Germans, as was their wont, burnt the château, but the new owner is restoring it. Left of the main gate stands the vaulted chapel with its weathered Renaissance doorway and richly decorated flamboyant east window. Only the main tower of the Renaissance château is in good shape; the block behind it is partially ruined and has lost its top storey. Although the château is closed to visitors, the dedicated tourist can plunge into the adjacent woods for a closer look at the structure, its dry moat and the splendid tripartite Renaissance windows. Fages is far from pretty, but it has a strong character of its own. Ninety years ago Edward Harrison Barker found it 'a very ghost-haunted place. The building had not fallen into ruin; it was still roofed . . . but there was no glass in the windows; all the rooms were silent with that silence so deep and sad of the long deserted house.' Despite the restoration now under way, its creepy atmosphere is unchanged.

Continue into Saint-Cyprien, which stretches out along the hillside like a sleeping cat. Stroll up through the steep streets to the large church, originally an Augustinian abbey. All around it are venerable stone houses with steeply pitched roofs, their façades lurking behind green and purple ivy and vines. The church is entered through a Gothic west door. The gloom of the interior is intensified by the sombre modern stained glass. When your eyes grow accustomed to the murk, you can see that the fourteenth-century church is nobly proportioned, with lean ribs curving elegantly from low supports to frame the vaulting. The exterior of the chancel, which, unlike the nave, is Romanesque at its most monumental, rises to form a mighty belfry. Just east of the town is the village of Castels, where you'll find a ruined Romanesque church and the eighteenth-century Château d'Argentonnesse in a park, and the curiously shaped Château de la Roque, which dates from the fifteenth and sixteenth centuries and rises above a rocky spur.

From Saint-Cyprien drive northwest to Campagne, which seems to contain more public buildings than private ones. There's a Romanesque church, long and low, a château, an

A simple Renaissance window at Limeuil, firmly shuttered against the elements.

inn, and not much more. From the grounds of the château there's a good view of the attractive chancel of the church. The fifteenth-century château itself consists of a massive machicolated tower and various later appendages in which medieval and Renaissance styles blend comfortably despite such signs of heavy-handed restoration as a new roof that appears to be made of plastic. The château is state property and the concierge seems to tolerate visitors who stroll through the grounds, though the interior is closed up. The busy little town of Le Bugue lies west of Campagne. There are numerous campsites and hotels and it is probably the best place to shop along the Vézère valley. There's one splendid old tower house built of rich golden stone on the Grand' Rue, a minute's walk from the bridge, but in general Le Bugue has little to recommend it. Just outside the town, however, is the curiously named cavern of Bara-Bahau, a relatively recent discovery, authenticated in 1951. The roofs are engraved with outlines of animals, including bears, bison and ibex, that are believed to be at least 20,000 years old.

Paunat, cupped in the hills north of the Dordogne valley, lies 8 kilometres west of Le Bugue. A village green – with a Calvary, a dovecot and a stone fountain for washing clothes – gives Paunat a cosy charm, but no one could describe the immense fortified church, a Benedictine foundation once attached to the abbey at Limoges, as charming. It's built like a fortress, with sheer unornamented walls, 3 metres thick in places, that rise to a great height and are broken only by narrow lancets. The abbey, founded in the eighth century, was frequently rebuilt, though the fabric, other than the fifteenth-century nave vaults, dates from the twelfth. The west entrance beneath the massive square belfry leads into a domed chamber preceding the nave, a rarity in the Dordogne. The lofty interior is more ingratiating, with its dignified vaulted chancel and domed crossing.

Continue south to the old walled village of Limeuil, which is packed down one side of an exceptionally steep hill. Limeuil has since Roman times occupied a position of strategic importance, for it overlooks the spot where the Vézère joins the Dordogne. Inevitably this little boat-building centre became involved in all the bloodiest episodes of local history, from the Hundred Years War to the Revolution. A thirteenth-century château once stood at the summit, the property of the powerful Vicomte de Turenne during the Wars of Religion, but it is now in ruins. Park by the river near the Pont Coudé, a pair of bridges that almost touch, one crossing each river. You'll see the medieval gateway, the Porte du Port, which leads into a lane that climbs steeply past numerous old houses. The Isabeau de Limeuil restaurant here is noted for the eccentricities of its *patronne*. When I lunched there those oddities were in abeyance, but I do recall being fed roast pheasant garnished with *morilles* as part of the 50-franc set meal.

After those five courses I needed the exercise of a climb up the lane to a section of the old ramparts; to the left you'll see another of the town gates. Bear right to the Place des Ormeaux and then left to the unremarkable church, a largely nineteenth-century building with a fourteenth-century chancel. Follow the lane up from the church to the Porte du Marquisat, the third of the old gateways in the town walls.

As in medieval times you step from the gate into open fields. Walk back down to the Place des Fosses close to the castle walls, then bear right and return to the Porte du Port. Just beyond the village, on the way to Le Bugue, stands the church of Saint-Martin. From inscriptions placed in the walls, historians have been able to date the church exactly. It was built at the order of Richard I in expiation for the murder of Becket and was consecrated in 1194. The interior is in terrible shape: the plaster is flaking, the masonry cracked, and the timber roof in a perilous state. The fifteenth-century frescoes of the Crucifixion and Deposition are of mediocre quality and in equally poor condition. Apparently this noble and historic church is to be restored. Soon, I hope.

It's a pretty drive west to Trémolat, a village dominated by its formidable church, a tall stark mass of stone topped by a twelfth-century belfry and an expanse of defensive chambers rising over the transepts and crossing. Only the mediocre classical porch and an inappropriate eighteenth-century bell gable distract from the power of this building. Inside, the eye is drawn down the dark narrow aisleless nave to the well-lit choir. The crossing, which like three bays of the nave is domed, rises to an immense height, as do the transepts. From the north transept steps lead to a very worn spiral staircase that climbs to the space between the roof and the rafters. Apart from the fine views through the windows of this defensive chamber, this is a rare chance to see a crossing dome from above. The choir, with its twelfth-century blind arcading between shallow rectangular columns and faded Gothic frescoes, adds a more elegant and less intimidating note. From the vault hang chains that once took the weight of a reliquary that contained the shirt of Jesus – or so the pious people of Trémolat were informed.

Although the church is austere, the village is not, so it's hard to recall that it was the setting for Claude Chabrol's frightening film *Le Boucher* (The Butcher). Bear left on leaving the church and you'll soon come to a lane that leads directly to the cemetery chapel of Saint-Hilaire. It has a fine twelfth-century west doorway beneath ornamented arches, and worn capitals carved with foliage and birds. Carved heads look down from the horizontal band above the entrance. The interior is lit by dark but luminous modern glass by the Parisian artist, Paul Becker, and, not

Above **The church and abbatial buildings at Cadouin fill one side of the market square.**

Left **From near Limeuil, the Dordogne begins another great loop as it flows to the west.**

surprisingly, the villagers prefer to worship at this warm little chapel than beneath the brutal masonry of the fortified church.

Church architecture is not the only attraction of Trémolat, for the village is situated by one of the spectacular loops (called a *cingle*) that the Dordogne makes in the course of its long journey. Take the road to the Belvédère de Racamadou to view this justly celebrated panorama. Tall cliffs overlook the north bank of the stately loop; to the south, within the collar of the river, lie rich flat fertile fields, while in the distance rise the hills of southern Périgord. On some occasions the water glitters with boats participating in the regattas held here. The road continues to wind along the cliffs until you come to a bridge that leads to Badefols-sur-

Dordogne. Tourism and tobacco-growing sustain the villagers, and though the setting of Badefols is pretty enough it doesn't excite my imagination or interest for long. There was a castle here from the ninth century, but it was frequently rebuilt and finally destroyed by Lakanal during the Revolution. It served as a hideout for brigands who used to ambush the river traffic and rob the barges. A few ruins remain on a cliff behind the village.

South of Badefols the road leads to Molières. Its spacious square and vestigial arcades and grid layout make it clear that the town is a bastide. Founded in 1284 by the English, its construction proved too costly and work was halted in 1318. The town still looks unfinished. The church is an imposing thirteenth-century Gothic structure with a tall square northwest belfry. From the north the thick walls of the tower protrude into the nave, while from the south corner rises a puzzling two-storey structure of similar design. Its lower level is vaulted and contains some lovely capitals. What is it doing here? Was the structure intended as the base of an unbuilt tower that was later turned into a baptistery or small chapel? Whatever its history, the eccentric design adds a graceful note to the church. The pentagonal chancel dates from the last century, and is a remarkably successful composition. Even the nineteenth-century stained glass is attractive, though the windows are placed in the wrong order, according to the sacristan, who happily grumbled to me about the expense of correcting the sequence.

Continue eastwards to Cadouin. This was once a major shrine and though pilgrims no longer crowd the lanes it is still worth coming here to admire the church and its cloisters, the finest in the Dordogne. The Cistercian foundation dates from 1115, though it was 1154 before the church was finally consecrated. The abbey had the good fortune to possess a linen cloth brought from Antioch that had once been wrapped around the head of Christ. A treasure indeed, and the Sainte-Suaire (as this cloth was called) attracted hordes of pilgrims, including kings of England and France. During the Hundred Years War the cloth was transferred to Toulouse for safe keeping. This was a tactical error, since the monks of Toulouse refused to return it, and the brothers of Cadouin had to resort to subterfuge and theft to regain their treasure. Thereafter they kept the reliquary firmly chained up, but there was a final obstacle that couldn't be surmounted. When the precious relic was subjected to scientific scrutiny in the 1930s, it was shown conclusively not only that it dated from the eleventh century but, ironically, that it was inscribed with Islamic texts! The pilgrim trade promptly dropped off, and Cadouin dwindled. The abbey dominates the *place*, and overlooks a fine covered market place. The west façade is in the Saintonge style, its width emphasized by blind arcades. Both the faces and the undersides of the arches are meticulously ornamented with motifs that keep the façade from any hint of stodginess despite its breadth.

As in all Cistercian abbeys, the interior design is austere, though there is more ornamentation within than first strikes the eye. Very shallow blind arcading decorates the nave arches, horizontal bands are embellished with nailhead and dogtooth ornament, and the capitals in the shallow transepts are carved with luxuriant foliage. In the north transept stands a large carved slab depicting monks at prayer — clearly not in situ. Both transepts are separated from the crossing by delicate iron screens.

Begun in 1468, the cloisters were not completed until the mid sixteenth century, and the decorative style ranges from flamboyant to Renaissance, as one might expect. Despite the presence of Renaissance detail, the overriding impression is of a late Gothic cloister, with flowing bulbous tracery in each bay. In the south gallery the ribs of the complex vault rise up from ledges, not columns, and below these ledges are remarkable carvings of heads. The east gallery is a riot of sculpture: canopied scenes are cut into piers on a number of levels, large figures are perilously suspended from bosses, some piers masquerade as battlemented towers with windows, and doorways almost sink beneath the weight of their ornament. Leading off from this gallery are the former chapter-house and other rooms that now contain vestments, plate, and a large nineteenth-century reliquary that contains the discredited shroud. The abbot's chair is built into the north gallery wall, and the cloister's finest sculpture is found on either side of it. From the left a procession of monks emerges from a tower-column, while to the right Christ carries his cross and a swooning Mary looks on. The naturalism of these carvings is striking, as is their exuberance and inventiveness. The solemn and the grotesque, the emotional and the comic, flourish side by side, conveying a sense of the richness of life, of the interpenetration of the religious world and the secular. To the right of this group of carvings is a faded but still beautiful fifteenth-century fresco of the Annunciation. Finally, along the west gallery are two beautiful Renaissance doors, their stylish restraint and precisely detailed medallions both a relief after the excesses of the flamboyant doorways, and just a touch prissy in their elegance, which seems self-conscious despite the impeccable craftsmanship.

Cadouin is situated in a shallow valley on the edge of the Bessède forest, which you must traverse to reach the charming village of Urval. When I first crossed the Bessède I was disappointed: it seemed somewhat desolate, and, for a forest, curiously lacking in trees. Weeks later, when reading a local newspaper, I learnt why. A few years ago a local farmer, enraged by what he regarded as the intransigence of a major landowner in the forest, set fire to a corner of the Bessède. The conflagration was easier to start than to control, and one whole third of the forest was destroyed. Urval itself clusters in a small nest of greenery. The unspoiled village is dotted with *manoirs* of various dates and styles as well as some charming cottages near the church. The church itself is an austere but beautiful Romanesque structure, containing finely carved capitals on the tall chancel arch, and additional capitals, though more crudely sculpted, in the eleventh-century chancel. Some of the columns in the church are of marble and it's possible that these were reused after a Roman temple that once stood nearby was dismantled. The west front is far taller than the nave, evidence of a large defensive chamber; indeed, the door giving access to it can be seen high on the north side. The chancel is also fortified, and these defensive measures were taken by the English during the Hundred Years War. Just north of the church, in the wall of the adjoining presbytery, is the communal bread oven, a delightful domestic relic from the fourteenth century, though none too popular with the villagers of that time, who preferred to use their own ovens rather than be compelled by the local seigneur to bake their bread communally.

From Urval head northwest along the Dordogne to Le Buisson. With its railway station, camping sites, hotels and restaurants, Le Buisson is a useful base for holiday makers, but in all other respects it is a drab place. On the opposite bank is the hamlet of Bigaroque, which saw grander days some centuries ago when the archbishops of Bordeaux built a château here. In addition to the pleasure of having a country retreat in so pleasant a spot, it also allowed these prelates to exercise considerable control over the watermen who plied the river with taxable cargoes. The château was razed by Richelieu in 1625, and a few ruins remain above the hamlet, which also contains some attractive Périgordin *manoirs* and a simple twelfth-century church. In the hills north of Bigaroque lies the little village of Saint-Chamassy, with its Gothic church, fifteenth-century *manoir*, and the dolmen of Cantegrel. It offers a fine view over the undulating countryside to the river valleys of the Dordogne and Vézère, as does the nearby hamlet of Audrix, set 200 metres high on a hilltop dominated by its fortified Romanesque church.

Audrix is only a few kilometres away from one of the great natural wonders of the Dordogne, the Gouffre de Proumeyssac. A tunnel leads to a platform that overlooks the huge cavern. Until this tunnel was built visitors had to descend a deep chimney to gain access to the cavern; long ago, law-breakers made a less enjoyable visit when they were hurled down the chimney as a means of execution. The cavern itself is shaped like a great dome with stalactites thickly clustered round the sides. Steadily dripping water forms pools on the uneven surface of the floor. The concretions formed by dripping limestone have been given fanciful names to match their fanciful shapes: the Medusa projects like a large nose from the curved roof and drips onto a table below. Thirty years ago the table was only 2.5 centimetres high, but is now about 15 centimetres thick thanks to the limestone deposits in the water. Opposite the Medusa is the Grande Cascade, a pale blue-grey mass that differs in colour from the ochre stalactites and emits a translucent glow when a light is held close to it. These formations are on a grand scale, but perhaps the most fascinating sight at Proumeyssac is an exercise in miniaturization: a small pool filled with tiny hollow triangular crystallizations, immensely delicate and precise – but no one can satisfactorily explain how they came to be formed. The guided tour of the cavern winds around the sides of the dome, and is enlivened by natural obstacles such as a drapery of stalactites that forces one to stoop low. I do wish the guardians of Proumeyssac were a little less theatrical with their electric lighting schemes, which add an obtrusively artificial note to a sight that is so astonishing because it is entirely natural.

From Proumeyssac it is a short drive north to Le Bugue, and back to Les Eyzies.

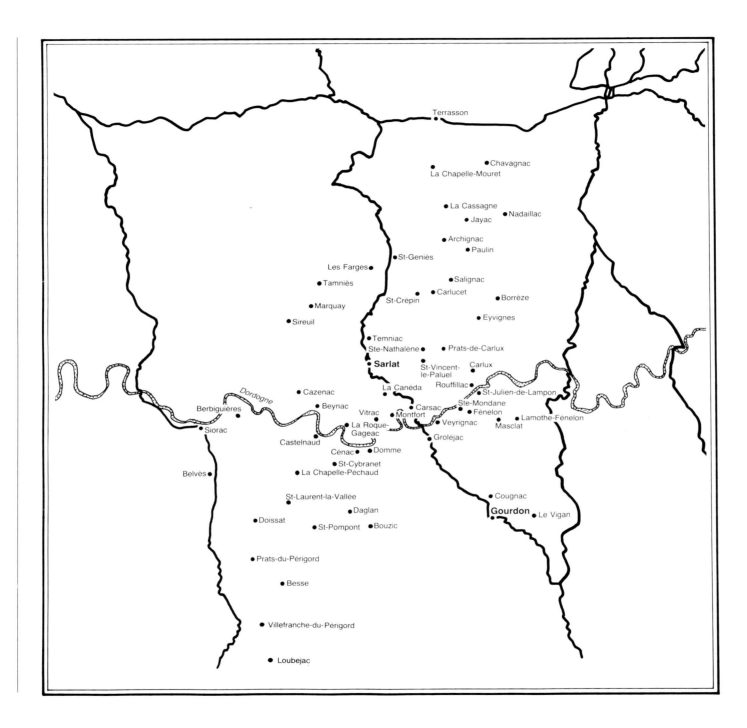

5
Périgord Noir

*Sarlat – Beynac – Castelnaud – La Roque-Gageac
– Montfort – Carsac – Fénelon – Commarque –
Salignac – Terrasson – Domme – Gourdon*

A Countryside of Castles: Sarlat and Périgord Noir
Thanks to human intervention rather than mere good
fortune Sarlat has managed to preserve, better than any
other town in the Dordogne, the atmosphere of a thriving
Renaissance community. Though often touted as a medieval
city, Sarlat is nothing of the kind. Its layout is certainly
medieval, but almost all its buildings are of a later date. The
sixteenth-century merchants' houses of Périgueux may
outclass those of Sarlat, but in Sarlat there is a wonderful
concentration of ancient buildings, whereas in Périgueux
the old town is embedded within an agreeable but
essentially nineteenth-century city. Sarlat is also an
excellent tourist centre, well stocked with a wide range of
hotels and restaurants. From Sarlat you can easily explore
the castles and churches of Périgord Noir; even the
prehistoric sites around Les Eyzies are easily accessible. Its
Saturday morning market is one of the best in the region,
and excellent shops specialize in local produce and wines. In
summer the tourists are joined by those who come to attend
Sarlat's renowned arts festival.

Sarlat originated as a monastery of the Benedictines, who
benefited from the gift of the relics of the local saint,
Sacerdos. In 940 the monks were granted land here by
Bernard, Count of Périgord, and the abbey, and of course the
town growing up around it, grew increasingly wealthy.
When in 1153 a papal bull brought the abbey under the
direct protection of Rome, its power grew even greater.

Throughout the thirteenth century the abbey clashed with
the bourgeoisie of the growing town. The bishops, even the
Pope, as well as the king became involved in the disputes. By
1298 the bourgeoisie had succeeded in divesting the abbey
of much of its power. In 1317, by way of compensation,
Sarlat became a diocesan seat and the abbey a cathedral; the
town was an increasingly wealthy market centre. During the
Hundred Years War, despite its vulnerable position in the
Cuze valley, Sarlat was never captured by the English.
Nevertheless the Treaty of Brétigny assured that Sarlat
became English territory, though only for a decade. The
Middle Ages brought not only war but famine, flood, plague
(Sarlat lost half its population of 6000 in 1521), and, of all
things, an earthquake. During the Wars of Religion, Sarlat
remained a Catholic town, though there was a brief
occupation in 1574 by the ubiquitous Protestant captain,
Geoffroi de Vivans (who roasted the body of poor St
Sacerdos and scattered his ashes), and an unsuccessful
attack in 1587 by the mighty Vicomte de Turenne. Once
peace was restored, Sarlat prospered anew, though it lost its
status as an administrative centre. It became what it has
remained, a thoroughly provincial town, which may explain
why it has preserved its ancient appearance so successfully.

The delights of Sarlat do not thrust themselves on the
visitor. A long thin town, it lies in a dip between hills,
sprawling unattractively to north and south. The main
thoroughfare, the Rue de la République, known by

Left Waving the flag at Sarlat, the most rewarding town in the Dordogne.

Above The cathedral at Sarlat peeks through behind a warm expanse of roofs and turrets.

133

everyone as La Traverse, brutally divides the town and gives little indication of the beautiful old city behind its modern shopfronts. Parking can be difficult, so it's best to leave your car on or near the boulevards that slip around the town. Make your way to the Place du Peyrou facing the cathedral. Turn your back on the large church and look at the astonishing house facing you: the Maison de la Boétie, birthplace of Étienne de la Boétie in 1530, a few years after the house was completed. It was Étienne to whom Montaigne addressed his celebrated essay on friendship. His house is thickly Renaissance in style, with carved transoms and broad rectangular columns decorated with roundels and lozenges and heads. Although there's an excess of ornament crowded over the narrow two-bay house, it does show how ardently the prosperous middle classes of Sarlat embraced the learned, liberating new style. Boétie himself took to the new learning with enthusiasm, and compiled translations of Xenophon as well as his own works of political theory before his early death.

Another Renaissance structure adjoins the cathedral: the bishop's palace (now a theatre), which is topped with the vestiges of a sixteenth-century loggia, a luxurious touch more reminiscent of northern Italy than France. Indeed, it was built for an Italian cardinal, Niccolò Gaddi, while he was Bishop of Sarlat. Of the Benedictine abbey little remains, for in 1504 Bishop Armand de Gontaut-Biron (see p. 107) tore the old cathedral down and began to build a new one. When the bishop was transferred to another see in 1519 work stopped; not until 1682 were the vaults built, and the dull doorway was added in 1706. There are older portions of the cathedral: Romanesque chapels and a chancel of the fourteenth and fifteenth centuries. The west belfry has a Romanesque base, though the upper stages date from various periods up to the eighteenth century. The interior of the cathedral is unenthralling, imposing enough but hardly distinguished. Nor are the furnishings of much interest: in the choir you'll find some rustic and cheerfully grotesque misericords, and some crudely carved fifteenth-century wooden panels in the chapels leading off from the choir.

Leave the cathedral by the south door. You'll pass the dignified twelfth-century Chapel of the Blue Penitents on the left before emerging into the grand little Cour des Fontaines, surrounded on all sides by plain old houses. Turn left into the charming Cour des Chanoines, with its fifteenth-century half-timbered houses adjoining the Chapel of the Blue Penitents. A curved passageway leads from the square into the area behind the cathedral chancel. Here a small garden is planted on the site of the old terraced cemetery, and a staircase leads to a small mutilated Calvary and the strange conical 'lantern of the dead', a grim structure shaped like a pointy-head from another planet. This lantern is far more imposing than those at Atur (see p. 69) and Cubas (see p. 84). It was built in 1180 but no one knows exactly why, though some historians claim it commemorates the visit to Sarlat of St Bernard and the miracles he wrought there. For whatever reason it was built, the lantern was later used as a funerary chapel and ossuary. Nearby a doorway leads into the Rue Montaigne. Note the tiny exquisite old house on the corner and continue straight through the alley and left down the Rue d'Albusse, which takes you back to the Rue Montaigne. Turn left and climb the street to the Rue Landry. Turn left again and you'll see through the railings of a thickly shrubbed garden the sixteenth-century courthouse known as the Présidial, with its irregular façade and bizarre octagon covered by a roof on stilts. Continue, then turn left when you come to an old galleried house, then right into the Rue de la Salamandre – named after the salamander that was the symbol of François I, an emblem frequently seen decorating the Renaissance houses of Périgueux and Sarlat. A flattened ogee doorway leads into the tall tower of the fifteenth-century Hôtel de Grézel. Here the alley opens into a charming little square, surrounded by ancient shuttered houses, some with old traceried arches concealed in the masonry, another with a timbered overhang. Continue down into the irregular Place de la Liberté which contains the secularized church of Sainte-Marie.

Sainte-Marie was built in spurts between 1365 and 1507 but was sold off after the Revolution and now contains offices. The old Gothic church is, apart from its tower and gable, scarcely visible behind the houses that have been attached to it over the years. Each Saturday the market is held in its shadow and in the neighbouring streets. Here you can find not only local fruits and vegetables and delicacies such as the wild mushrooms called *cèpes* and *morilles*, but also live trout and crayfish; *biologiques* (organic) goat cheeses from Belvès; baked goods such as *tourtières de*

Quercy (a cake of flaky pastry made with apples, plum liqueur and rum); live poultry; preserved poultry, terrines and *confits*; and herbs and spices.

On the other side of the church is the Place des Oies, packed on all sides with old houses and turrets. The mansion with three prominent Gothic windows on the first floor is the fourteenth-century Hôtel Plamon. The former cloth merchant, Guillaume Plamon, was town consul in the 1330s and his family name appears over an archway. The Gothic windows are mostly rebuilt and mix oddly with the fifteenth-century windows above. Walk into the courtyard of the mansion to see the splendid seventeenth-century open wooden staircase. Opposite the hôtel is the dank fifteenth-century fountain of Sainte-Marie. Bear left on leaving the hôtel and you'll come to the Traverse. Turn left and left again at the brief Rue du Minage. In front of you appears an archway that leads into the Place Lucien de Maleville. Look behind you and looming above is the large tower of the Hôtel de Maleville, an agglomeration of mostly sixteenth-century houses. Medallions portraying Henri IV and his mistress Gabrielle d'Estrées were placed above the door in tribute to his powerful patrons by Jean Vienne, who built the mansion.

Turn right into the narrow Passage Henry de Segogne, which leads into delightful courtyards full of medieval houses. Discreetly restored, this succession of alleys and courtyards gives a fine idea of how this proud little town, with its assertive towers and lofty houses, must have appeared centuries ago; while the bustle of its main shopping streets, just a few metres away from here, is a reminder that Sarlat is far from fossilized. Return to the Traverse and walk up it till you see the Rue des Armes on the left. Turn into it and you soon come to a charming group of houses, some of which date from the fourteenth century. A covered archway leads to the fourteenth-century north gate and a segment of the former ramparts. Return to the Traverse and bear right up the ramp that leads to the Chapel of the White Penitents, with its heavy but striking baroque doorway. The chapel now contains a display of religious art. A lane passes alongside the chapel into a quarter dense with medieval houses and eventually to the ramparts again. This west side of Sarlat has been less thoroughly restored than the east side and is comparatively uncharted, so visitors who

like to discard their guidebooks from time to time should wander at leisure through these unspoiled streets, for what the west side lacks in grandeur it makes up for in authenticity. When weary of sightseeing, make your way to the public gardens southeast of the cathedral. They were designed in the seventeenth century by a pupil of Le Nôtre's and are the perfect place in which to unwind.

Sarlat is the gateway to the Périgord Noir, that most sumptuous of all the regions of the Dordogne. In the nineteenth century its forests were more menacing. Edward Harrison Barker observed that it was 'one of the few districts in France which still draw a sum from the Government yearly in the form of prize money for the wolves that are killed here'. Ten kilometres southwest of Sarlat the village of Beynac huddles beneath its castle. It lies along a stretch of the Dordogne packed with splendid castles, but for the magnificence of its site Beynac, in my view, wins hands down. Perched on a limestone crag 150 metres above the river, it is visible from far around and presents a marvellous silhouette from all sides. There are two principal structures: the massive keep and subsidiary buildings of the castle itself, and the spacious chapel, now the parish church, daringly positioned on a sheer rock. On one side a crenellated curtain wall soars away from the castle, extending the courtyards and enclosures within. It is possible to drive up to the castle, but I strongly recommend leaving your car by the river and walking up through the little town. The alleys are very steep but you will pass dozens of lovely houses with tiny gardens. The path to the lauze-covered twelfth- or thirteenth-century church lies to the right of the castle, and there is a splendid view from its terrace.

Richard I captured Beynac in 1189, and this was one of the castles sacked by Simon de Montfort, who dismantled it in 1214. The present buildings date from the thirteenth to fifteenth centuries, when Beynac was a French stronghold. The main buildings form a squarish mass, stark and seemingly impregnable. Those parts of the castle open to the public are at present unfurnished, a good thing, as it enables visitors to appreciate the layout and defensive strength of the fortress. Many of the tall chambers are entered by ramps rather than staircases, thus enabling men on horseback to ride right into the château. The greatest room at Beynac is

Left Every street in Sarlat is packed with houses of historical and architectural interest.

Below Beynac, perched high on bare rock over the Dordogne, must be the most dramatically sited castle in the region.

the large thirteenth-century Salle des États where the States-General of Périgord used to meet, for Beynac was one of the four baronies of Périgord; indeed, the baronial flags still hang in the barrel-vaulted hall. Just off the hall is a small oratory which contains fifteenth-century frescoes of the Last Supper, primitive but sharply drawn, a precious survival.

It's worth climbing up to the steep castle roofs, as the view, from almost 200 metres above the river, is stunning. Instead of looking across the river, you find your gaze directed upstream towards Castelnaud, the great rival of Beynac. You then descend into the inner courtyard. The roofs were designed so that rainwater would flow down into this yard and thence into the cisterns which once provided the sole water supply for the garrison. You will also be shown the barbican where unfortunate invaders were trapped once they'd breached the outer ramparts and the drawbridge was raised by the garrison; unable to escape, the invaders were stoned from above. After the enemy had been destroyed, the defending soldiers, who hated to throw anything away, would haul the precious rocks back up by pulley and put them away until next needed.

Every stone of Beynac reeks of war, but drive a kilómetre or so into the hills and you find yourself in tranquil unspoiled country. The other village in the commune of Beynac is Cazenac, a hilltop hamlet with fine views of these peaceful woods and farms. Its church is a particularly attractive and well looked after fifteenth-century building, with a simple and elegant interior that is entirely vaulted; clear unleaded glass keeps the church light and airy. A visit to Cazenac is, however, a detour, for the main road continues westwards along the Dordogne valley past Saint-Cyprien (see p. 124) to the unexciting town of Siorac – its seventeenth-century château is one of the dullest in the Dordogne. From here bear left along a riverside road crammed with châteaux. The first is Berbiguières, a stern grandiose building that utterly dominates the small village at its foot. The mostly seventeenth-century château is in a poor state of repair and is not open to the public. The village church, rebuilt in 1745, is of no interest, but it's pleasant to walk along the lane that hugs the château walls; it leads past sturdy stone houses and barns, and the simple elements of these structures – their stone walls and tile and slate roofs –

are in perfect harmony with the tranquil green hills around the village.

A few kilometres further on is the romantic Château des Milandes, built in 1489 by François de Caumont. Unlike Fages on the other side of the river, Milandes was a Protestant base. It acquired fresh fame in 1948 when the cabaret star, Josephine Baker, bought the château and brought up a multi-racial clan of adopted children there. Milandes (open to the public) is more a country house than a castle, despite its hodgepodge of towers and pepperpot-roofed turrets, some of them nineteenth-century embellishments. The dormer windows are as elaborate as ornate headdresses, and the whole building is surrounded by lovely gardens and terraces. The château contains a collection of fine furniture, much of it Louis XV (eighteenth-century), and memorabilia of its former inhabitants. The adjoining church has a delicately carved late Gothic entrance, with niches and canopies for statues long vanished.

Just beyond Les Milandes stands the moated Château de Fayrac, a splendid pile of grey and yellow limestone, with a drawbridge, massive guard tower and a host of pepperpot towers, crenellated ramparts and gables. The earliest buildings here date from the fourteenth century, but it was added to up to the seventeenth and imaginatively restored in the nineteenth. Fayrac was the home of the Protestant Vivans family, one of the few places in the vicinity Geoffroi de Vivans didn't need to take by force. A balustraded terrace looks out onto the river and faces the even more formidable castle of Beynac. The road continues to the ruinous castle of Castelnaud (not to be confused with the equally magnificent Château de Castelnau many kilometres upstream). Despite its condition, Castelnaud is well worth a visit. Its site is almost as staggering as that of its rival Beynac; it seems to grow out of the sheer rock on which it is perched. Thick windowless round towers and a stern machicolated central tower with a pretty asymmetrical roof look down on visitors tramping up to the castle. From close up the initial

---

Les Milandes is probably more celebrated for its former owner, Josephine Baker, than for its architectural delights.

impression is confirmed: the blocks of yellow masonry do indeed rise straight from the sheer rock. Castelnaud appears impregnable, but it was not. The ferocious Simon de Montfort captured it in 1214, though the castle he besieged was, in physical terms, substantially different from the one we see today. His occupation lasted a year. An archbishop of Bordeaux later occupied Castelnaud and burnt it, and by the fourteenth century it had been considerably altered and strengthened, just in time for the Hundred Years War. Castelnaud was, for much of that time, an English stronghold and thus there was constant skirmishing between Castelnaud and French-held Beynac. During the sixteenth century Castelnaud was the girlhood home of Anne de Caumont, but not for long, as she was kidnapped by her uncle Jean de Cars to keep Anne, and her considerable fortune, out of the hands of the Gontauts of Biron (see p. 107). At the age of seven she was married to

Cars' son, himself a venerable thirteen. Widowed at twelve, Anne was kidnapped for a second time and married to a nine-year-old. Her third and last marriage at the age of eighteen, to François d'Orléans, was disastrous and after she left him Anne understandably threw in the towel and retired to a convent.

Castelnaud is undergoing long-term restoration, and will eventually be reopened to the public. Some of the earlier restorations have been excessive. Smooth new stone rises patchily over the old, and it's clear that much of the château has been recently rebuilt. Be sure to walk to the terrace as there is a stunning view over the river. The bend is filled with rich farmland while to either side the river banks are thickly wooded beneath cliffs. To the left juts the awesome profile of Beynac, and on a hillock on the far side of the river loop rises the Château de Marqueyssac. This seventeenth-century château has exceptionally fine gardens, laid out by Le Nôtre, and is open to the public during the summer.

From Castelnaud, cross the river and drive to the exceptionally picturesque village of La Roque-Gageac. Tall cliffs overhang its steep terraces and not long ago part of the cliffs crumbled away, destroying some of the houses and their inhabitants. Some of the houses were sensitively rebuilt so as to blend perfectly with their more ancient neighbours. At one end of the village stands the handsome nineteenth-century Château de la Malartrie. As fakes go, La Malartrie is a very good one; there's a small shop there where you can sample *eau de noix* and buy truffles and *foie gras*. From the riverside road steps and covered alleys lead up to the terraced houses along the cliff face. Strolling through these lanes you'll pass the small Château Tarde, where the mathematician and chronicler Jean Tarde was born in the 1560s. Further along stands the small sixteenth-century church, which seems about to topple over the edge. All along the path palms and ferns and cactus improbably bloom, a tribute to the sheltered, if perilous, position of this very lovely village. See it if you can at the end of the day, when many of the tourists have left and La Roque-Gageac

Near La Roque-Gageac a farmer disposes of a bumper crop of walnuts by selling them to passing motorists.

Right **Many visitors consider La Roque-Gageac the prettiest village in the Dordogne.**

recovers its tranquillity and contemplates its own reflection in the steady but placid motion of the Dordogne.

The next riverside village to the east is Vitrac. Old Vitrac is hidden away, while a new section of the village consisting entirely of hotels and restaurants has sprouted along the river road. If you find Sarlat too crowded as a base, and Beynac and La Roque-Gageac too expensive, then Vitrac could be ideal. The hotels are welcoming, reasonably priced, and offer acceptable if not distinguished food. Old Vitrac, with its ugly nineteenth-century château and thick-walled church, is not of especial interest. The road continues to wind along the river bank towards Montfort, while lanes lead north towards La Canéda, worth visiting if you enjoy fortified churches, for La Canéda has one of the most uncompromising, a tall barn-like structure built by the Templars. Montfort itself is everything a medieval castle should be. Its stout tower and turrets and gables pierce the sky and its massive main block glowers on top of the craggy rock that plummets down to the loop of the river known as the Cingle de Montfort. Its advantageous position surveying a large stretch of the river made it the inevitable target of innumerable assaults. Simon de Montfort began the process by destroying the castle early in the thirteenth century, and Montfort repeatedly changed hands during the Hundred Years War. The last of many destructions took place at the order of Henri IV; consequently, the surviving buildings date mostly from the sixteenth century, with considerable nineteenth-century restorations. The castle is closed to visitors, and you can only walk as far as the crenellated walls that tower over the modest compact village. Yet close up Montfort is something of a disappointment, and my favourite view of it is from the road to Carsac.

On entering Carsac from Montfort you will pass the well restored Romanesque church. The imposingly recessed west porch leads into the broad-aisled interior that makes Carsac memorable. The nave was embellished in 1542 with a most lovely vault, composed of carved bosses and finely moulded ribs that rest on charming projections. The domed crossing

---

The almost impregnable Château de Montfort looms over the village it dominates.

has exceptional purity of line. Both chancel arch and apse are lined with double columns, and the capitals are carved with stylized foliage and lions. Not all the decoration is ancient, for the windows are filled with modern stained glass by Léon Zack. Less sombre are the abstract Stations of the Cross by the same artist. West of the church, against a hillside, rise the evocative ramparts and restored watchtower of what must have been a commanding medieval château.

From Carsac head south towards the river. On the far side of the ugliest bridge over the Dordogne is the straggling village of Groléjac. Approaching the bridge you see the large château up on the cliff, and next to it stands the *lauze*-roofed church with its Romanesque apse and rugged crossing tower. From Groléjac take the river road to the left past the church and château and on to Veyrignac. Here, too, there is a Romanesque church and a château in a park overlooking the river. The largely eighteenth-century Château de Veyrignac was burnt down by German troops in 1944 but has since been rebuilt.

The next riverside village is Sainte-Mondane, from which signs direct visitors to the Château de Fénelon. This great building was long the home of the Salignac family, whose most famous member was born there in 1651: François de Salignac de La Mothe-Fénelon, who became Prior of Carennac (see p. 178), Archbishop of Cambrai, and in 1689 tutor to the Duke of Burgundy, Louis XIV's grandson. Fénelon, as this cultivated and humane prelate is simply known, won lasting fame with *Télémaque*, an account of the adventures of the son of Ulysses. He wrote this for the edification of the young duke, though it was suspected that the tale, which exhorted his pupil to be as virtuous as men had been in the past, was also a satirical look at the court of the Sun King. Its publication, together with his unorthodox theological views, earned him banishment from court in 1697 and Fénelon lived out his days at Cambrai, where he died in 1715. A vivid account of Fénelon's activities at court, especially his relationship with the young duke and with the theologically controversial quietists, can be found in the memoirs of the Duc de Saint-Simon.

Later the castle became the property of the Maleville family of Sarlat. A drive lined with chestnut trees leads to the modest fortified gatehouse set into the first line of

143

ramparts. Another set must be penetrated before you reach the main entrance. As you circle these ramparts past pepperpot towers and a huge sequoia tree, the complex of castle towers rises threateningly behind the walls. The path passes a shallow basin where horses' legs were bathed, and soon you approach the second gatehouse, next to which stands a thriving cedar of Lebanon, planted, it is said, when Fénelon was born. Passing through the gatehouse, you confront the mass of the château, with its fourteen towers, many abutting each other. The oldest section of the castle is the twelfth-century keep. After the castle was burnt by the French in 1375, the stout round towers were added. There is far more to the castle than is immediately visible: subterranean chambers and passages burrow through the rock, and the kitchens are gouged out of the cliff too.

Unfortunately the living quarters are closed to the public, but visitors are shepherded into other rooms, one of which contains memorabilia associated with the archbishop: books, prints, busts, vestments. You will also be shown a collection of antique cars, of which the present owner of Fénelon seems more proud than of his great castle. The innermost entrance to the château is approached up a curving pair of steps and across a drawbridge. The doorway leads into a seventeenth-century arcade which adjoins the principal courtyard (*cour d'honneur*). You can visit the small fourteenth-century chapel, which contains a fine modern walnut crucifix. Not surprisingly, the view from this highest level of the château is magnificent. Despite the alterations and restorations over the centuries, Fénelon is one of the most evocative and perfect of the great castles of the Dordogne.

From Fénelon head east to Masclat. I have a soft spot for this dispersed agricultural village in gentle farmland. Its shops and restaurant are friendly and its principal buildings modest but appealing. The Romanesque church is quite devoid of ornament, but the proportions of its simple vaulted interior and dignified little chancel are most attractive. Close by stands the château. Occupied by the English for much of the fourteenth century, it passed through many hands in the succeeding centuries. It was heavily repaired in the nineteenth century, and stylistically the modified sections now overwhelm the medieval parts, even the two truncated round towers. Nevertheless, the setting of the château in its palm-studded garden is pleasing without being especially picturesque or imposing. The countryside south of Masclat appeals in a similar way: unpretentious, not forcefully picturesque, yet authentic, in the sense that the landscape and its villages cater not to tourists (who are scarce in this area) but to the needs of the local population. Fields are separated by chestnut woods, and tobacco leaves are hung up to dry in drying-sheds (*séchoirs*). The only other village of interest in the area is Lamothe-Fénelon. Its fortified church has a handsome west

Near Sarlat a dangerous drug is hung up to dry in a farmer's *séchoir*.

Left **The square crossing tower and rounded apse of the church at Carsac are typical of the local Romanesque style. The church contains splendid twentieth-century church art as well as Romanesque capitals.**

145

front and Romanesque apse, and around it stand attractive houses and *manoirs*, many with decorated cornices and attached dovecots.

Return to the Dordogne valley and the village of Saint-Julien-de-Lampon. The chancel of the otherwise drab church contains sixteenth-century frescoes of unusually high quality, depicting God the Father and saints and prophets carrying scrolls. On the opposite bank stands the hamlet of Rouffillac, the scene of German wartime atrocities but now no more than a crossroads lined with hotels and a few houses, though high above the village looms the magnificently sited seventeenth-century château. Take the road to the substantial village of Carlux, passing an exceptionally fine group of farm buildings. A steep lane leads to the clumsily rebuilt Gothic church and the ruins of the twelfth-century château, which was destroyed by the English during the Hundred Years War. Only part of the walls and the ruins of a single grim tower remain. Northwest of here is the unpretentious rural hamlet of Prats-de-Carlux. A pleasant group of farmhouses arranges itself around the twelfth-century church, which has a distinctive *lauze*-covered west porch.

West of Prats-de-Carlux is the village of Sainte-Nathalène. Its church is a patchwork structure, though the interior is more coherent: note the carved capitals beneath the twelfth-century chancel arch. Visitors to this village will probably be more drawn to the nearby Moulin de la Tour, a walnut oil mill that sells its delicious product directly to the public. To the south is the village of Saint-Vincent-le-Paluel. Its fifteenth-century château was burnt by the Germans in 1944 but is happily restored. Nearby is the hamlet of La Salvie, where you can see some *cabanes*, stone huts that may date from Gallo-Roman times.

Continue westward to the hillside village of Temniac. The *lauze*-covered and much rebuilt church shows signs of the damage it repeatedly suffered during both the Hundred Years War and the Wars of Religion. The interior is domed

Although much repaired and added to over the centuries, this grand riverside farmhouse retains enormous charm.

and the west bay of the nave has a curious passage high up supported by arches and grotesque corbels. Notre-Dame-de-Temniac drew pilgrimages from nearby Sarlat, especially when drought hit the town in 1627, followed by an epidemic in 1688. Near the church are the ruins of a château which used to be a palace of the bishops of Sarlat. The views from Temniac are splendid, for the village overlooks the Cuze valley and Sarlat itself.

Forgotten Manors, Dozing Hamlets: North of Sarlat

Tucked into the hills north of Sarlat are not only many fine châteaux but some of the loveliest countryside in all the Dordogne. Set off along the road to Les Eyzies. After a few kilometres a lane on the right leads up to the Château de Puymartin (open to the public). This Renaissance structure was largely rebuilt in the nineteenth and early twentieth centuries, but, with its powerful keep and pepperpot roofs, it still has a picturesque appearance. The interior is notable too, for the chapel and the seventeenth-century murals and Renaissance chimneypieces, as well as for furnishings and tapestries that have been here for centuries. The road continues to the imposing seventeenth- and eighteenth-century Château du Roc, laid out on a grand terrace. Soon after Le Roc (Le Roch on the Michelin map) you'll see a garage. Turn right and follow signs for Paradoux and Les Cabanes. After 4 kilometres you reach a farm with a remarkable group of low stone huts, some with rough conical *lauze* roofs. It was pleasant to be greeted warmly by the farmer, his wife, and his dogs, and invited to wander over his property at my leisure to inspect the *cabanes*. These are found in various parts of the Dordogne, but this particular grouping, known as Le Breuil, is among the most substantial and accessible. These huts date, many claim, from the Stone Age. Although others dispute the exact degree of antiquity (some *cabanes* are thought to be medieval shelters built for shepherds rather than Stone Age homes), these huts are nevertheless the earliest human habitations still intact in this ancient region – with the obvious exception of excavated *abris* or cave shelters.

Return to the main road and bear right to Sireuil, a hilltop village with a good but unremarkable Romanesque church.

However, not far from the village along the road to Marquay, a steep path leads down the slopes of the Beune valley to the ancient Château de Commarque, surely one of the most dramatic and romantic ruined châteaux in the Dordogne. Built in the twelfth and thirteenth centuries, it was sold off by the Templars (to whom an early lord of Commarque had pledged it in order to raise money for a crusade) to the Baron of Beynac; in the early fifteenth century it was occupied by English troops – until it was retaken by the French. It was destroyed some time during the sixteenth century. Commarque, embedded in a tangle of greenery, still preserves the stark outlines of its extremely tall and thick-walled keep and fortifications. Nearby, though rarely open to the public, are some troglodytic dwellings and caves with prehistoric engravings. The Commarque family still lives in the region, and the present marquis owns the Renaissance Château de la Bourgonie above Le Buisson as well as another château near Urval, and actively participates in the region's archaeological and cultural life through his field centre at Sireuil. From the awesome ruins you can look across the Beune valley to the more demure Château de Laussel, a stylish building dating from the fifteenth and sixteenth centuries. Nearby was discovered the famous Aurignacian carving known as the Venus of Laussel. Also close to Laussel is the important cave known as the Abri du Cap Blanc, which contains a magnificent Magdalenian frieze of horses, as well as reliefs of deer and bison that, as at Lascaux (see p. 119) and Font-de-Gaume (see p. 116), exploit the contours of the cave walls to flesh out, as it were, the outlines of the animals.

To visit Cap Blanc, you must return to Sireuil and cross the River Beune. From Commarque continue east to Marquay, where there is a plain barrel-vaulted Romanesque church. The west wall rises straight up to a crenellated top; defensive loopholes peer out from below the roofline. The wooded countryside around Marquay is gratifyingly empty and one can drive back to Sarlat down the D6 without seeing much sign of human habitation. Resist that temptation, however, and continue north and over the Beune to Tamniès, perched high above the valley. The Romanesque church, which has seventeenth-century polychrome statues within, juts over the edge of the hilltop. The views are splendid. From Tamniès drive east along the valley, past a

lovely *manoir* at Les Farges and immediately after it the tall Château de Pelvézy before reaching the pretty little town of Saint-Geniès. The *lauze*-covered church here dates from the twelfth century, though there are many later additions, including the impressive west door and sixteenth-century belfry. The apse is lined with arcades that rest on carved capitals, and on the exterior some entertaining grotesque projections work their way around the apse. Adjoining the church is a fine château with an ovoid tower. The château dates from the thirteenth century, though most of the buildings visible today are sixteenth-century, while the machicolations on top of the tower are relatively recent.

At the souvenir shop next to the post office you can pick up the key to the Chapelle du Cheylard. This curious chapel of 1329 sits on a nearby hillock. Although only two bays long, the yellow-stone chapel is as tall as a major church. The frescoes within are of particular interest. Above some well-defined portraits of saints, including Francis of Assisi, Peter, and George slaying a rather miserable puppy dog, are some large-scale compositions: a Last Supper, much faded apart from the central figure of Christ, and vestiges of a Last Judgment. The style is linear and somewhat crude, but the more lively panels (St Catherine, the two figures above the west door, an angel balancing souls) have considerable grace and vigour. From Saint-Geniès drive south to the utterly charming hamlet of Saint-Crépin. Attached to an old gabled house is the Romanesque church, with its very steep roof and stark crossing tower. Just beyond the cemetery is the enchanting sixteenth-century *manoir* of La Cipière. How perfectly the old weathered buildings blend into the rich gentle hills that rise up behind them! No doubt centuries ago Saint-Crépin was as war-torn and troubled as any other hamlet hereabouts, but now it breathes a rare tranquillity. And so, too, does Carlucet, just east of here. It's easy to mistake Carlucet for a farmyard, for its church is located within a farm enclosure. Nothing here can have altered in 200 years. Adjoining the church is the old walled cemetery, with stone tombs along the sides and more graves placed under arches along the walls. The unenclosed west belfry of

The *manoir* of La Cipière dozes in the depths of the countryside.

the church is a crude but effective wooden structure, doubtless a specimen of local carpentry; it supports a solitary bell. All around is the particularly lovely countryside, small-scale in its undulations and valleys, and profoundly rural.

Beyond Carlucet lies the little town of Salignac. The Gothic church is of little interest, but there is an important château here, which may be visited. It was once the property of the Salignac family to which Fénelon (see p. 178) belonged, and some objects associated with the writer are on display. The tall towers, two of them with pepperpot roofs, and stern living quarters were built from the fifteenth to seventeenth centuries, though the ramparts and the chapel date from the thirteenth. Inside the large hall is a stupendous fifteenth-century fireplace, and the vaulted cellars are most impressive too. Although so many of the adjoining structures that make up the château are of different heights, they are united by the great expanses of *lauzes* that roof them. From the château terraces there are good views of the countryside, and before leaving Salignac it is worth strolling through the ancient town, where some of the houses date from Gothic times. There are other charming *manoirs* and farmhouses to be relished at the unspoiled hillside hamlet of Paulin to the north, and Archignac, just west of Paulin, is full of *lauze*-covered houses and has a fine Romanesque church with excellent carved capitals. Paulin is also dominated by its Romanesque church, which is tall and severe. The interior has been severely scraped and the grey mortar glares from the yellow and pink stone of the walls.

Further north another fine Romanesque church can be seen at Jayac. The oldest part of the much restored church is the eleventh-century choir, which is enlivened with blind arcades resting on carved capitals. The south transept contains a damaged stone pietà, probably late Gothic. East of the church stand a ruined twelfth-century keep and the remains of what must once have been an impressive fifteenth-century château. Rejoin the main road to the northwest at La Cassagne, where you will find an attractive

---

The severe Château de Salignac shows that most castles were built for defence rather than to make picturesque contributions to the landscape.

lauze-covered church. The interior is less rewarding than the exterior, which is made even more delightful by the presence of a sixteenth-century priest's house next to it. And in the cemetery stands a sixteenth-century cross. In the village itself is a barn with a vaulted lower chamber that is traditionally supposed to have had some connection with the Templars. Continue north through this pleasant countryside to the sleepy hamlet of La Chapelle-Mouret. The west door of the twelfth-century chapel is ornamented with carved capitals of almost pagan crudity depicting human figures; small heads, not unlike Easter Island statues, line the underside of the innermost arch. The interior of the chapel, with its three small windows in the square chancel, is utterly plain.

Sadly, this land of dozing villages with their stone-covered houses and churches comes to an end when you reach the valley of the Vézère. At this point the Vézère is not the lively river that trills past Saint-Léon and Tursac but a stretch that has been exploited for industrial purposes around Condat to the west. The road approaches Terrasson from the south, but it is best to cross to the north bank and park in the large square near the war memorial, from which there's a fine view of the town. To the right the Vézère is spanned by a modern road bridge, while to the left is a charming but more frail twelfth-century bridge. On the other bank, behind the quai with its shops and tall balconied houses, cliffs rise sharply to the upper town, clustered around the fifteenth-century church. Cross the medieval bridge and walk straight up the narrow Rue Margontier towards the church. To the right you'll see a fine old hôtel, partially half-timbered; a Renaissance dormer is incongruously placed next to the dovecot. From the terraces laid out above the former ramparts fine roofscapes spread out below. Although the west front of the church has been renewed, it still has part of its flamboyant doorway, though in battered condition. The polygonal choir, with its strong buttresses and medallions along the cornice, is the finest part of the church. The broad interior has a certain grandeur, but it's awfully dull.

The attraction of Terrasson lies in its setting more than in the quality of its buildings or amenities, so it will not be a terrible wrench to drive southeast over the hills to Chavagnac, which is graced with a Romanesque domed

Those who died in two world wars are remembered in every village and town, as here at Terrasson.

wooded hills, and the bulk of the sixteenth-century château, darkly roofed with *lauzes*, is massive and imposing.

A pleasant cross-country drive via Sainte-Nathalène (see p. 147) returns you to Sarlat.

via Sainte-Nathalène (see p. 147)

Strongholds and Forests: South of Domme

Domme may not be as classic or complete a bastide as Monpazier or Beaumont, but who would deny that it is the most attractive and dramatic of them all? The site is responsible both for its deviations from the norm and for the powerful impression it makes on visitors. From the valley it appears that only a few buildings and terraces overlook the Dordogne from a rocky crag; the rest of Domme slopes steeply down the other side of the crag. Because of this commanding position, the builders of Domme could not adopt the usual rectangular plan, and the layout is roughly trapezoid. Nor is there a central market square with arcades; instead the *place* is situated at the top of the town. One side of the square opens onto the terraces known as the *barre* from which the townspeople, as defenders, could survey the valley below.

Domme was founded in the 1280s by Philip the Bold of France. Its construction took decades, for the early settlers found the physical obstacles to building on this terrain hard to overcome. The irritated French king responded by fining the inhabitants, thus adding to their burdens and grievances. Eventually Domme was completed and settled down to enjoy its considerable privileges, for it had jurisdiction over much of the surrounding area and the right to coin its own money. Inevitably, as a fortified town in a vital strategic position, it repeatedly changed hands during the Hundred Years War. During the Wars of Religion Domme was Catholic, which was why the irrepressible Geoffroi de Vivans decided to capture it. He attempted to besiege the town in 1572 but its formidable defences were too much even for him. On his next attempt, in 1588, he

church, and then south to Nadaillac, an enchanting village. The twelfth-century church here was a priory dependent on Saint-Amand-de-Coly, and like its mother church was heavily fortified, especially over the beautiful crossing and apse. The south side of the nave is enclosed within a small yard from which a gate leads into the village. This is packed with delightful medieval houses, many roofed with *lauzes* and attached to towers. Continue south to the Borrèze valley and the village of the same name. Its houses, lining the lanes around the thirteenth-century church, are modest but characteristic of the Quercy. A large tower dominates the west end of the church, which was much altered in the late Gothic period. Southwest of Borrèze lies the pretty agricultural hamlet of Eyvignes, with its long church backing into the fields. Sadly, the splendid Château du Claud is not open to the public, for glimpses of its romantic profile from the lanes north of Eyvignes suggest it must be a fine building indeed. Its pepperpot towers glower over the

From the Belvédère at Domme, the town defenders enjoyed a commanding view of the Dordogne river.

adopted the guile for which he was celebrated and one dark night sent a platoon straight up the cliff face to the *barre*. The townspeople had considered the climb impossible and so hadn't bothered to defend the cliffs. They learnt of their error too late, for once inside the bastide the Protestant forces were able to open the gates and admit the rest of the troops. Vivans only held Domme for four years, and having demolished sections of the town that displeased him, such as the church, sold it to the king's representative and left.

Two roads lead up to Domme from the valley, one from Cénac, the other from Vitrac. The latter route brings you to the more spectacular of the two town gates, the Porte des Tours, guarded with massive round towers, their masonry broken only by arrow slits, while on either side ramparts rise up over the harsh rock. These towers were used, most effectively I'm sure, as a prison during the Hundred Years War, while the English held Domme from 1417 to 1438. A hundred years earlier captured Templars were held in those towers, and left graffiti still visible today. Both town gates lead into the spacious Place de la Rode, where it is best to park. Walk up the main street, the Grand' Rue, lined with shops specializing in local foodstuffs and wines. I often stocked up with fresh sausages from the butcher near the Esplanade, as well as bottles of Pécharmant wine from the merchants of the Grand' Rue. Some of the shops encourage visitors to taste the sticky nut liqueurs of the region without charge. Although it would be an exaggeration to say that Domme has been spoiled, it has grown self-conscious and is not immune from touches of gentrification. At the top of the main street you will pass on your right the sixteenth-century Maison du Gouverneur with its awesome tower, in which the town museum is now installed. Opposite stands the galleried seventeenth-century covered market, and from here you enter the grottoes beneath the town – for Domme cleverly combines almost all the attractions of the Dordogne in one spot. The caves at Domme are as lurid and splendid as most of those in this limestone region, complete with stalactites and curious *excentriques*.

Just beyond the market you'll find the church. It had to be rebuilt after the Huguenots had finished with it, and it's a building of little distinction. However, a side chapel contains a small collection of relics and carvings removed from neighbouring churches, assembled here to protect them from thieves and vandals. Most of those churches, such as the chapel at the charming dead-end hamlet of Turnac (which overlooks the Cingle de Montfort to the northeast), are kept more or less permanently locked, so the authorities extracted their modest treasures and display them here. From the church walk onto the Belvédère. From the *barre* you can relish one of the finest of all Dordogne views (and, incidentally, eat superbly at the adjacent restaurant). To the west, Beynac and La Roque-Gageac are visible on a clear day and you can follow the loops of the river past Vitrac – more or less opposite – and east towards Montfort and Groléjac. Below you is the contrast typical of this stretch of river. The flat fertile plain is couched among the loops of the meandering Dordogne and beneath the harsh limestone cliffs that loom over them, wooded and inhospitable – and of course ideally suited to the building of castles. Of this view the romantic Henry Miller wrote: 'Just to glimpse the black, mysterious river at Domme from the beautiful bluff . . . is something to be grateful for all one's life.'

Follow the path to the left to the public gardens where you'll find a useful *table d'orientation*. Just before the tennis courts turn left along a track that winds around what's left of the ramparts. Continue along the Rue Guibert de Dome, which takes you through a quiet corner of the town. Turn right at the Rue Porte del Bos for a look at the second major gateway; then follow the signs for Centre Ville, back to the Place de la Rode. Domme is a town to be wandered through and savoured, for it is dotted with attractive streets and well-tended balconied houses of golden stone. In the Rue de l'Abbaye you will find the ruins of a medieval abbey; down the Rue des Consuls stands the restored Hôtel de Ville, with its Gothic windows and crenellated top; and in the Rue Eugène Le Roy you pass the house where the celebrated novelist once lived. In the Place de la Rode itself is the oldest house in Domme, the Hôtel du Batteur de Monnaie, the mint built in 1282 and distinguishable by its Gothic arcades.

The bastide of Domme is still guarded by the medieval gateways that permit access through the town walls.

A winding road leads down to Cénac. Nearby are caves that were inhabited in Palaeolithic times and a Gallo-Roman site, testimony to the thousands of years of habitation this valley has known. The church is just west of the village along the road to Saint-Cybranet. It's a hefty tall structure, mostly rebuilt during the nineteenth century, for the bulk of the church was razed by Geoffroi de Vivans. The twelfth-century section that survives – the apse and its side chapels – is certainly remarkable and, inside and outside, displays a wealth of carving from about 1130. Stylistically, the carvings are related to those of the school of Moissac. Moissac, a Cluniac foundation located on the Tarn northwest of Toulouse, was the base for one of the finest schools of Romanesque art in Europe. The distinctive carvings that characterize the Moissac style are found not only in the justly celebrated porch and cloister at Moissac itself but in many other churches that fell within its orbit. In the Dordogne examples can be seen here and at Souillac (see p. 166) and Carennac (see p. 178). The Souillac and Carennac carvings, even more than these at Cénac, display the restless arrangement of figures, the energetic movements, and the highly evolved realism of the Moissac style. The capitals here depict biblical scenes and animals, while the exterior medallions exhibit a profusion of vivid grotesques: ferocious animals and soldiers, a contortionist, dancing men and women, some of them naked. These are among the most sophisticated and vigorous examples of Romanesque sculpture to be found in the Dordogne. Admire, too, the fine lofty proportions of the chancel, with its elegant arcades and balanced mouldings over each window.

Continue westward to La Chapelle-Péchaud, an attractive hamlet from which there are pleasant views over the hills. The Romanesque church has a dignified chancel, though decidedly modest after the splendours of Cénac. From here zigzag to Belvès, a marvellously situated town on a high spur above the Nauze river. The road winds up for 2 kilometres to reach the town from the valley. The principal church, Notre-Dame-de-Montcuq, is set on the edge of town on the way to Cadouin (see p. 127). Founded as a Benedictine priory in the thirteenth century, it's a large Gothic pile with a tall fifteenth-century west belfry propped up by hefty angle buttresses. The broad interior is of little interest, except for enthusiasts for *art populaire* (rustic art), who will find plenty of crude baroque work to satisfy them. From here a road leads to the shrine of Notre-Dame-de-Capelou. The church had to be rebuilt in the last century to accommodate the hordes of pilgrims who came in search of miraculous cures. The only attractive feature for the non-pilgrim is the sixteenth-century Virgin in the sanctuary. As prominent as the belfry of Montcuq is the octagonal tower in the Place de la Croix des Frères, all that remains of the Dominican church founded here in 1321. Adjoining it now is an attractive block of municipal buildings. Walk from here to the main square, the Place d'Armes, down the Rue Manchotte, along which lies the much altered former château and an excellent butcher. A square belfry of twelfth-century origin overlooks the Place d'Armes and the fifteenth-century covered market on rickety wooden columns; here you will find the vestiges of a medieval pillory. Crime does not seem to be a major problem in this bustling market town, which is a centre for the cultivation and marketing of walnuts.

Indeed, at Doissat, a few kilometres southeast from Belvès, flourishes the largest walnut plantation in all Europe; the small trees stride in neat rows over 65 hectares of slopes. There used to be a sixteenth-century château here, but it was destroyed during the Revolution and replaced by a nineteenth-century building. However, some of the old outbuildings survive, and one of them contains a small museum dedicated, appropriately enough, to the local nut. The famous warrior, Geoffroi de Vivans, whose exploits so enliven the history of the Dordogne, is, as a plaque on the museum wall records, buried at Doissat. Continue south to the rambling village of Prats-du-Périgord, overlooked by a sixteenth-century château with a fourteenth-century battlemented tower. There's an astonishing Romanesque church here; heavily fortified, its rounded chancel and the belfry are taller than the nave. The belfry itself is half-timbered and capped with a very steep roof. The nave and the lofty west front are windowless, except for a single slender south lancet. Which village needs a donjon when it has a church as formidable as this?

Further south lies the thirteenth-century bastide of Villefranche-du-Périgord, which was built by Alphonse de Poitiers. The main square contains, as every bastide should, a handsome covered market and many arcaded houses. From the market square turn into the Rue Saint-Georges, where you'll pass a few old houses, though, compared to other bastides of southern Périgord, Villefranche is a disappointment. The town layout remains authentic, but many old houses have vanished and the replacements are for the most part graceless. Return down the parallel Rue Notre-Dame. Turn right down the short Rue Sully to glimpse a fine tower house; then turn left and continue to the main square down the Rue Saint-Martin. The town church is a hideous example of nineteenth-century pastiche Romanesque, but at Loubejac to the south there's a handsome twelfth- or thirteenth-century church with a splendid octagonal belfry in the Limousin style.

From this most southerly point in the department head north again towards Besse, a village buried among thick woods and gentle hills in this sparsely populated area, where many local people earn their living, appropriately, from the lumber industry. Besse is justly famous for the elaborately carved Romanesque west front of its church. Compared to Cénac, the carvings at Besse are crude, for some of them date from the eleventh century, but they are well-preserved and full of interest. Not only are the capitals carved, but the arches around the doorway are filled with sculpture. There is a mixture of decorative palm-leaf and knot designs and panels depicting animals and human figures, including a fine St Michael poking away at a dragon, a mounted hunter on a stag hunt (a visual allusion to St Eustace in pursuit of Christ), the Temptation of Eve, and the Expulsion from the Garden. To the casual observer, the arrangement of the carvings is somewhat chaotic, though the distinguished art historian, Jean Secret, discerns Christ's redemption of mankind as an underlying theme.

Saint-Pompont, northeast of Besse, lies in a charming position astride a weed-choked stream which is overlooked by frail galleried houses. Cross one of the many footbridges into the nameless little streets of the tiny old town. Here you'll find more galleried houses, a medieval gate with a wooden balcony above its pointed arch, and a rather scrappy church with a rebuilt but still impressive belfry. Nearby stand the remains of the fifteenth-century château, its broad tower glowering beneath machicolations. It seems probable that church and château once formed complementary parts of the same system of fortifications, originally built by the English. Cross the main road near the church and you will reach a small square with a remarkable Périgordin house on the corner: arches screen storage areas on the ground floor, shuttered windows light the living quarters above, while the top storey is entirely open, a kind of primitive loggia. Through the upper windows of many of the barns scattered around Saint-Pompont you can see tobacco hanging up to dry in the autumn.

Just off the main road to Prats-du-Périgord stands the splendid Château de Mespoulet, framed by thick twelfth-century towers, a structure both formidable and visually beguiling. Unfortunately it is closed to the public and hardly worth a special journey, but look out for it if you are driving this stretch of the D60. Another detour could be made northwest to Saint-Laurent-la-Vallée, a village set in undulating Quercy countryside among small fields lined with tall poplars and pines. Attractive houses stand close to the church, which has a fine though weathered twelfth-century west doorway. Behind the altar in the tall rounded apse is a thoroughly rustic seventeenth-century screen, with statues of saints in unusual attitudes. John the Baptist, for instance, is scratching his groin, doubtless made itchy by the stylish animal skin he's wearing.

From Saint-Pompont drive northeast to the large well-tended village of Daglan. There are some curious houses here in a debased Renaissance style, such as the former town hall. The rebuilt church is of little interest, but one corner of Daglan has abundant charm. A lane leads down towards the river. You'll pass on the left a house with a curious corner window decorated with what look like masonic hieroglyphics and the date 1634, and a sadly dilapidated galleried house. The lane is blocked by a wall, lapped by convolvulus, where you can sit and be refreshed by the bickering of the little River Céou. I wouldn't want to make great claims for Daglan, but it is a tranquil and distinctive little town. The road follows the winding Céou valley east to Bouzic, set in a Quercy valley surrounded by thickly wooded hills. Here you can stroll past some typical *manoirs* and a church with a fifteenth-century flamboyant west doorway and some interesting carved capitals. Continue along the Céou valley, then branch off towards Gourdon.

From its hilltop Gourdon commands a part of Quercy known as the Bouriane. The old town is circled by boulevards that replace the former ramparts. Park in the

Above Serene and sheltered, the Dordogne flows towards the bridge at Cénac.

Right The apse of the church at Cénac is adorned with some of the liveliest Romanesque carvings in the Dordogne.

large square near the post office and walk up the Rue du Corps Franc Pommies, past some pleasant old houses; follow the signs to the Esplanade. From this terrace over 300 metres high there are marvellous views over the town and the surrounding countryside. By all accounts the castle of Gourdon, which once stood here, was one of the great fortresses of Quercy, but it was dismantled in the seventeenth century. Descend to the small square behind the chancel of the church where you'll see a group of medieval houses, one of which has a charmingly carved wooden door. The west door of the fourteenth-century church of Saint-Pierre is framed by a much-moulded surround; small figures and heads adorn the pinnacles that flank the porch. The interior is surprisingly broad and spare. The first chapel on the left has attractively carved doorways and niches and a delightful window with geometric tracery over the side wall. On leaving the church, walk under the arcades of the Hôtel de Ville (town hall) and turn down the Rue Majou. Turn left again into the tiny Rue des Consuls for a glimpse of some galleried houses before returning to the Rue Majou, which is crammed with ancient houses, some dating from the thirteenth century. No. 24 has the accidental charm of its assorted masonry. Continue either by taking the Rue Zigzag to the left as it meanders past mostly ruined houses, or by descending Rue Majou to the old town gate. Turn left along the boulevard to the austere Cordeliers, a fine late thirteenth-century church that contains an exceptionally well carved font of the same period. By continuing along the boulevard you will reach the post office square.

The special quality of Gourdon is its compactness, the way its ancient houses pack themselves in around the steep hill. This little-frequented town would make an excellent base for excursions and for walks in the lovely Bouriane. Such excursions are plentiful. A short distance southeast of the town is the rebuilt fourteenth-century church of Notre-Dame-des-Neiges, worth a visit for its mediocrity more than its merit. Beneath the belfry is a porch constructed of as primitive a pile of seventeenth-century masonry as you're likely to come across. The south door exhibits more fifth-rate carving. To visit the interior, you must get the key from the Syndicat d'Initiative at Gourdon (this also applies to the Cordeliers). Five kilometres east of Gourdon is the town of Le Vigan, with its splendid priory church. The priory was founded by the Bishop of Cahors in 1083, though the surviving buildings date from the late fourteenth century; their stylistic cohesion suggests that construction proceeded rapidly. The priory was extremely powerful in the Middle Ages, but suffered from the usual vicissitudes during the Hundred Years War and subsequent disturbances. After the Revolution the monastery was disbanded. A large recessed rose window looks out from the west front, and a tall crossing belfry rises over the complex chancel. The interior is elegantly vaulted and the chancel is exceptionally well proportioned. Just south of the church stands an extremely peculiar fountain, modelled, it would appear, on a wet stalagmite.

From Gourdon it is a short drive north to the caves at Cougnac, where you can see both fanciful limestone concretions and some prehistoric paintings of animals, mostly ibex, as well as humans. The principal wonders of Cougnac, however, are the extraordinary stalactites of needle-like thinness, packed closely together to form what in some cases look like lampshade fringes or sheets of rain, and in others like some ghastly device created by Poe for efficient impalement. For visitors staying south of the Dordogne valley who nevertheless wish to sample the kind of limestone caverns so common north of the river, Cougnac is more than worthwhile. The caves are close to the main Sarlat road, so you can return swiftly to Sarlat or Domme.

At Gourdon, machicolations between the towers helped deal with visitors who came to fight rather than pray.

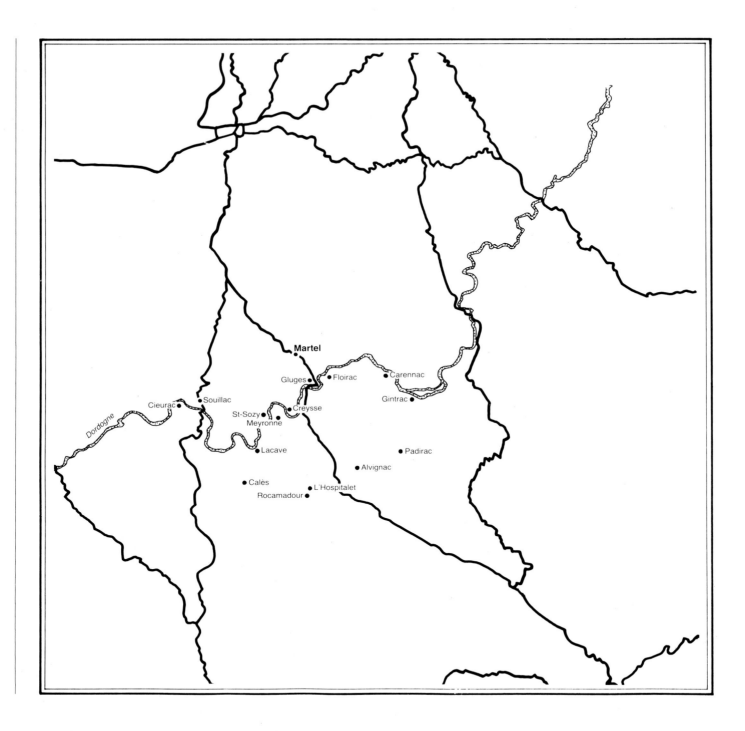

Martel

Gluges • • Floirac • Carennac

Cieurac • • Souillac Gintrac •

St-Sozy • • Creysse
Meyronne •

Dordogne

Lacave •

• Padirac

Calès • • Alvignac

Rocamadour • • L'Hospitalet

6
The Causses: Clifftop Shrines, Subterranean Caverns

Martel – Souillac – Rocamadour – Padirac – Carennac – Creysse

The eastern part of the Dordogne region is not in the department of that name but in the Lot. As you leave ancient Périgord and begin to penetrate ancient Quercy, differences in landscape and architecture become increasingly apparent. The upper Dordogne is a land of great plateaux and astounding underground caverns beneath the surface of the limestone hills, and the site of a shrine that was once one of the most holy spots in Christendom. Nor is there any shortage of great churches and of enchanting villages filled with *manoirs* and the dovecots that are a hallmark of Quercy. Martel makes an excellent base for exploring the region, though Souillac has a better supply of hotels and restaurants. The best reason for staying in Martel is that it is a marvellous little town, less overrun than Sarlat, more ambitious than Gourdon.

The town is named after Henri Martel, the hammer of the Saracens, who built a church here in the eighth century to celebrate his great victory over the Islamic forces threatening to overrun Europe. Many centuries later, another Henri, Henri Court Mantel, son of Henry II of England, came to Martel, only he came to die, and with his death Richard Lionheart became heir to the English throne and the great French territories that were then part of the English domains. Young Henri was in rebellion against his father but his campaign was faltering through lack of money. To rectify the situation Henri plundered every abbey and shrine within sight, including Rocamadour, which he sacked just before arriving in Martel, where he was taken ill. Stricken with remorse, Henri begged his father for forgiveness, and though Henry Plantagenet was unable to deliver it in person (he was occupied waging war near Limoges), he did send a messenger with his pardon shortly before his son died. History, then, has taken peculiarly dramatic form in the streets of fish-shaped Martel.

Make your way to the large fourteenth-century church, easily identified by its magnificent belfry, which was completed in 1514; it's a massive fortified structure with large angle buttresses and an octagonal turret. The wall to the right is protected by machicolations, and above its Gothic doorway a modern coat of arms carries the Martel crest: three hammers. The west tower forms an open porch below, protecting the twelfth-century sculpture over the doorway preserved when the tower was built. This sculpture represents a seated Christ in Majesty, his arms outstretched, flanked by four angels, two holding the Instruments of the Passion, two blowing long trumpets, while at their feet the dead are pushing up their coffin lids. The interior is a disappointment: a spacious hall church vaulted with garishly painted ribs. However, the east window is exceptionally fine, filled with fifteenth-century stained glass attributed to Arnaud de Moles. Medieval glass is extremely rare in the Dordogne, and this window, illustrating the life of Christ, is not only ancient but of good quality. There is another item of interest on the north wall,

Left The sixteenth-century belfry dominates the delightful town of Martel.

Below These shallow domes float over the east end of the abbey at Souillac, which contains superb Romanesque carvings.

an eloquent and graphic sixteenth-century crucifix.

On leaving the church, take the Rue Droite, passing the much altered Maison du Silence as you walk into the town. Continue through the small Place de la Bride past many medieval houses to the Hôtel Vergnes de Ferron, a turreted house with a classical doorway. Then turn right into the Place des Consuls with its imposing eighteenth-century covered market, a square dominated by the Palais de la Raymondie, built in the thirteenth and early fourteenth centuries by the immensely powerful Vicomte de Turenne. (During the Crusades the then Viscount imaginatively decreed that Martel citizens convicted of adultery were to be dragged naked through the streets.) Note the fine Gothic arcades at ground level and the half Gothic, half Renaissance windows along the Rue Senlis. The corners of the building are, inevitably, turreted and towered, giving the palace dignity and panache. From the courtyard there is a good view of the principal tower and access to the museum, which contains Gallo-Roman remains found at Puy d'Issolud, a plateau about 8 kilometres to the northeast where the Petrocorii (see p. 20) fought their last battles. Also facing the Place des Consuls is the greatly altered Maison Fabri, where Henri Court Mantel died in 1183. Facing the Raymondie is the Hôtel du Chauffoir, behind which rises the Tour des Pénitents, one of the many medieval towers that still dominate the ancient streets. Return to the Rue Droite and walk west. On the left you'll see the charming Petite Raymondie, with its small courtyard garden spilling out onto the street through the grilles of its arcade. Cross the little Place Meteye and walk east along the lane past the Maison de Mirandol with its elegant turreted tower, until you emerge again into the Place de la Bride.

Although Martel is, deservedly, much visited, come nightfall the town empties rapidly. After a standard six-course dinner at one of the friendly restaurants one can stroll through the quiet lanes, footsteps reverberating on the ancient paving and scarcely any other sound troubling the night air. Just a few kilometres from Martel you can find countryside that is, compared to the Périgord, positively desolate. Parts of the Périgord are certainly remote, but rarely far from woods or streams. But north of here lies a limestone plateau called the Causse de Martel, one of a number of *causses* in the Lot. These plateaux are almost treeless, and only really suited for the grazing of sheep. In summer these high expanses of scrubland are as hot as the Midi, while in winter the exposed plateau can be bitterly cold. It is a harsh land to which we shall return later in this chapter. For now, however, drive west to Souillac.

Virginia Woolf stayed here in 1937 and was delighted to find 'no tourists . . . England seems like a chocolate box bursting with trippers afterward'. The English traveller, Arthur Young, was equally entranced in 1787: 'a delicious little valley . . . scattered with fine walnut trees; nothing can apparently exceed the exuberant fertility of this spot'. A mighty Benedictine monastery once dominated this meeting point of two rivers, the Borrèze and the Dordogne, but it suffered severely during the Wars of Religion. All the monastic buildings were destroyed, though fortunately the twelfth-century abbey church survived. In 1632 the abbot began to restore the ancient building, and work continued until 1712. After the Revolution the monks were expelled and the abbey secularized. It was reopened in 1801, and restored once again. Fortunately those who maintained the church fabric carefully preserved its unique features.

Most visitors approach the abbey from the spacious square to the east, and are confronted by the extraordinary chancel with its descending scallop-shell roofs and its ornamental cornices sheltering the numerous windows; blind arcading keeps the rhythms of the building lively despite its great breadth. Above the broad mass floats the great dish of the *lauze*-covered main dome, crowned with a small pine-cone turret pierced with openings. Like Saint-Front at Périgueux, Souillac has been heavily restored, but how much more tactful is the hand that retouched Souillac! Although much of the texture is recent, the east side still preserves an authentically Byzantine atmosphere, incorporating eastern vocabulary into a fundamentally Romanesque utterance. From the north, in contrast, the abbey appears tall and austere, with its plain round-headed windows below the roofline, and the square tower that, at its base, dates from the tenth century, making it one of the oldest structures in the region.

Enter through the southwest door, a remnant of the seventeenth-century reconstruction. Try to avoid the temptation to look behind you at the west wall as you enter the nave. This first glimpse of the interior is magical: the space is simple and elegant, but lifted by the immense domes that support the nave and crossing and give the whole church an almost weightless floating quality. The nave is divided into only two bays, each lit by two windows on either side. A gallery runs along the base of the windows and below it soars a tall blind arcade of three arches per bay, two slender ones flanking a larger one. This gives a vertical lift to a building that is exceptionally broad. In the choir the sanctuary is ringed by an alternating broad and narrow arcade, which rests on numerous capitals, some splendidly carved with foliage and birds, others with biblical scenes. My favourite is a particularly delicate Annunciation. The abbey is furnished with seventeenth-century stalls and religious paintings, of which the most interesting is a sixteenth-century Spanish polyptych.

But the glory of the church lies against the west wall, a group of carvings that would originally have been found on the exterior, as at Moissac (see p. 156), where the sculptures are clearly related to these at Souillac and may well be by the same artists. The carvings were wisely moved inside the church during the seventeenth century, since enough damage had already been done to them during the Wars of Religion. The main panel, flanked by statues of St Benedict and St Peter, crams in various episodes in the life of the monk Theophilus, who, unjustly sacked from his post as church treasurer, made a pact with the devil and so got his job back; but remorse stricken, he appealed to the Virgin Mary, who appeared to him in a dream and gave him back the incriminating parchment the devil had made him sign. The sculpting of all these episodes within one panel requires the viewer to accept the convention of simultaneity; fortunately the vigour and clarity of the carving make it fairly easy to make out the various overlapping scenes. The great carved pillar on the right must originally have been the central pier of a large doorway. A tour de force of ferocious energy, it shows animals devouring their prey, but that phrase only lamely describes the way the pillar is clotted with interlinked carvings. As the art historian, Meyer Schapiro, observes, 'The beasts are twisted, entangled, and unbalanced by their own rapacious energy. . . . We cannot isolate the figures without disrupting the architecture.' Depictions of lustful embraces suggest that the ensemble is a warning against the consequences of sin. Yet paradoxically its joyful barbarism undermines the sternness of its apparent message. Among this seething mass of carving there are also signs of intense humanity. Observe the figure of Abraham, eyes piercing and haunted, preparing to sacrifice Isaac, whose eyes are closed but whose mouth is anxious: the gestures are tender, the feeling behind the flowing rhythms of the brilliantly carved stone deep and compassionate. By the arch you will have doubtless noticed the famous striding figure of Isaiah, sinuous yet dramatic. See how carefully the hems of the draperies are decorated, though this detail doesn't impede the flow of the figure. These great carvings have all the panache, attention to detail, virtuosity and depth of feeling of the highest art.

East of the church a tall tower rises over the small Place Saint-Martin. This is the belfry of the former parish church, now disused. There's a damaged early medieval carving of Christ in Majesty over the door, thin gruel after the abbey. Indeed, apart from the abbey, Souillac has little to offer. The ancient Hôtel Dufour in the Rue de la Halle (reached via the covered market visible from the Place Saint-Martin) has been restored and there are a few other attractive houses nearby. Because Souillac is a popular base from which tourists explore this stretch of the Dordogne, the town is invariably overrun in summer. I used to contribute to the overcrowding by patronizing a *charcuterie* on the main street that made the loveliest pâté I have ever eaten, a sumptuous melange of duck livers and truffles. Souillac, then, is represented in my mind by fine examples of the most enduring art, namely architecture, and the most ephemeral, the preparation and consumption of food. Of the nearby villages, only one is memorable: Cieurac, on the south bank of the Dordogne. Here a short drive up an unpromising lane leads to some old turreted *manoirs* and a large, mostly nineteenth-century château guarded by vicious dogs behind the walls and by a squad of peacocks on top of them.

Leave Souillac by the winding D23. After a lovely drive of 5 kilometres, you'll spot a fine château on the south bank of the Dordogne. A casualty of the Wars of Religion, when it was burnt down by the Catholics, La Treyne is nevertheless a most attractive building. The massive central keep, built by the Rouffillac family, dates from the early fourteenth century. The bulk of La Treyne is seventeenth century and was built by the de la Ramière family. It is now a luxurious

hotel. A terrace overlooks the river and the gardens are especially attractive. Three kilometres further on the strategic confluence of the Dordogne and the Ouysse is overlooked by a castle that rivals Beynac and Castelnaud in the drama of its site. Belcastel (which can be visited in the summer) is perched on a crag about 300 metres high, and the labour involved in transporting building materials to the summit must have been extraordinary. Most of the castle, sadly, is a nineteenth-century rebuilding, and only the chapel and part of one wing are medieval, so the view from below is far more satisfying than the view from close up; on the other hand the panorama from the terrace by the ancient ramparts is staggering.

The road twists along the hillside to the village of Lacave, named after its sole attraction. You are now approaching another of the *causses*, the Causse de Gramat, and beneath this plateau lie two of the most magnificent caverns in France; Padirac is the more spectacular, but Lacave is well worth visiting too. Prehistoric remains have been found here, but no paintings or engravings, and the appeal of these caverns is their extraordinary formations, eerie in their resemblance to identifiable animals and structures. Underground rivers and pools and bizarre glowing light add to the strangeness, like a scene from a Jules Verne novel. From Lacave drive south onto the *causse* to the spruce village of Calès, with its restored Romanesque church and attractive houses. Continue towards Rocamadour, and after about 5 kilometres bear left along the lane that leads to the fourteenth-century fortified mill of Cougnaguet, set in a dramatic little canyon of the Ouysse. It's well worth the detour, not just because of the intrinsic interest of this rare medieval survival, but because the lane takes you through typical *causse* landscape, remote, parched, and strangely beautiful. Return to the main road and L'Hospitalet, a village overlooking Rocamadour. Here I suggest you leave your car and take to your feet. For centuries pilgrims approached the shrine on foot, and the visitor short-circuits the experience

---

Left **The Château de La Treyne, overlooking a turbulent stretch of the Dordogne, is now a luxury hotel.**

of Rocamadour by driving straight into the village, quite apart from the fact that it is almost impossible to find a place to park.

Major shrines such as Rocamadour strike visitors in very different ways. Rocamadour, I confess, leaves me cold, though no visitor to the area should fail to go there, for it is unique. Shrines always speak to me of desperation, of the sick and wretched people who travel there often at vast expense and inconvenience in a last bid to solve a problem. Perhaps the allegedly miraculous cures are genuine, but the vast majority of supplicants leave with their prayers unanswered. Still, Rocamadour, unlike Lourdes, is not as active a shrine as it once was, and tourists far outnumber pilgrims. Some denigrate Rocamadour as too commercialized, but that is foolish, for shrines have been commercialized since the Middle Ages. Where pilgrims come in their thousands, there is a need for services and provisions and accommodation. Nor are commemorative medallions and trinkets an invention of the advertising age.

The publican, Zacchaeus, a disciple of Christ and husband of St Veronica, came to France, it is said, to escape religious persecution. After St Veronica died, he came to this cliff where he lived as a hermit for the rest of his days. When in 1166 a perfectly preserved body was found in a grave high on the rock, there was speculation as to its identity. In time the theory that it was Zacchaeus took the lead. In any event, St Amadour, as the corpse became known, gave his name to the cliff (Roc Amadour), and it soon attracted a major pilgrimage. Saints Bernard and Dominic, and the kings of England and France, made their way up to the chapels on their knees. The pilgrimage became recommended as a penance for the severest offences. The other attraction here was the Black Virgin, a twelfth- or early thirteenth-century image that can still be seen. Then, as now, Rocamadour attracted hostelries and souvenir sellers, and the town thrived, despite the ravages of the Hundred Years War. In earlier conflicts Henri Court Mantel sacked Rocamadour, and in later ones the Huguenots, under Captain Bessonies, did great damage, as did the revolutionaries in 1793. Bessonies even tried to cremate the saint's body but, *mirabile dictu*, it wouldn't burn, so the enraged Huguenot had to be content with hacking it to pieces. Thanks to these desecrations most of what remains at Rocamadour is a

Left **From the top of a pillar of rock, the Château de Belcastel surveys the River Ouysse and the** *causse*.

Above **One of the mills along the Ouysse near Lacave.**

171

Below A Quercynois tower on the *causse* near Calès.

Right The vertiginous cliffs at Rocamadour, a place of pilgrimage for hundreds of years.

nineteenth-century reconstruction undertaken with the intention of reviving the pilgrimage.

From L'Hospitalet, where the shrine hospital used to stand, there is an unforgettable view onto the town that hugs the sheer cliff in tiers along narrow terraces. To have built houses and churches there at all seems an act of defiance against nature. Take the lane down to the thirteenth-century Porte du Figuier, which guards the lowest of the town's three levels. Every hundred metres or so this street, the Rue de la Couronnerie, is interrupted by other medieval gates, until you finally reach the Porte Basse. Lining this street are shops and restaurants; on the middle level are clustered the chapels, while at the top are the town ramparts 200 metres above the valley. Two structures are worthy of attention among the razzmatazz below: the Couronnerie, the heavily restored fifteenth-century town hall, and, beyond the Porte Basse, the tall handsome fourteenth-century fortified mill of Roquefrège. Retrace your steps to the Grand Escalier. A lift ascends to the higher levels, but it is expensive and quite contrary to the spirit of the place. So unless you are feeling very weary, follow the example of kings and walk up the 216 steps. At the first terrace you'll see the former palace of the bishops of Tulle, a vast over-restored turreted structure that later became a fort. Before entering the fort – the steps continue through it – walk along the oldest street in Rocamadour, the Rue de la Mercerie, where medieval pilgrims bought badges to wear in their hats, to the square fourteenth-century Maison de la Pomette. The steps through the fort lead up to the Parvis des Églises and the seven chapels of the shrine.

As you enter the Parvis you will see opposite you Saint-Sauveur, a basilica built in 1913 in a pure Romanesque style. Wooden galleries lead from here to the venerated chapel of Notre-Dame, which was rebuilt in the nineteenth century. The dark chapel flickers with the candles of the faithful, and ex votos (plaques from grateful pilgrims) line the walls. From the roof, barely visible in the gloom, hangs an eighth-century bell, which is said to ring of its own accord (actually on the prompting of angels) when a miracle is imminent. Behind the altar is the walnut Black Virgin and Child, a stark slender carving trimmed with silver and lightly embroidered with jewels, the patina of its antiquity lending the calmly gazing figure dignity and power. Next to the chapel

entrance, traces of a fifteenth-century fresco depict the Dance of Death, while on the other side of the door is the spot where the body of St Amadour was discovered, and nearby, embedded in the chapel wall, is a great iron sword. This, you will be told, is none other than 'Durandel' and belonged to the eighth-century warrior, Roland; sadly the legend is untrue. Opposite the chapel door, over the apse of St Michael's chapel, are superb frescoes, probably twelfth-century, of the Annunciation and Visitation. It's worth visiting as many of the chapels as are open, for their atmosphere more than for any architectural distinction. Then return to the Parvis, where you'll find the museum, full of reliquaries and vestments and other church treasures.

A tunnel under Saint-Sauveur leads onto a broad terrace. From here take the path up to the nineteenth-century Calvary, zigzagging past various Stations of the Cross and grottoes. Finally, ascend to the ramparts, which jut right out from the cliff and offer stupendous views down into the

The venerable and venerated statue of the Black Virgin at Rocamadour.

Alzou gorge. These fortifications are mostly fourteenth-century, though the buildings up here are much more recent and house the guardians of the shrine. A level road leads from the ramparts over the clifftop to L'Hospitalet. If you can arrange it, visit Rocamadour early in the morning, when the light is at its best and the shrine is relatively uncrowded. You can lunch at Rocamadour itself or at Alvignac, and then spend the afternoon at Padirac to the northeast, the other unmissable sight on the Causse de Gramat.

Even the 100-metre descent into Padirac is exciting. A lift takes visitors to a platform above a vast hole in the ground, and a second lift descends to the foot of the chasm. It's like dropping into the mouth of a wet volcano, for water drips and cascades down the sheer rock, and ferns and lichen cling to ledges. You will enter a long narrow cave flanked on either side by overhanging cliffs. The walkway is built above an underground brook, but after 300 metres the passage becomes impassable on foot and visitors must take to boats. It's an eerie experience, squeezed between the cliff walls and the rough vault of the roof, with the voice of the guide and the sound of the paddle breaking the silence. The chilly water is crystal clear, but there are no fish: the darkness and lack of oxygen make this an unpromising habitat. The river broadens into the Lac de la Pluie (Rain Lake), aptly named, as water dripping from the roof now scores a direct hit on the boats. Come prepared. Immense stalactites as thick as Muhammad Ali's thighs descend from the roof but fail to touch the cavern floor. The river flows for more than 10 kilometres before emerging near Montvalent, but the boat journey ends by the lake shore and you must walk from here to the largest of the caverns, the Grand Dôme. All around are bizarre rock formations, some of them horizontal, like stacks of pancakes. Other concretions mimic the undersides of mushrooms. Culinary comparisons are unavoidable, though there's little that's appetizing about these weird formations. The texture of these contorted rubbery rocks resembles plasticine. The constancy of these caverns is equally unreal. The water temperature is 8 degrees Centigrade, and the air 13 degrees Centigrade, unchanging the year round. Underground caverns pay no heed to seasons.

The chasm of Padirac has been a well-known local hazard for centuries, and legends ascribe its presence to a contest

The village alarm clock at Lavergne near Gramat.

between the devil and St Martin, in which Satan dared the saint to leap over the chasm he conjured into being with his foot. But it was only in 1890 that the speleologist, E. A. Martel, discovered the Grand Dôme. It must have been an astonishing moment when he crawled into this vast chamber 91 metres high, with pools for a floor and an undulating, barely discernible rock vault for a roof. Amazingly, only 7 metres of rock separate the roof from the open air of the

Left Pastures and *causse* in a valley near Rocamadour.

Above This barn near Gintrac is a likely candidate for conversion into a town-dweller's summer cottage.

177

causse. Plunging stalactites and overhangs confuse the eye, so it's difficult to gauge the cavern's dimensions. No matter, for this is the moment to forget the statistics and luxuriate in the awesome immensity of the place. Of all the caverns of the Dordogne, the Grand Dôme is surely the most splendid. Walking along the passages that wind around the caverns I could imagine how Jonah must have felt inside the whale.

From Padirac turn north to the Dordogne valley, pausing at the typical Quercy village of Gintrac, which enjoys a lovely cliffside setting. Pretty half-timbered houses line one side of a stream, while the church stands opposite, with galleried houses and dovecots for company. A few kilometres downstream is the wholly delightful little town of Carennac. Famous for its local greengages, its associations with Fénelon, and its enchanting roofscapes, it huddles on the south bank of the Dordogne. The solid masonry of the much rebuilt deanery faces the river; against a wall stands a bust of Fénelon, for he became Prior of Carennac in 1681 and stayed for fifteen years and, it is said, wrote *Télémaque* on the little island called the Île Barrade.

In a letter of May 1681 Fénelon described his arrival here:

'I arrived at the harbour at Carennac to find the quayside crowded with people. Two boats, filled with the town dignitaries, came towards me, and at the same time I realized that some very warlike local soldiers had cunningly hidden themselves in a corner of the pretty island that you know: from there they emerged in battle formation to greet me by firing their muskets. Adding to the sound of the volleys was that of the drums. I crossed the lovely Dordogne river, which was packed with boats escorting mine, and was met by solemn ranks of venerable monks.'

Adjoining the rather stern deanery is a medieval archway, the last remnant of the fortifications. Through this arch can be seen the great entrance of the priory, with its mid twelfth-century carving over the door in the style perfected at Moissac (see p. 156). A Christ in Majesty, his right hand raised and his left holding the Book of Judgment, is seated within an oval of light. His eyes look sternly down. At the corner of the oval are the symbols of the Evangelists, and the remaining panels are filled with lively representations of the Apostles and two adoring angels. The border of the sculpture is particularly well carved with a stylized frieze within which small animals scamper, just as they do along

Above **Fénelon, the nobleman, prelate and writer, who spent much of his life at the priory of Carennac.**

Right **The porch at the priory church at Carennac shelters a fine Romanesque carving.**

the edges of illuminated manuscripts of the period. On either side of the portal climb three mythological creatures, all that remains of what must once have been a richly entertaining group of carvings.

The tall barrel-vaulted nave has four bays supported on piers of varying design that rest on fairly primitive capitals. The domed crossing leads into a vaulted chancel marred by an east window stuffed with bad pictorial glass. Of the cloister, only one Romanesque gallery, with characteristic round arches resting on twinned columns, remains, and the three other galleries are in a late fifteenth-century highly decorated flamboyant style; most of the tracery has been destroyed, though other flamboyant embellishments, such

Left Carennac, once a major ecclesiastical centre, now a village of irresistible charm.

Above If you sense the overhanging cliffs at Gluges are too close for comfort, you'd be right.

as the vaults, survive. There are a number of first-rate sixteenth-century sculpted Entombments in the Dordogne, but the group at Carennac, placed in a room off the cloister, is one of the very finest. The draperies are exquisitely carved and the still, mourning figures are dignified and deeply expressive.

The priory at Carennac is a solemn building, but the village around it is bright and cheerful, a perfect balance of yellow stone and the liveliness and greenery that proximity to a river lend a village. The houses have the irregular charm so often found in Quercy: undercrofts are packed with firewood and straw, while above them turrets peer down under their perfectly shaped roofs of grey-brown tiles that blend so beautifully with the ochre stone and dark shutters.

If you can resist the temptation to linger in Carennac indefinitely, continue west along the shady river road to Floirac. A mass of buildings on the horizon seems to indicate a fortress church in the distance, but not so: the impression is created by the presence of a tall fourteenth-century donjon adjoining the church, a lumpish eighteenth-century building that does contain a crude but moving sixteenth-century pietà. Beyond Floirac begins a dramatic loop of the river called the Cirque de Montvalent. Easily the best view of the Cirque and its ring of high hills is obtained from the Belvédère de Copeyre, reached by crossing the river just beyond Floirac, then turning immediately right until you see an iron cross on a clifftop. From here the panorama is superb. There is a striking contrast between the placid settled quality of the farmland close to the water and the wilder, more desolate cliffs rising up to the *causses*.

Backtrack to the remarkable village of Gluges, cowering beneath overhanging cliffs near the river. The astonishing thing about Gluges is not its picturesque quality, for it's not especially lovely, but the fact that anyone chose to build in this spot in the first place. La Roque-Gageac was partially destroyed by falls of rock, and Gluges seems an even more likely candidate. The drive from Gluges towards Creysse takes you along one of the more harrowing roads in the region. To the right the yellow-grey cliffs rise sheer above you, while to the left swirls the forceful river. It is a constantly enjoyable feature of the Dordogne that within a few minutes the landscape can alter so suddenly, as it does here from the farmlands of Floirac to this dramatic riverscape. Where there's water there must be Creysse and you soon reach this gem of a village, which Cyril Connolly described as a 'water-bound rival to Carennac'. Cross two small bridges on foot and climb the path up to the church past delightful stone houses, old and new.

The church is remarkable on account of its paired Romanesque apses, a unique feature. However, the 'apses' have now been demoted to a pair of south chapels. Nevertheless it's apparent that, when the church was the chapel of the nearby castle, the apses truly were apses and terminated the chancel, but that at a later date the building was expanded into its present form. The irregular exposed masonry gives the church a rough-hewn look matching its craggy site. Note the ancient font carved with a primitive Crucifixion, and the fragmentary frescoes. From the church terrace there are fine views of the village, the wooded hills, and the river. Walk down to the village hall and the charming small *manoir* screened by palm trees. A lane to the right leads alongside the old ramparts to the remains of the château. Bear right under the stern walls of the tower and take the first left past some old cottages to another *manoir*, for in its garden stands a splendid Quercynois dovecot.

The attractive D23 leads directly back to Martel, but those with time to spare can return via Meyronne and Saint-Sozy. Meyronne was once the seat of the bishops of Tulle, though nowadays there's little to indicate its former eminence. The best thing to do at Meyronne is pause for refreshments at the Hôtel de la Terrasse above the bridge and enjoy the view of the Dordogne and the limestone escarpments near Lacave. Saint-Sozy lies on the other side of the river. Stroll up to the old *manoirs* and towers set along the hillside. From Saint-Sozy you can drive north to Martel or take a narrow but very lovely road over high hills back to Souillac.

The pepperpot tower of a manor pokes above the wooded banks of the Dordogne near Meyronne.

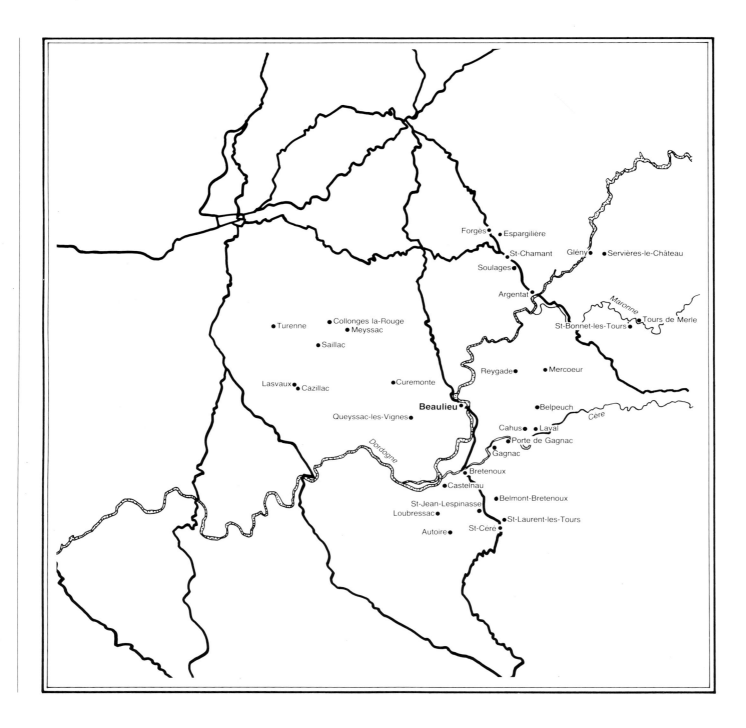

Forgès • • Espargilière

St-Chamant • Glény • • Servières-le-Château

Soulages •

Argentat • *Maronne* Tours de Merle •

St-Bonnet-les-Tours •

• Turenne • Collonges la-Rouge
• Meyssac

• Saillac

Reygade • • Mercoeur

Lasvaux • Curemonte •
• Cazillac

Beaulieu •

Queyssac-les-Vignes • • Belpeuch
Cère

Cahus • • Laval

Dordogne • Porte de Gagnac
• Gagnac

• Bretenoux

• Castelnau

St-Jean-Lespinasse • • Belmont-Bretenoux

Loubressac • • St-Laurent-les-Tours

Autoire • • St-Céré

7
The Upper Dordogne
Beaulieu – Castelnau – Montal – Argentat –
Collonges – Turenne – Curemonte

Romanesque Sculpture, Renaissance Busts:
South of Beaulieu

Beaulieu, which means beautiful place, was so named by a
ninth-century prelate. The praise is justified, for Beaulieu is
not only of great architectural interest but is delightfully
situated along the banks of the Dordogne. There's excellent
bathing and camping here, which makes it a good base for a
holiday as well as for sightseeing. The old town is, like
Martel, ringed by a boulevard, from which lanes and alleys
plunge into the centre of medieval Beaulieu and up to the
great abbey. Although the present abbey buildings were
erected by Cluniac monks in the twelfth century, the
foundation dates from the ninth century. The Cluniacs were
never self-effacing, and the church is on a large scale; above
it rise both a Limousin-style octagonal crossing tower and a
tall fourteenth-century west belfry. But it was on the broad
south doorway that the monks lavished their greatest care,
importing sculptors from Toulouse to carve the sculpture
over the doorway, and on the piers and arcades. The
carvings were completed in the 1120s and are stylistically
related to those at Souillac and Moissac.

Beaulieu is an enjoyable place to visit on bustling market
days, but to see the carvings at their best come here at
lunchtime, when the only sound in town is the clinking of
cutlery. You'll have the place to yourself, though of course
the interior of the abbey remains closed until the custodians
have finished their coffee and *digestif*. In the sculpture over
the doorway, a seated Christ surveys the Last Judgment, his
hands outstretched as if acclaiming the moment at which the
trump is sounded by the angels placed beneath his arms. The
apostles stand in a row behind Christ, while at their feet the
dead are pushing up their gravestones. What gives the
composition its serenity is that it omits the drama of the
Judgment itself. Here are no devils inflicting tortures on the
damned, as portrayed at, for instance, Conques, the great
pilgrimage church about 70 kilometres southeast of here.
The Beaulieu carving is a positive glorification of Christ's
power, not a lesson in the doctrines of the Church to keep
illiterate peasants in line. In the two horizontal bands below
the sculpture there are indeed monsters and chimeras,
including some in the act of devouring men. Yet these are
not devils so much as an apocalyptic portrayal of a rapacious
inhuman energy. How effortless and accomplished these
carvings are: the serene might of the large-eyed bearded
Christ, the marvellous many-headed monsters prowling
along the lintel set against a background of rosettes, and,
equally arresting, the sinuousness of the prophets on the
central pier of the doorway, their hands and arms straining
under the weight of the majestic carvings above them. The
sides of the porch are more weathered, though some of the
carvings, such as those depicting Daniel in the lions' den,
can be clearly identified.

Enter by the west door. As your eyes move down the great nave to the lofty chancel arcades, you'll notice the sculptural quality common to the best Romanesque architecture: the stately progression of the bays, the rhythmical alternation of semicircular column set against square pier, the great height of the domed crossing, lifting up the whole church, and the tall chancel piers, providing space so that the ambulatory windows can light the east end. Only the windows of the chancel, battling against the curvature of the roof, seem clumsy. There are some carved capitals and lintels inside the church, but nothing comparable to the south porch. The church treasure, with its Romanesque Virgin and numerous relics, is worth inspecting. On leaving the church by the west door you will face a tall house that is in effect a lapidary museum of Renaissance carvings set into the façade. Turn right down the Rue de la République, then down the alley on the right to a peaceful square, from where you can see what remains of the monastic buildings before completing the circuit of the church. Before leaving the town, walk to the twelfth-century Chapel of the Penitents down by the river. Over sixteen years I've made four attempts to get inside it, but always without success. The walk there is never wasted, though, for from the chapel terrace is a delightful and tranquil view of the river.

A fast road leads south from Beaulieu to Bretenoux, a bastide founded in 1277. Bretenoux is less spectacular than the bastides of southern Périgord, but it does have considerable charm. A fine stone mansion, now the Hôtel de Ville (town hall), stands along the main street, its façade interrupted by a broad tower. Behind it is the cobbled Place des Consuls, which is partly arcaded. From here you can walk into the town along the Rue Manoir de Cère. To the right a Gothic arch breaks the ramparts and frames a view of the River Cère, into which weeping willows reach down from the bank opposite. Walk through this arch and turn left along the river, then left again until, after passing some attractive houses, you eventually come to what appears to

be a dead end. A narrow passage on the left allows you to cut between two houses and walk down the Rue du Pressoir à Huile (Olive Press Road). You'll pass more vestiges of the ramparts, and as you cross the Rue Pierre Loti, you'll see a lovely group of houses. Two doors along stands the modest house where the exotic novelist Pierre Loti spent his childhood holidays from 1861 to 1864. Continue down the Rue du Pressoir à Huile to a house with a slender tower. Turn left until you cross the Rue du Pressoir à Vin, a charming Gothic alley roofed with flat wooden beams.

A few kilometres downstream from Bretenoux the Cère joins the Dordogne, and commanding this strategic spot is the magnificent Château de Castelnau, once the seat of the most powerful nobles of Quercy. Squatting on its hilltop, Castelnau is a beautiful yet sinister castle, for it is built of red ironstone, the colour of which ranges from ochre and orange to dried blood. A keep was built here by Hugues de Castelnau in about 1080, and the château was frequently enlarged until by the seventeenth century it had attained its present triangular shape broken by round towers at the points. In the eighteenth century it suffered from neglect and a fire of 1861 – possibly started with the intention of collecting the insurance – proved very destructive. Fortunately, Jean Mouliérat, an actor from the Opéra Comique, bought Castelnau in 1896 and spent the next thirty-six years restoring it. Walk round the ramparts and it soon becomes apparent that much of the formidable castle is a shell. Predictably, given Castelnau's varied history, the buildings show the influence of many periods and styles: the rough thick walls of the eleventh-century keep, the Renaissance windows and dormers, and the fake Romanesque arcades of the restoration.

The castle gate opens into an arcaded courtyard containing a lapidary collection. There are some good pieces here: a late Gothic pietà, Romanesque capitals, Gothic Madonnas and effigies. Since Castelnau had to be fully restored, it has the air of a museum more than a home. Rooms are cluttered with huge Louis XIV and Louis XV wardrobes, Louis XIII chairs that no one has sat in for decades, ancient portraits no longer identifiable, Aubusson and Beauvais tapestries, and a collection of porcelain. Still, some original elements remain: the shields bearing the crest (lions and towers) of the lords of Castelnau, some heavy Renaissance

---

Monsters devour men and the dead raise their tombstones in the magnificent Last Judgment at Beaulieu.

Left The Chapel of the Penitents at Beaulieu, often overlooked by tourists who come to see the more spectacular abbey.

Above The mighty château at Castelnau, glowing on its hilltop in the evening sunshine.

fireplaces and patterned frescoes, and best of all, the wonderful chapel, with its fifteenth-century altarpiece, its Madonnas from the thirteenth and fifteenth centuries, both under original canopies, and glorious fourteenth-century stained glass. Many of the castle windows are studded with fragments of medieval glass and Renaissance roundels, but in the chapel you can see an intact Crucifixion, worn but still glowing with colour and emotion. The other Gothic chapel at Castelnau, on the other side of the main courtyard, is less interesting: once frescoed, the paintings have now faded. Also dating from this period is the church at the foot of the ramp leading up to the castle. Built from the same stone as the château, this is a noble building, but it seems permanently closed – a pity, since it apparently contains fine stalls and statues.

From Castelnau turn south and drive up the winding road to the lofty village of Loubressac. Park in the square by the war memorial. Facing the village, bear right till you reach a viewing platform with its splendid panorama over the Dordogne valley. To the right you can see the towers of Saint-Laurent-les-Tours behind Saint-Céré, while almost straight ahead Castelnau sprawls on its hilltop. Walk back to the square and through the stone arch that leads to the church, with its mutilated yet still elegant doorway of 1520. Inside, the roof is painted in rustic fashion, as are some of the projections supporting the roof in the chapels. In the chancel behind the altar there's an elaborate eighteenth-century screen of wood painted to resemble marble, primitive to be sure, but all of a piece and redeemed by the grandeur of its design. Continue into the village and on the right you'll see some handsome old houses and the château gatehouse surmounted by a heraldic device. The seventeenth-century château itself is hard to see from the village, but you will have caught repeated glimpses of the striking building with its pepperpot roofs during the drive up to Loubressac.

Even more appealing than Loubressac is the nearby village of Autoire on the edge of the Causse de Gramat. For its size it contains a surprising number of *manoirs*, most of them entirely typical of Quercy, with their turrets and small towers decked in vines and ivy. Dovecots stand like sentinels in the fields or are attached to the village houses. Autoire's attractions are enhanced by its setting deep in a cliff-lined valley. The Romanesque church is embellished with entertaining grotesque corbels that line the stately little chancel. From the village a lane leads to a waterfall, from which a steep path climbs to the *cirque*, an amphitheatre offering splendid views over the surrounding Quercy countryside. By continuing up the valley and then bearing northeast you will come to the Grotte de Presque, caves that burrow deep into the rock. Here moisture has helped to form astonishing concretions, mostly pillars and columns that glow with colour. Continue north to Saint Jean-Lespinasse, a peaceful village bypassed by the traffic rushing along the valley road. The chunky Romanesque church is built in the form of a Latin cross; medallions around the chancel cornice depict acrobats, trumpeters, wolves, and owls. Close to the church stands an old barn with a half-timbered and steeply roofed dovecot above it, a typical example of the unassuming yet fitting domestic architecture found in so many Quercy villages. Across from the village a lane leads to the Château de Montal.

However many châteaux you may have visited by now, it is essential to visit Montal, for it is unlike any other domestic building in the region. There are a number of châteaux in the Dordogne, such as Monbazillac and Puyguilhem, that were evidently designed more as ostentatious country retreats than as fortresses. Yet they maintain a show of military preparedness, even though some of those defensive features are fake. Montal is to the outside world a fortress château, but its courtyard and interior display a refinement and sophistication unequalled by any other Renaissance structure in the Dordogne. Only two sides of the courtyard were constructed, though Jeanne de Montal, who built the château, had plans for other wings that never came to fruition. This great lady, widow of the Governor of Haute Auvergne, built Montal in the 1530s for her eldest son, Robert, but he was killed in battle. Although he never saw the splendid gift his mother had devised, his initial and hers ('I' in sixteenth-century French) are carved on the château walls. His brother, Dordé, became head of the family, but it

---

The hilltop village of Loubressac offers some of the best views onto the Dordogne valley.

Left A galleried house at Loubressac, tucked behind the village gateway.

Above Autoire. A delectable village nestling in a quiet valley just south of the Dordogne.

Below Behind this formidable medieval tower at Montal is the loveliest Renaissance courtyard in the Dordogne.

Right Part farm, part manor, part fortress, this house at Autoire is typical of the domestic architecture of Quercy.

The graceful, gracious Renaissance courtyard at Montal, one of the gems of the Dordogne.

seemed inevitable that he would be the last of the Montals, since he was a priest. To Dordé that was a trifling consideration, and he obtained a papal dispensation so that he could marry and breed.

Running the length of the L-shaped building is a lovely frieze, delicately carved in bas-relief with figures on horseback, satyrs, shields, arabesques – just about the entire repertoire of Renaissance motif and decoration. The letters I and R punctuate the line, of course, and above are equally elaborate dormers. Then, too, there are seven superb busts of the Montal family, stern but elegant in their elaborate hats, marvellous in their naturalism. All this ornament is unquestionably lavish, but it is also decorous and controlled, forming an exquisite and refined composition, easily the best of its kind in the Dordogne. Its survival, though, is close to miraculous. The château was partially dismantled during the Revolution, and its contents sold off by an unscrupulous owner during the last century.

A new owner, Maurice Fenaille, came to the rescue, recovered many of the missing contents, restored the building, and, in a final act of munificence, left the resuscitated château to the nation in 1913. The interior is thus the creation of M. Fenaille, and so, like Castelnau, Montal inevitably has the atmosphere of a museum more than a home. Hardly any of the original decoration remained when he bought the château; some faded silk Italian wallpapers hung on the walls, and the magnificent Renaissance fireplaces – many embellished with the family initials and with scallop shells, the family crests – were also still in place. Everything else was acquired by M. Fenaille, though he managed to recover some of the original furnishings. The tapestries are especially fine; those depicting tournaments and a Renaissance garden are exquisite in colouring, detail and workmanship. Less exquisite is the fireplace in the *salle d'honneur*. Here the almost perfect taste of Jeanne seems to have deserted her, for seated above the fireplace is a life-size stone stag, both splendid and absurd. There are paintings too, a Flemish triptych and a Catalan polyptych, but the most beautiful interior feature is the magnificent stone staircase that rises to the full height of the house. The underside of each step, visible from the flight below, is carved with geometric and animal forms; each step is differently sculpted, and all with the same elegance as the exterior frieze.

From Montal travel east along the Bave valley to Saint-Céré. Like Sarlat, the town is bisected by a Rue de la République, and most of the attractive streets and houses lurk behind this main drag. On one side of it stands the uninteresting Gothic church with its large seventeenth-century belfry porch. On the other side is the parallel Rue du Mazel and the winding Rue Saint-Cyr. The latter is full of lovely houses, stone *manoirs* and more modest shuttered houses of brick and timber. Just as attractive is the Place du Mercadial, grouped around a fountain. The town is overlooked by the two ruined but still domineering

A half-timbered house blocks one end of the main square at Saint-Céré.

Left **South of Saint-Céré.**

Above **The towers of Saint-Laurent-les-Tours have kept watch over Saint-Céré since the fourteenth century.**

fourteenth-century towers of Saint-Laurent-les-Tours on top of a steep hill. These sombre, forbidding ruins flank a château, which appears to have been medievalized in the nineteenth century. Although the château is private property, you can drive up to the ramparts and walk around them to enjoy the fine views over the heavily settled Bave valley and the wooded hills.

Indeed it is always a relief to escape into these hills from the valley. Take the road north to Belmont-Bretenoux, from which there are splendid views back onto Saint-Laurent-les-Tours. North of the village on the road to Cornac is the hamlet of Lavayssière. This small group of *manoirs* and farms, all turreted and gabled, is delectable, a perfect example of how functional buildings can blend into the countryside and acquire, almost inadvertently, great charm and beauty. Continue north over the hills and then descend to Gagnac. North of the church, which has a fine vaulted chancel, are numerous attractive old houses, many galleried and with overhanging roofs. On the war memorial a plaque reminds visitors that this unspoiled village was the home of 'martyres de la sauvagerie nazies'. On the other bank of the vigorous Cère is the hamlet of Porte de Gagnac, with its spacious houses and hotels lining the river bank.

From here you can either drive up the narrow Cère valley to Laval or, after a few kilometres, turn left towards Cahus. The first time I drove into the main square of the village, I asked an old man whether this place was Cahus. 'From time to time these things change,' he shrugged, 'but for the time being this is Cahus.' It is not a particularly interesting village, despite the eccentricities of its older inhabitants, though I enjoy the chandeliers in the rather bizarre little church; they look as if Pierre Loti brought them back from an Istanbul brothel. But the steep drive up to Cahus and then down again is dramatic and the views over the Cère gorges are splendid.

From Laval the railway line burrows far up the gorges, but not the road. For motorists this is the end of the line. Smoke pours from the chimneys of this small industrial town and railway depot, a deeply unattractive settlement in this wild and beautiful spot. On the opposite bank of the river stands the château of La Borie, with its massive fifteenth-century round towers with their pepperpot roofs. A machicolated polygonal tower with Renaissance windows overlooks the

living quarters of the château, which faces a small park. From Laval head north towards Mercoeur via the old shrine of Belpeuch, to which pilgrims have come for a thousand years. The object of the pilgrimage nowadays is an eloquent fifteenth-century pietà above the altar of the older of the two chapels that stand here. My own pilgrimage was clearly insufficiently devout, for shortly after Belpeuch the exhaust dropped off my car. Mercoeur is a compact little village on a hillside. The tall granite Romanesque church is a dignified building, with a broad crossing tower and pentagonal chancel roofed with *lauzes*. From Mercoeur there's a lovely drive across the high meadows and conifer woods of the Xaintrie plateau to Reygade, a dim little village with a dim little church. It's worth coming here, though, to see the splendid fifteenth-century Entombment placed in a chapel

Right **The rolling hills of the upper Dordogne near Mercoeur.**

Below **The Romanesque church at Mercoeur, built of granite and roofed with** *lauzes.*

beside the church. For 20 francs, no mean sum, you can see it accompanied by *son et lumière*, complete with heavenly choirs and deep emotion. You can see it plain and unaccompanied for nothing, which is rather better value. The seven figures around the bier, including a Mary almost collapsing with grief, are composed with variety and character and retain almost all their original polychrome colouring. From Reygade a winding and picturesque road will take you back to Beaulieu.

The Lords of Turenne: North from Beaulieu

From Beaulieu the Dordogne valley winds northeast towards Argentat, and beyond Argentat the river valley entirely changes character, for immediately above the town begins a series of major dams, which have transformed over 60 kilometres of the upper Dordogne into long finger lakes and reservoirs. These stretches are, however, virtually inaccessible by road, and so our exploration of the Dordogne must end just beyond Argentat. The charm of this little town lies in its riverside setting, not in the merits of its buildings. Surrounded by the thickly wooded hills of the Corrèze, Argentat straddles the river. On one side modest old houses with wooden balconies are built right up against the river bank. Opposite, a short esplanade welcomes strolling pedestrians. Although Argentat is an excellent base for exploring the upper Dordogne, there is little here to detain visitors for long.

It is not only the river that changes above Argentat. The landscape is noticeably different too. You have left the gentle hills of Périgord or Quercy for the wilder country of the Corrèze, and beyond, should you follow the river to its source, you would reach the mountains of the Auvergne. Splendid country it is too, but beyond the range, both geographical and topographical, of this book. Nevertheless there are fine excursions to be made into this countryside. The road along the south bank takes you into the gorges of

---

Argentat. Upstream from here the Dordogne has been dammed and resembles lakes more than a river.

the upper Dordogne. Just beyond the Argentat dam you'll glimpse the Château du Gibanel behind the trees on the opposite bank. Of the church at Glény, only a single bay and a Romanesque apse survive. The quality of the exterior and interior carvings suggests there was once a fine building here, and the remnant, with its crenellated belfry, is still picturesque. The next dam upstream is Le Chastang, and it's worth driving up to the belvedere that overlooks it. The view of the 85-metre-high dam, and the still body of water beyond it, is undeniably impressive, as are the wild hills hemming it in. Yet recalling the lively Dordogne that flows past Carennac or Limeuil, it's hard to realize that this is the same river. Technologically it's admirable, but as a river the Dordogne is no longer alive at this point.

From Chastang a winding road leads to Servières-le-Château. Its castle was destroyed in 1916 and rebuilt as a grim institutional building; the church, too, with its exceptionally tall apse, has been rebuilt. Servières is a depressing place, though marvellously situated high above the Gorges de la Glane. From here you can either return to Argentat along the main road or continue south to the Maronne gorge and the thrilling fortress of Merle. The tall straight towers, all that remains of this once mighty stronghold, were once attached to a complex of fortresses. Perched on an awesomely steep rock, the seigneurs of Merle successfully withstood English attacks throughout the Hundred Years War. However, their position deep in a valley made them vulnerable once artillery warfare became the norm. When it became clear that the Tours de Merle were no longer secure, they were abandoned by their garrisons, and have been dramatic ruins ever since. The road westwards to Argentat passes the nondescript village of Saint-Bonnet-les-Tours and the thickly massed medieval Château du Rieux.

The area west of Argentat is less spectacular in its landscape but richer in history and architecture. From Argentat drive north towards Saint-Chamant; 2 kilometres before the village you'll pass the fine château of Soulages. Saint-Chamant itself is of little interest apart from the church's west porch sheltered beneath a handsome wooden belfry, which is itself covered with a large steep roof of *lauzes*. A Christ in Majesty, flanked by adoring angels, dominates the twelfth-century carving above the west door,

Above **The stately little town of Collonges is built entirely of red sandstone.**

Right **At Le Chambon south of Argentat a bridge crosses a turbulent stretch of the Dordogne.**

while beneath him are ranked the apostles on either side of Mary, all vivaciously carved and characterized. The two busts on either side of the angels probably represent the donors, the local seigneur and his wife. Further up the road is the village of Forgès, enlivened by a fine *manoir* and some substantial houses. From the main square take the narrow road to Espargilière; a short path to the left brings you to a Calvary of 1893. On all sides there are splendid views of the wooded Corrèze, which can be enjoyed in deep tranquillity, for the only sounds to be heard are of birdsong and the barking of dogs from nearby farms. Return to Forgès and follow the signs for the Cascades de Murel. The road takes you high into a narrow valley until you reach a dead end. Follow the path alongside the rushing stream to the cascades – no different from streams and rapids elsewhere in mountainous country, but a welcome hint of wildness after the civility of much of the Dordogne valley.

Drive in a southwesterly direction to the Roche de Vic. A path winds through heather and bracken to the summit of this 636-metre hill. The views are magnificent, not just over the Dordogne and Corrèze but of such distant landmarks, identified by a *table d'orientation*, as the Puy de Dôme and the mountains of Cantal. With lizards and butterflies for company and a statue of the Virgin Mary surveying the scene, this is a splendid spot, offering a panorama less intimate and touching than, say, Espargillière, but unquestionably grand. Continue southwest to Meyssac, which, built largely of red sandstone, is like a dress rehearsal for nearby Collonges. Though eclipsed by its more spectacular neighbour, this pottery-making town should not be ignored. Enter the elaborate doorway of the sixteenth-century church, which is guarded by a massive fortified west belfry with a broad wooden roof. The nave would appear quite harmonious if only it were possible to see it properly, for dark stained glass keeps the church perpetually gloomy. The north transept contains a late medieval gilt Madonna and Child of considerable poise and dignity. Around the church stands a pleasant group of red houses, most with balconies, some with turrets, and half-timbered houses overlook the eighteenth-century covered market.

Despite its attractions, unpretentious Meyssac pales beside Collonges-la-Rouge, perhaps the most visually arresting town in the Dordogne. The entire place is built of red sandstone, and in the afternoon sun the hillside glows with the rich colour, though under heavy skies the stone is a leaden russet and the town can appear sombre and oppressive. Even the loveliest villages of the Dordogne are patchy; a continuous history cannot guarantee stylistic perfection. But Collonges is all of a piece, with a unity of style and atmosphere unmatched in the region. It was a satellite town of the viscounty of Turenne, and the seigneur, Gédéon de Vassignac, was also a captain-governor of the viscounty. Indeed, Collonges was a country retreat for grandees loyal to Turenne, which explains its unusually high proportion of fine *manoirs*. As Freda White has observed, there is something comic as well as vainglorious about the presence of so many proud houses in this one village. Clearly the grandees of Turenne kept up with the Vassignacs as assiduously as we keep up with the Joneses. Now, however, the viscounty has been defunct for centuries, the nobles have long vanished, and this petrified town stands as a unique survival, bizarre, lovely, and, one hopes, imperishable.

Park along the main road, for the lanes of the village are narrow, and walk down the main Rue de la Barrière. The walking tour suggested by the Michelin guide is thoroughly sensible and my own suggestions scarcely deviate from it. On the corner after the tower house with Renaissance dormers, you'll see the Maison de la Sirène, named after the prominent corbel that depicts a siren holding a lute. At the foot of the street is the Hôtel de la Ramade de Friac, with its two round towers and irregular pepperpot roofs. Continue under the covered passage and bear right to the Château de Beuges, with its aggressively fortified tower. Return to the Hôtel de la Ramade de Friac. The half-ruined Porte Plate opposite leads to the covered market and the main square overlooked by galleried houses.

Dominating the square are a chapel and a church built on the foundations of an eighth-century Benedictine priory. Unusually, the church has two naves, for when the Vicomte de Turenne became a Protestant in the sixteenth century, the Catholics made the right nave available to his co-religionists, retaining the left for their own rites. The broad fortified west tower was also built in the sixteenth century, and beneath it is placed a Romanesque carving. During the

Wars of Religion the sculpture was dismantled in order to protect it; not until 1923 was it restored to its original position. Four angels kneel before a Christ ascending, while below him Apostles and the Virgin Mary stand beneath arcades. The frieze around the sculpture is decorated with medallions of small heads. The complex early twelfth-century belfry, with its square open stages followed by octagonal stages, is, like Beaulieu, in the Limousin style. Stand beneath the beautiful eleventh-century domed crossing and look up: through a hole in the roof you can see into the belfry itself. The church furnishings are not especially interesting, with the singular exception of a twelfth-century wooden effigy of Christ placed in the south chapel. Southeast of the church is the Castel de Vassignac of 1583, once the home of the seigneur. With its living quarters guarded on all sides by towers and turrets, the splendid Castel is a mixture of *manoir* and castle. North of the church the fifteenth-century Chapel of the Penitents, now deconsecrated, contains a seventeenth-century walnut crucifix and a small town museum. North of the chapel a lane wanders past modest well-restored houses. The lane emerges by the Castel de Maussac; for some reason half the red stone has been obscured with stucco.

Beaulieu and Collonges are worldly towns, and the sculptures adorning their churches derive from the sophisticated school of Moissac. Yet at Saillac, just south of Collonges, we are, aesthetically, in a different world. There the entrance chamber of the Romanesque church is furnished with an ancient carved holy water stoup and a red sandstone font, and has a polychrome sculpture that depicts the Three Kings and Joseph kneeling before the Virgin and Child. To the left of the kings stand their tethered horses. Below, on the lintel, a griffin is devouring what looks like a baby, and a green dragon breathes fire. The lintel of the west door rests on a pillar of twisted columns and bands up which men chase animals, and vice versa. These graphic, elemental images are remote from the majestic Christ figures we have been seeing throughout the Dordogne valley. Here the style is earthy, the gestures large, the outlines vivid and immediately comprehensible. The interior of the church is worth a glance too, for below the domed chancel are some capitals carved with biblical and legendary scenes. The road west, towards Turenne-Gare, traverses a landscape of lovely hillside meadows and passes the curious château of Le Peuch. Its principal tower, encrusted with gables and turrets, resembles the Castel de Maussac at Collonges.

For some time you have been crossing the domains of the once mighty viscounts of Turenne. As you approach Turenne itself, huddling around the remains of a fortress, it may seem hard to realize that this sleepy little town used to control one of the most powerful fiefdoms in France. Seen purely in terms of the picturesque, Turenne, its castle perched over 300 metres up, is a superb sight, with the houses of the town tumbling down the steep hillside. But dozy Turenne must be imaginatively reconstructed by the visitor, for from the shadowy fifth century onwards, its seigneurs ruled most of Haut Quercy, Bas Limousin and Périgord Noir. Originally their fortress occupied a neighbouring hilltop, but in the eleventh century they moved their headquarters to the present site. By the fifteenth century the viscounty controlled 1200 villages and hamlets as well as the towns of Martel, Beaulieu and Argentat. The viscounts of Turenne acted like monarchs – they had their own coinage and created their own nobles – because in effect that's what they were. During the Wars of Religion, Turenne was a noted Protestant centre, and in the seventeenth century Henri de la Tour d'Auvergne, who owned the viscounty, was hailed as an outstanding soldier and rejoiced under the appellation of 'the Great Turenne'. Until his death in 1675 he fought at every important battleground in Europe in defence of Protestantism and King Louis XIV. The dynasty came to an end after 1300 years, when Charles Godefroy, laden with debt, sold his viscounty to Louis XV in 1738. With this transaction vanished the last independent sovereignty within France.

Park and walk down the Route du Château. The present church replaced one burnt down in 1575. The new church was begun in 1593 and completed in 1661. The doorway sheltered by the west belfry has flat classical surrounds beneath a statue of the Virgin and Child. The interior is impressive and the flat low vaults contribute to a sense of breadth and amplitude, an openness appropriate to the Protestant worship for which the church was intended. The lavish golden nineteenth-century altarpiece in the choir is a reminder that Catholicism has returned to this building. Below the south transept altar is placed a simple and

Above **At Saillac a weathered millstone has come to resemble avant-garde sculpture.**

Right **Now a sleepy village, Turenne was once the seat of a viscounty that controlled 1200 villages and towns.**

Left The hamlet of Saint-Michel-de-Bannières west of Queyssac-les-Vignes.

Below Guarding a property at Saint-Michel-de-Bannières.

dignified twelfth-century wooden figure of the dead Christ. Follow the road into the lane marked as a cul-de-sac, bearing right at the end up a steep path. As you pass between some fine old houses, you'll see the tall cylinder of the thirteenth-century (some say earlier) Caesar's Tower looming above you. Bear right under the cliff supporting the castle walls and circle the walls until you reach the entrance to the castle ruins. Pass through the ramparts to the red stone clock tower of the thirteenth century, the former guardroom and now a small museum. Surprisingly, the steps lead to a garden terrace, and at the far end rises Caesar's Tower. Climb to the top for a fine view. Sadly these two towers are all that remains of the once mighty château, which was destroyed during the Revolution.

South of Turenne stretches the Causse de Martel, and a number of attractive villages such as Lasvaux and Cazillac. At Lasvaux there are some fine stone houses and a worthwhile Romanesque church, decorated with grimacing heads above the thirteenth-century west porch. The interior, with its pentagonal chancel, is equally enjoyable. Note the font, which rests on a reused capital with carved scenes depicting the Annunciation and the Journey to Bethlehem. There are grand views over the *causse* from the hillside church at Cazillac, and at the top of the hill stands a handsome old presbytery. But the most interesting village of the region lies to the east at Curemonte. From the eleventh century onwards this proud village owed allegiance, inevitably, to Turenne. Curemonte's two magnificent castles, Château Saint-Hilaire and Château de Plas, stand side by side within the same ramparts guarded by the same watchtowers. The fifteenth-century Château Saint-Hilaire is flanked by two stern square machicolated watchtowers. The second château is a more recent structure, from the sixteenth century, but it is now in ruins. South of the irregularly shaped and much rebuilt church, formerly a chapel of one of the châteaux, stands the early nineteenth-century covered market, and opposite is the weathered base of a sixteenth-century Calvary. Below the east wall of the châteaux are some delightful, if over-restored, old houses and a turreted sixteenth-century *manoir*. A third château, La Johannie, a fortified cluster of tall buildings less conspicuous than the other two, stands close to the market. Colette, a native of Burgundy, spent the summer of 1940 here, and hated it.

'We've now been in this green tomb for a month,' she complained to friends, 'without letters, telegrams, telephone, petrol, or newspapers.'

South of Curemonte is another little hilltop town, Queyssac-les-Vignes, with splendid views over the *causse* from the top of the old donjon that now stands in the grounds of the Hôtel Vin Paillé. *Vin paillé* is an extremely sweet dessert wine, made from ripe grapes left on beds of straw for months until they have shrivelled and their sugar content has reached very high levels. Philip Oyler wrote rapturously about this wine a few decades ago, in a book that now seems to be describing another world. The wine was rare then, but seems unobtainable now in the Dordogne, even at the hotel named after it. No doubt some of the things that we now regard as indestructible in the Dordogne will also vanish as the years pass, but the region as a whole should be able to retain its personality. For the Dordogne is large and diverse, a well-packed suitcase rather than a single gem, a dazzling collection of mini-regions, loosely linked though not defined by climate, landscape and architecture, and united solely by the great river that flows through its midst. Though no part of the world is immune from change – even the wild gorges of the upper Dordogne have been utterly transformed in recent decades – this region is so rich and varied that its appeal should remain constant. Few parts of Europe have so much to offer, and it is hard to think where else so many enthusiasms – whether for food, architecture, bathing, drinking, walking or plain escaping – can be so easily satisfied.

Index